RASACHANDRIKA

Late Smt. Ambabai Samsi
The author of original *Rasachandrika*

Born : 29th October 1879 Died : 17th December 1938

RASACHANDRIKA

SARASWAT COOKERY BOOK

with Notes and Home Remedies, Useful Hints and Hindu Festivals

The Saraswat Mahila Samaj
Bombay

Popular Prakashan
www.popularprakashan.com

Published by
Asmita Mohite for
POPULAR PRAKASHAN PVT. LTD.
301, Mahalaxmi Chambers
22, Bhulabhai Desai Road
Mumbai - 400 026
info@popularprakashan.com

The Saraswat Mahila Samaj
B/1 Saraswat Co-op. Buildings
Dr. Kashibai Nowrungay Marg
Gamdevi, Mumbai - 400 007

First published June 1988
Second edition, June 1991
Reprinted 1994
Reprinted 1997
Reprinted 1998
Reprinted 2001
Reprinted 2004
Reprinted 2008
Reprinted 2009
Reprinted 2011
Reprinted 2015
Reprinted 2018
Reprinted 2020
Reprinted 2024
Reprinted 2025

(3339)
ISBN 978-81-7154-290-1

Cover painting by
P. G. Sirur

Inside coloured photographs by
Nandan Balwalli

PRINTED IN INDIA
by Manipal Technologies Limited
Manipal, Karnataka - 576104

Preface

The Saraswat Mahila Samaj was founded on September 6, 1917. The publication of the first edition of Marathi *Rasachandrika* was undertaken during its Silver Jubilee year and it was brought out on October 30, 1943. Only a thousand copies of this edition were printed which were sold out within a month.

Several members of the Samaj made additions and alterations which were incorporated in the future editions. The fact that the Marathi *Rasachandrika* went into its ninth edition evidently shows its popularity among the Saraswats as well as other communities. The Saraswat Mahila Samaj is very grateful to all the members of the Samaj and other friends for their contribution to this book.

The metric system of weights and measures was introduced in 1958 in this country. So this was introduced in the cooking section from the seventh Marathi edition onwards. This conversion was done by Smt. Shalini G. Sirur and Late Smt. Shreemati M. Nadkarni.

As the book was found to be so popular it was translated in Hindi and published in 1958.

The late Smt. Kalyanibai Samsi had the idea of publishing the English edition of *Rasachandrika* as far back as twenty years ago, but the project did not materialise at the time. So it was decided to publish it this year when the translation has been fully completed.

The English translation of the cookery section has been done by Smt.Mira G. Hattiangadi and Smt. Neela C. Balsekar. The simple remedies given in the Home Remedies Section and Some Useful Hints originally furnished by Smt. Hira Nadkarni have been translated with necessary modification by Dr. Smt. Suniti T Mukerjee. The Festival Section has been translated by Shri Mangesh Rao Sujir.

The Saraswat Mahila Samaj is grateful to the renowned artist Shri P. G. Sirur for the painting of a Saraswat kitchen in 1940s on the front cover done by him free of charge for the first Marathi edition of *Rasachandrika* published in 1943 and to Shri Nandan Ballwalli for the inside coloured photographs.

Editing of this book with corrections, translation-modifications and changes wherever necessary have been carried out by Smt. Sarala B. Kalthod and Smt. Kunda M. Kagal. Also Smt. Shalini G. Sirur and Smt. Shaila S. Hemmady have assisted.

Our thanks are due to all the above mentioned persons as well as to Shri Sadanand and Smt. Nirmala S. Bhatkal, to Shri Ramdas G. Bhatkal and Shri Raghunath N. Gokarn of Popular Prakashan and to several others for their valuable advice and help in bringing out the first edition in response to the great demand from the younger generation which is more conversant with English than Marathi.

We are glad to mention that, as we hoped, all 2000 copies of the first edition of English *Rasachandrika* printed in June 1988 were received with tremendous enthusiasm and appreciation. Hence, we are glad to bring out the second edition to meet the increasing demand.

In this edition we have added a few more typical and popular Saraswat recipes which were not included in the previous editions of *Rasachandrika* so far. Also, the proportion of chillies in the curries has been reduced taking into consideration the diet consciousness of the present generation. Improvements in some recipes have also been incorporated.

Thanks to the sincere efforts and unstinted co-operation of all the members of Managing Committee of The Saraswat Mahila Samaj, we are proud to present to you this revised second edition, which we hope will be received with greater enthusiasm.

Vijaya S. Yederi
President

Shaila S. Hemmady
Vice-President

Sharayu A. Bijurkar
Chairman

The Saraswat Mahila Samaj,
Gamdevi, Bombay 400 007
Date : 1st March 1991

Foreword to Marathi Edition

Cooking is an art and both men and women should be proficient in it as it becomes a necessity in this age of small families and self-reliance. Although cooking is so essential, the importance given to this art is much less than to that given to others and the enthusiasm to teach it, is utterly lacking.

This book was, therefore, written by my mother-in-law, the late Smt. Ambabai Samsi, to make up for just this lack of enthusiasm. Both she and the rest of us hoped fervently that the book would be published in her lifetime, so that she could see the utility of it, but unfortunately this was not to be as she passed away very suddenly on December 17 , 1938, without being able to see the publication of this book.

I had also hoped that it would be published at least before her first death anniversary, but although the manuscript was ready, it had to be edited, which took some more time. The editing was done with the help of Smt. Indirabai Kallianpurkar, Smt. Aparnabai Jathar, and Smt. Rukmabai Tallur to whom I am greatly indebted for their help and their willingness to spare their valuable time.

My mother-in-law also wished to include a section of home remedies in this book. This idea was fully supported by two members of the Saraswat Mahila Samaj, namely, Smt. Sitabai Padbidri and Smt. Kamalabai Dongerkery. The actual writing of the home remedies was a team effort by many friends but the methodical arrangements of the matter and preparation of the glossary was done by Dr. Smt. Girijabai Heble.

Finally I wish to express my deep gratitude to the Saraswat Mahila Samaj, who undertook the responsibility of publication.

This book is the result of long perseverance and intense hard work on the part of my revered mother-in-law and the enthusiastic follow-up by the members of the Saraswat Mahila Samaj. I feel very happy, therefore, to present this masterly work to the readers.

KALYANIBAI SAMSI

October 30, 1942

Author's Note to Marathi Edition

The most important thing to sustain life is food. There are several ways of cooking it, which may not necessarily be beneficial to the eater. The method of cooking may destroy the essential nutrients of the food. Cooking, therefore, should be such that food remains wholesome and nutritious, leading to increased vitality and long life.

Diet varies according to climate and locally available ingredients. This is why cooking differs in different places.

A large number of cookery books have recently been published, depicting a great variety of cooking. Housewives can, therefore, learn and select recipes from different parts of the country or the world, belonging to different climates and different groups of people. In this process, Saraswat women have learnt a large variety of dishes not typically their own, and it was felt that other housewives may also like to experiment with Saraswat dishes. Hence the inspiration to compile and write this book.

Since formal academic education has now become more widespread than in my time, girls cannot devote much time to cooking till they are about 20. As a result it becomes very difficult when they first undertake the responsibility of cooking. Under these circumstances Saraswat girls can refer to this book and start cooking typically Saraswat dishes without much difficulty. Traditional Saraswat cooking is not very spicy and is therefore nutritious and good for health. I have laid special stress on such recipes and methods of cooking. However, some select dishes belonging to other communities, which may be popular amongst Saraswats are also included in this book.

For novices learning to cook for a household, measures and directions are required. In this book I have used measures in all the recipes to help them. With this as a guideline, weights and measures can be altered to suit individual requirements.

I sincerely hope that all readers and potential cooks, whether young or old, will benefit by this book and will be able to prepare tasty, wholesome and nutritious food by using it.

AMBABAI SAMSI

October 1938

Contents

RASACHANDRIKA

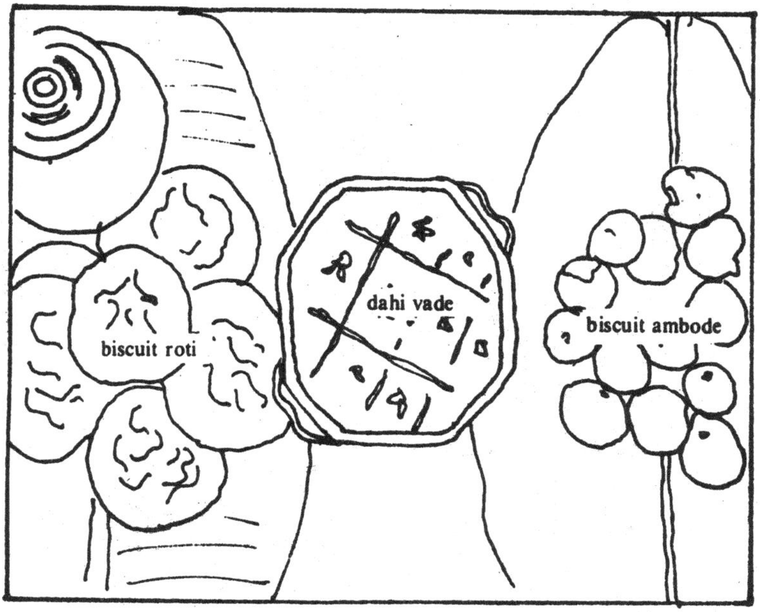
biscuit roti
dahi vade
biscuit ambode

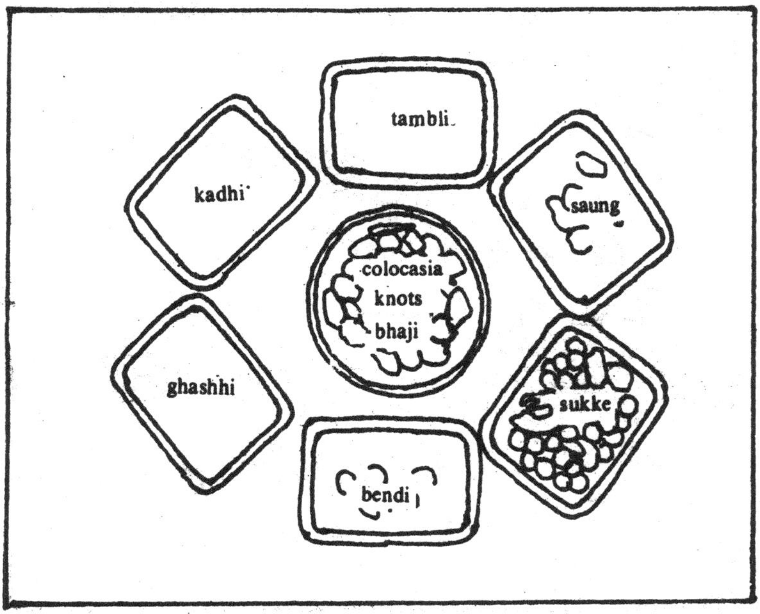
tambli
kadhi
saung
colocasia
knots
bhaji
ghashhi
sukke
bendi

vayana
ambat
vari gruel
patholyo
kaap
kochholi
alani upar - saltless

nevaryo
modak
arati
khotte
ghashhi
kaap
madgane
sukke
katla (salad)
aluwadi

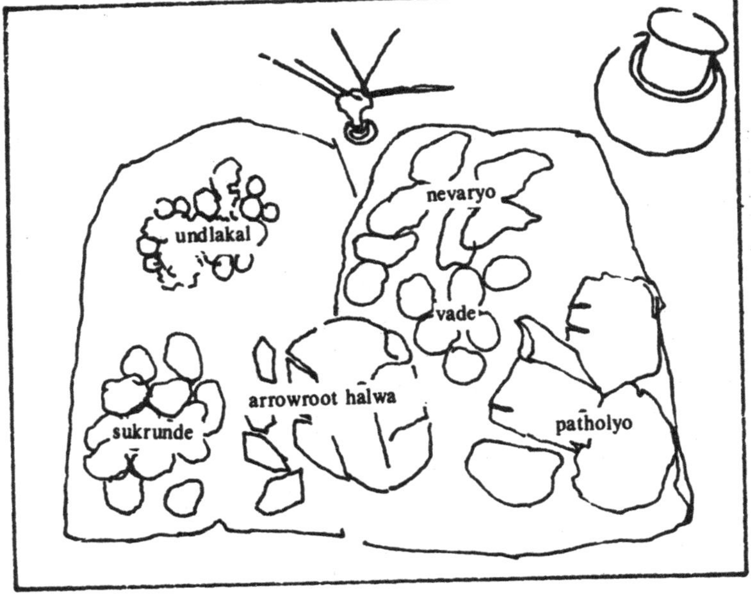
undlakal
nevaryo
vade
sukrunde
arrowroot halwa
patholyo

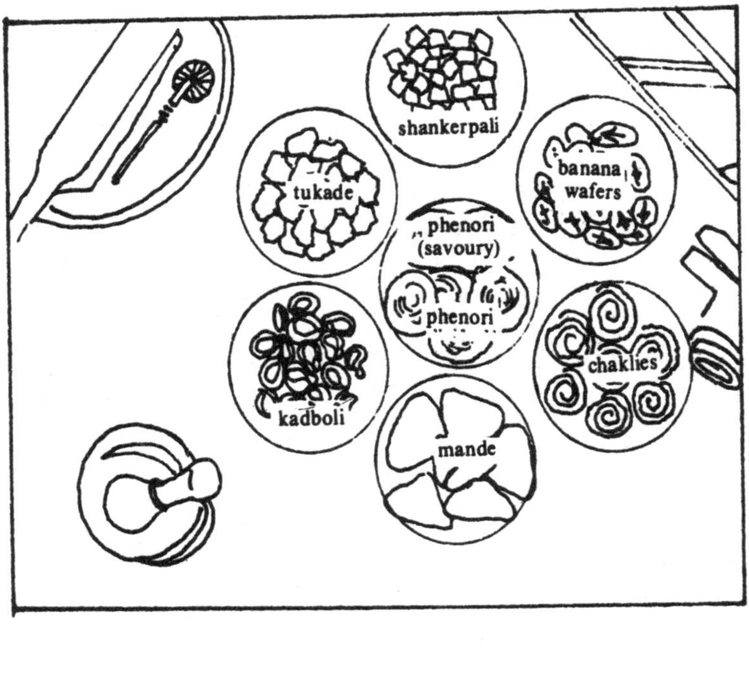
shankerpali
tukade
banana wafers
phenori (savoury)
phenori
kadboli
chaklies
mande

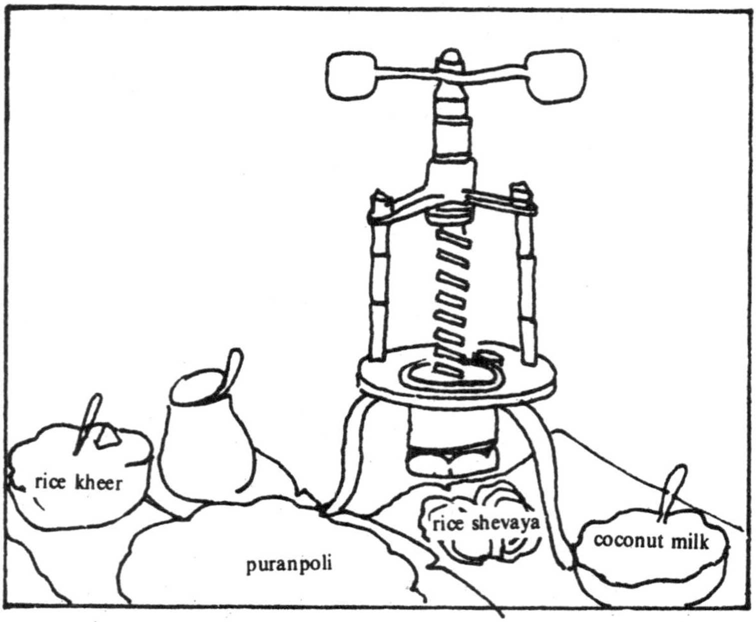
rice kheer
rice shevaya
coconut milk
puranpoli

khotte
black gram appe
jaggery appe
idli
jaggeryless appe
patholyo

prawns pickle
fried fish
hugga
spicy fish curry

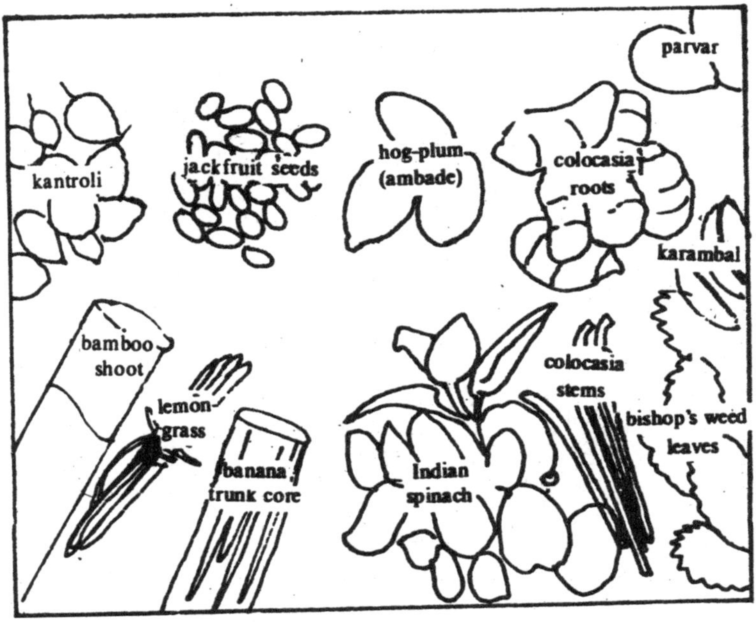
parvar
kantroli
jackfruit seeds
hog-plum (ambade)
colocasia roots
karambal
bamboo shoot
lemon-grass
banana trunk core
Indian spinach
colocasia stems
bishop's weed leaves

dodhak
surnolyo
dudhi sandan
blackgram
pancake
panpole

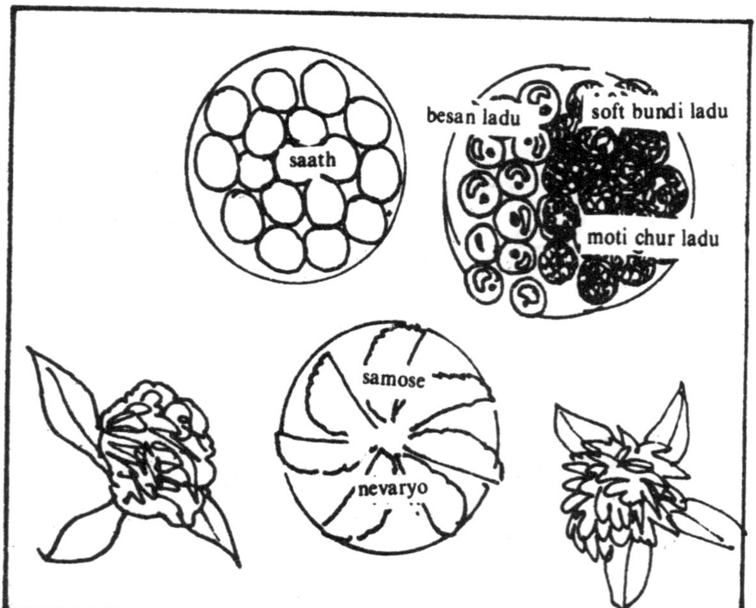
besan ladu
soft bundi ladu
saath
moti chur ladu
samose
nevaryo

sukrunde
papad
rice
saar
vade
seasoned varan
pickles
chutney
koshimbir
sukke

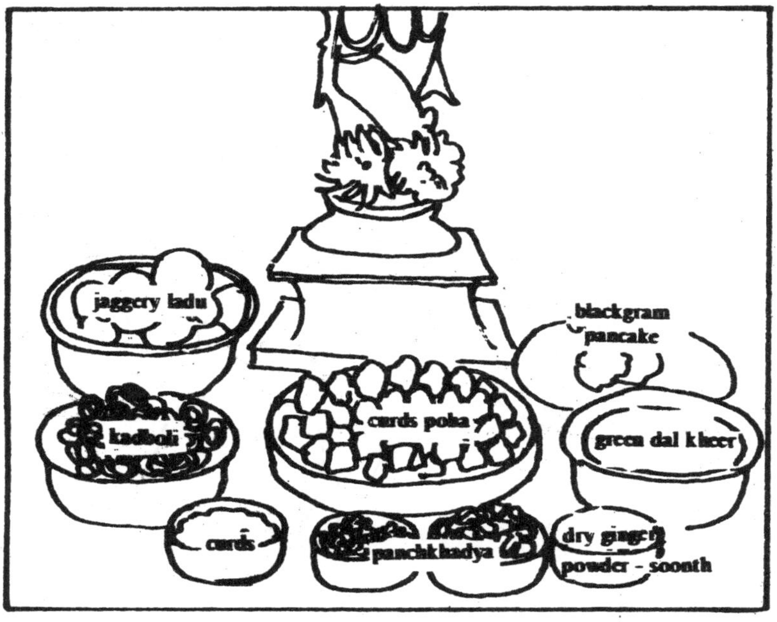
jaggery ladu
blackgram
pancake
kadboli
curds poha
green dal kheer
curds
panchkhadya
dry ginger
powder - soonth

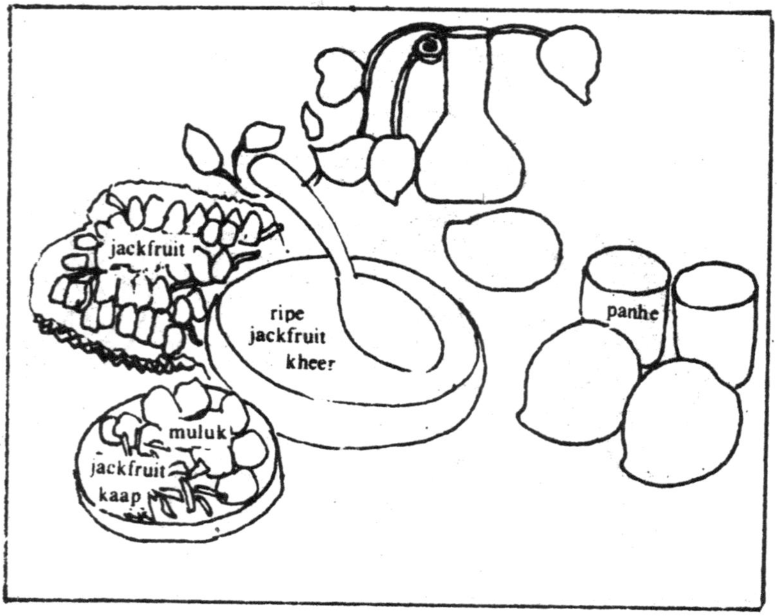
jackfruit
ripe
jackfruit
kheer
panhe
muluk
jackfruit
kaap

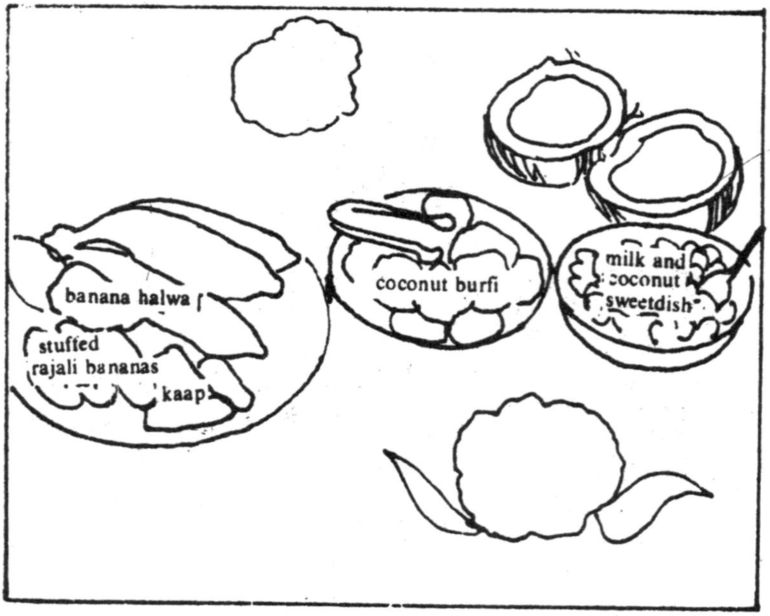
banana halwa
stuffed
rajali bananas
kaap
coconut burfi
milk and
coconut
sweetdish

Masalas

1. Amti masala

1 kg coriander seeds
½ kg red chillies
125 gms turmeric pieces
250 gms bengal gram dal (soaked and parched)
250 gms white sesame seeds
20 gms asafoetida
250 gms groundnut oil
100 gms cumin seeds
250 gms poppy seeds
100 gms mustard seeds
50 gms pepper corns
50 gms cloves
50 gms cinnamon
50 gms cinnamon leaves
50 gms badian
50 gms caraway seeds
50 gms big black cardamom (with skin)
50 gms jai patri
50 gms dagad phool

1. Keep ready an iron frying pan, flat ladle and 2 thalis. 2. Hand-pick and clean all the dry ingredients. 3. Pound turmeric and asafoetida into small pieces. 4. Remove stems of the chillies. 5. In an unlined vessel, pour 4 teaspoonfuls of oil and fry the chillies on a low flame, stirring constantly, until they are crisp. 6. Take an iron frying pan, pour sufficient oil in it and keep it on a stove; when the oil is slightly heated, deep fry the ingredients separately in the following order – turmeric pieces, asafoetida, pepper corns, cloves, cinnamon, cinnamon leaves. 7. In the remaining oil fry the coriander seeds on a low flame until they are light reddish brown. 8. Later fry the gram dal, cumin seeds, aniseed, and caraway seeds and big black cardamom similarly. 9. Roast the sesame seeds on a dry hot plate. 10. Pound together all the first group of fried ingredients. 11. Then pound the chillies. 12. Mix the coriander and sesame seeds with dal and pound together. 13. Mix and blend together all the pounded ingredients, sieve through a medium fine sieve, and store the masala in a glass jar with a tight lid.

NOTE: Using the above recipe as a guide, vary the quantity proportionately according to requirements. If desired, ½ kg grated dried coconut, roasted and pounded, can be mixed in the masala.

2. Kholamba masala

½ kg coriander seeds
250 gms red chillies
20 gms turmeric pieces
40 gms black gram dal
40 gms bengal gram dal
groundnut oil for frying
20 gms black pepper corns
40 gms fenugreek seeds
20 gms asafoetida
50 gms mustard seeds
50 gms cumin seeds
2 handfuls curry leaves

1. Handpick and clean all the ingredients. 2. Pour sufficient oil in a frying pan, heat it slightly and fry all ingredients, separately on a low flame until they are light brown. 3. Pound them together and sieve. 4. Blend the masala well and store in a glass jar with a tight lid.

3. Rasam masala

250 gms coriander seeds
125 gms red chillies
125 gms dried coconut
20 gms turmeric pieces
groundnut oil for frying
20 gms cumin seeds
20 gms fenugreek seeds
20 gms asafoetida
2 handfuls curry leaves

1. Handpick and clean all the ingredients. 2. Pour sufficient oil in an iron frying pan and heat it slightly. Fry all the ingredients separately on a medium flame until they are golden brown. 3. Mix the ingredients and pound them together to a fine powder. Sieve it through a medium sieve. 4. Blend the masala well and store in a glass jar with a tight lid.

4. Tamil saar masala

200 gms coriander seeds
20 gms turmeric powder
20 gms cumin seeds
10 gms fenugreek seeds
groundnut oil for frying
5 gms asafoetida
50 gms red chillies
50 gms dried coconut
20 gms curry leaves

1. Handpick and clean all the ingredients. 2. Take an iron frying pan and pour sufficient oil and heat it slightly. Fry all the ingredients separately stirring constantly, until they are light brown. 3. Pound them together to a fine powder and sieve through a medium sieve. 4. Blend the masala well and store it in a glass jar with a tight lid.

5. Sambar masala

½ kg coriander seeds	20 gms asafoetida
250 gms red chillies	20 gms cumin seeds
50 gms turmeric pieces	20 gms pepper corns
100 gms black gram dal	20 gms mustard seeds
100 gms bengal gram dal	100 gms whole wheat

1. Handpick and clean all the ingredients. 2. Heat an iron frying pan on a medium flame and roast all the ingredients until they are brown. 3. Pound them together to a fine powder, sieve it on a medium sieve and blend the masala well. 4. Store it in a glass jar with a tight lid.

Method of grinding masalas containing coconut gratings

1. Masalas for semi-dry dishes should be ground coarsely. 2. Masalas for chutneys should not be too fine. 3. Masalas for stuffing vegetables and for raitas should be ground fairly fine. 4. Sambar, ambat, and cold curry masalas should be ground to a very fine paste. 5. The curries prepared with ground coconut masala should not be boiled too much. Excess boiling results in curelling and separation of oil from coconut which spoils the flavour and taste of the curry.

Dishes served with Rice Gruel

---

1. Indian spinach curry (liquid)

1 bunch Indian spinach	1 tspful washed rice
1 small ball of tamarind	1 tbsp ghee
salt and jaggery to taste	½ coconut gratings
6-8 garlic cloves for seasoning	4-6 red chillies

1. Sort out leaves and stems of the spinach, wash them, cut the leaves to small pieces and the stems 5 cms long. 2. Put the stems in a vessel, add a little water and cook them with some salt and

jaggery. 3. When they are half cooked add the leaves. Continue boiling until the leaves are also cooked 4. Remove the vessel from the stove and keep it aside. 5 Grind grated coconut, rice, tamarind and red chillies. Add the masala to the cooked spinach and bring it to boil on a medium flame. 6. In an iron seasoning ladle pour ghee and heat it. Add the crushed garlic and fry, stirring constantly, until reddish brown. Add the seasoning to the dish and cover it with a lid.

NOTE: As variants, raw papaya or raw tender jackfruit may be added to spinach or used separately. In the latter case, prepare the dish as described above, but use less jaggery.

2. Bottle gourd curry

½ kg bottle gourd (remove the core and seeds, and peel off the skin)
7-8 kokum or gamboge rinds
½ tsp mustard seeds
a few curry leaves
salt to taste

½ coconut gratings*
4-6 green chillies*
1 tsp washed rice*
1-1½ tbsp ghee or coconut oil for seasoning

*Grind together

1. Cut the gourd into small pieces (2.5 cms long and ½ cm thick). 2. Put the pieces into a vessel, add 3 measures of water, salt to taste and kokum or gamboge rinds. Bring them to boil on a medium flame and cook them till soft. 3. Grind the masala and add it to the cooked gourd pieces. 4. Allow to boil for some more minutes, and remove the vessel from the flame. 5. Heat the oil in an iron seasoning ladle and add the mustard seeds. Allow them to splutter. Put in the curry leaves and fry them for a minute or two. Add the seasoning to the gourd curry.

NOTE: As variants, instead of bottle gourd, vegetables like cucumber (*Maggen*), tender plantain-stem or cabbage may be used.

3. Leafy vegetable curry

2-3 bunches of any leafy vegetable
1 handful coriander leaves
salt (and jaggery if desired to taste)

½ coconut gratings*
4-6 red chillies*
1 tsp washed rice*
tamarind*

*Grind together

1. Sort, pick and clean the leaves from the stems. Sprinkle a little salt on the leaves and shake them well with a whisk. (This helps to

remove small worms, if any.) 2. Wash the leaves and tender stems thoroughly and cut them into small pieces. 3. Put the cut leaves and tender stems into a vessel, add a little water and boil them on a medium flame until well cooked. 4. Add salt to taste and boil for 5 to 10 minutes. 5. Grind the masala and mix it with the leaves and bring it to boil. (Instead of tamarind, 7-8 gamboge rinds can be used.) 6. Add the chopped coriander leaves and remove the vessel from the flame.

NOTE: Similarly, any leafy vegetable can be used for curries served with rice gruel. Fenugreek leaves, aniseed leaves and spring onion stalks should not be used. Leafy vegetables like Amaranth (green or red) should be used as far as possible.

4. Colocasia stem curry

½ kg colocasia stems (peel off skin and cut into thin rounds)
½ litre water
2 tspfuls grated jaggery
6 green chillies, sliced
salt to taste
4 kokum rinds
6 garlic cloves
1 ½ tbsp ghee or coconut oil
6-8 garlic cloves for seasoning

1. Wash the cut colocasia stems, put them in a vessel with the water and boil. 2. Cook until the pieces are soft. 3. Add salt, jaggery, green chillies, kokum rind and crushed garlic. Allow it to cook until the pieces are very soft. 4. Prepare a seasoning with garlic (which is crushed slightly) and add it to the curry.

5. Raw mango chutney

Green mango, green mango preserved in salt water, or green mango steamed in salt water and preserved are generally used to prepare semi-liquid chutneys to be served with rice gruel.

½ green mango (either raw, preserved in salt water or steamed in salt water
½ coconut gratings
2-3 green chillies
4 garlic cloves
salt to taste

1. Grind the masala coarsely with coconut gratings, green chillies, salt (necessary only in case of fresh green mango), and garlic. 2. Add the mango pieces and grind further to a semi-liquid consistency.

6. Raw mango raita (variety 1)

2 steamed and preserved green mangoes (remove the seed)
3 red chillies
salt and jaggery to taste
½ coconut gratings
1 tbsp ghee or groundnut oil for seasoning
½ tsp mustard, a few curry leaves

1. Grind the coconut gratings and red chillies coarsely. 2. Cut the mangoes into small pieces and mix them with the masala. 3. Add salt if necessary and jaggery to taste. 4. Prepare a seasoning with mustard seeds and curry leaves and add it to the raita.

7. Raw mango raita (variety 2)

2 raw green mangoes
water enough to cook mangoes
jaggery equal in quantity as the mango pulp
salt to taste
½ tsp mustard seeds
2-3 red chillies
a few curry leaves
1 tbspful ghee for seasoning

1. Wash the mangoes, cut and remove the seeds. 2. Boil and cook the mangoes with water in a vessel. 3. Allow it to cool slightly, and make a pulp of the mangoes with the water left after cooking. 4. Add jaggery, salt to taste and cook well by boiling. 5. Heat ghee in a seasoning ladle on a medium flame, put in the mustard seeds and allow them to splutter. Add pieces of red chillies and fry them for a minute or two. Lastly add the curry leaves. Add the seasoning to the raita. The raita can be preserved for 4 or 5 days.

8. Indian gooseberry Hindi

1. Take 1 cupful of preserved Indian gooseberries (Amla) 2. Grind together 2-3 green chillies and a few coriander leaves, to blend it with the Hindi. 3. Serve it with rice gruel.

NOTE: Instructions for preparing salted mango and Indian Gooseberries preserves are given under the heading "Pickles"

Potatoes

1. Sukke (variety 1)

½ kg large potatoes
1 tsp salt
water enough to boil and cook potatoes
1-1 ½ tsp coconut oil to fry spices
½ tsp black gram dal*
¼ coconut gratings*
1 small ball of tamarind*
¼ tsp turmeric powder*
5 red chillies*
1 tsp coriander seeds*
¼ tsp fenugreek seeds*

*Fry in coconut oil

1. Wash the potatoes well, peel off the skin and cut them into pieces (3.5 cm or 2.5 cm long and 2.5 cm broad). 2. Put them in a vessel, add a little salt and sufficient quantity of water to boil and cook the potato pieces. 3. Keep them aside when well cooked. 4. Heat the oil and fry the spices individually until reddish brown.. 5. Grind together coarsely the coconut gratings, tamarind and turmeric powder. 6. Add the fried spices and grind further until fairly fine. 7. Pour the masala into the cooked potatoes, (if necessary add some water and salt to the masala) and mix well. 8. Keep the vessel on a medium flame and cook until the masala comes to boil.

2. Sukke (variety 2)

½ kg potatoes
250 gms onions
¼ coconut gratings
1 small ball of tamarind
¼ tsp turmeric powder
1 ½ tsp coconut oil to fry spices*
5 red chillies*
1 tsp coriander seeds*
5 cloves*
2 pepper corns*
1 pinch asafoetida*

*Fry in coconut oil

1. Boil and cook the onion pieces in a little water. 2. Wash, peel and cut the potatoes into large pieces. Add a little salt and sufficient quantity of water to the potatoes and cook them until soft. 3. Heat coconut oil and fry the spices individually. 4. Grind coarsely the coconut gratings, tamarind and turmeric powder and the fried spices and gruel further until fairly fine. 5. Pour the masala into the potato and onion pieces. Add salt if necessary. Stir well and bring to the boil.

3. Sukki bhaji (variety 1)

½ kg potatoes (boiled and peeled)
550 gms onions chopped
1 handful chopped coriander leaves
pulp of a small ball of tamarind
7-8 green chillies sliced
1 handful coconut gratings
2 tbsps ghee or groundnut oil
salt to taste
¼ tsp turmeric powder

1. Cut the potatoes into big cubes. 2. Mix together coriander leaves, tamarind pulp, turmeric powder, green chillies, coconut gratings and salt. 3. Add this to the potato cubes, mix and press slightly so that the masala is well blended with the cubes. 4. Heat the ghee or oil in a vessel and fry onions to a light brown colour. 5. Put the potato mixture with it and cook on a low fire until the dish is fairly dry.

4. Sukki bhaji (variety 2)

½ kg potatoes
250 gms onions
250 gms tomatoes (sliced)
1½ tbsps ghee or groundnut oil
1 handful coriander leaves
8 green chillies
1 tsp sugar
salt to taste

1. Wash, peel and cut the potatoes into large pieces. 2. Chop the onions and fry them in ghee or oil for a few minutes. 3. Put in the potato pieces and some water to cook. Add salt, chopped chillies and coriander leaves, tomato slices and sugar. 4. Cook for some more minutes until the potatoes are tender. 5. A handful of grated coconut may be added (optional). The dish should have a thick gravy when ready; it can be served with puris.

5. Sukki bhaji (variety 3)

½ kg potatoes
250 gms onions
250 gms ripe tomatoes (sliced)
8 pepper corns; powdered
salt and sugar to taste
1-1½ tbsps ghee or groundnut oil

1. Wash, peel and cut the potatoes into large pieces. 2. Heat the ghee or oil and fry the chopped onions for a few minutes. 3. Put in the potato pieces, tomato slices, powdered pepper, salt and sugar and cook until the potatoes are tender.

6. Sukki bhaji (variety 4)

250 gms potatoes
250 gms tomatoes
125 gms onions
6 green chillies – sliced
2 tsps flour (maida)
1½ tbsps ghee
salt to taste

1. Wash, peel and cut the potatoes into long and fairly broad pieces. 2. Cut tomatoes into 4–6 pieces. 3. In a vessel put the potato pieces and sliced chillies and add enough water to cook the potatoes. 4. When well cooked, add salt. 5. In another vessel or a small frying pan pour in ghee and when heated fry the chopped onions to light brown colour. 6. Add the flour and fry slightly. 7. Add this to the cooked potatoes and cook for a further period until the gravy thickens slightly.

7. Sukki bhaji (variety 5)

½ kg potatoes
250 gms onions chopped
1 tbsp groundnut oil
½ tsp mustard seeds
1 pinch asafoetida
¼ tsp cumin seeds
3-4 green chillies
½ tsp turmeric powder
salt to taste

1. Heat oil in a vessel, put the mustard seeds and allow them to splutter. 2. Then add cumin seeds, chillies, turmeric powder, asafoetida and fry them slightly. 3. Add the chopped onions and fry them for a few minutes. 4. Mix salt in water and apply it to the potato pieces and add them to the seasoning. 5. Cover the vessel with a lid and cook potatoes until soft, stirring them from time to time.

8. Sukki bhaji (variety 6)

½ kg potatoes boiled, peeled and cut into small pieces
250 gms onions, chopped
salt to taste
a few coriander leaves
1 ½ tbsps groundnut oil
½ coconut gratings*
4–5 green chillies*
5 garlic cloves*
½ tsp turmeric powder*
1 tsp poppy seeds*

* Grind fairly fine

1. Heat the oil in a vessel and fry the chopped onions to a light brown colour. 2. Put in the potato pieces and salt. 3. Add the ground masala and bring it to boil. 4. Chop the coriander leaves and put them into the masala. Remove the vessel from the stove.

9. Saung

½ kg. potatoes (boiled, peeled and cut into small pieces)
4 tbsps coconut oil
10-12 red chillies*
250 gms onions, chopped
1 ball tamarind (size of small lemon)*

* Grind

1. Heat the oil in a frying pan or a vessel and fry the chopped onions until light brown. 2. Put in the potato pieces, salt and ground masala with some water to form a thick gravy. 3. Simmer on a medium flame for 10 minutes.

10. Talasani

½ kg potatoes peeled & cut into flat "fingers" 3.5 cms
1 tbsp groundnut oil
1 pinch asafoetida
¼ tsp cumin seeds
½ tsp turmeric powder
2 tsp chilly powder
1 tsp salt

1. Heat the oil in a frying pan and prepare seasoning with cumin seeds, turmeric powder, asafoetida and chilly powder. 2. Put the potato pieces and stir well. Lower the flame. Cover the pan with a lid and allow it to cook on a low flame. 3. Add salt when the steam starts issuing, and cook further, stirring the dish from time to time, until the potato pieces are dry, soft and ready.

NOTE : For seasoning garlic, black gram dal and red chillies can be used instead.

11. Upkari (variety 1)

½ kg potatoes
1-1½ tbsps ghee or coconut oil
½ tsp mustard seeds
a few curry leaves
1 tsp chilly powder
1 tsp salt
1 small piece of jaggery
1 handful coconut gratings

1. Boil, peel and cut the potatoes into small pieces. 2. Heat the ghee or oil in a vessel and prepare a seasoning with mustard seeds allowing them to splutter, curry leaves and chillie powder. 3. Put in the potato pieces, salt and jaggery and stir well. 4. Allow it to cook for a few minutes and add the coconut gratings. Remove the vessel from the flame.

12. Upkari (variety 2)

½ kg potatoes
1-1½tbsps ghee or coconut oil
½ tsp mustard seeds
3-4 green chillies, chopped
1 tsp salt
1 tsp sugar
1 handful coconut gratings

1. Boil, peel and cut the potatoes into flat fingers. 2. Heat ghee or oil in a vessel and prepare a seasoning with mustard seeds. When they splutter, add chopped green chillies and fry for a minute. 3. Put in the potato pieces, salt and sugar. Stir well and allow it to cook for a few minutes. 4. Add the coconut gratings. Stir again. Remove the vessel from the flame.

13. Koshimbir (variety 1)

½ kg potatoes
2 onions
½ tsp cumin seeds
1 small ball of tamarind
1 tsp salt
¼ coconut gratings
3 red chillies
2 tsps coriander seeds

1. Boil, peel and cut potatoes into small pieces. 2. Chop onions fine. 3. Grind together the remaining ingredients. 4. When the chutney is ready, mix the potato pieces and chopped onions into it and serve.

14. Koshimbir (variety 2)

½ kg potatoes
1 tsp salt
juice of ½ lemon
Oil for deep frying
4 green chillies*
1 onion*
a handful of coriander leaves*

*chop finely

1. Wash the potatoes, peel off the skin and cut them into small pieces. 2. Heat oil in a frying pan and deep fry the potato pieces until light brown. 3. Mix together all the chopped ingredients, add salt and lemon juice. 4. Lastly add the fried potato pieces and blend them well before serving.

15. Bhareet

½ kg potatoes
½ coconut gratings*
3 red chillies*
1 tsp salt
2 onions chopped fine
pulp of a small ball of tamarind

*Grind finely

1. Boil, peel and cut the potatoes into small pieces. 2. Mix the tamarind pulp and salt with the ground coconut and chillies. 3. Add the chopped onions and the potato pieces and blend well.

NOTE: Instead of chopped onions, a seasoning of mustard seeds and asafoetida may also be used.

16. Raita

250 gms potatoes
3-4 green chillies
½ tsp mustard seeds
¼ coconut gratings
250 gms curds
1 tsp salt
½ tsp mustard seeds and a few curry leaves for seasoning

1. Boil, peel and cut potatoes into small pieces. 2. Grind the coconut gratings into a fine paste, add the fried chillies and mustard seeds and grind again. 3. Mix the ground masala with curds, salt and the potato pieces. 4. Give a seasoning of mustard seeds and curry leaves fried in ghee or oil.

17. Patal bhaji (variety 1)

250 gms potatoes
125 gms onions
250 ml water
6 kokum rinds (or lemon juice)
1 tsp salt
1-1 ½ tbsps ghee or groundnut oil

¼ coconut gratings*
4-5 green chillies*
6 garlic cloves*
1 small piece of ginger*
½ tsp turmeric powder*

*Grind to paste

1. Wash, peel and cut potatoes into cubes. 2. Chop onions and fry in ghee or oil until light brown. 3. Add the potato pieces and water and salt and cook until the pieces are soft. 4. Put in the ground masala, add kokum rinds and boil for a few minutes until the masala simmers. This **Bhaji** should be served with puris.

18. Patal bhaji (variety 2)

250 gms potatoes (peeled and cut into cubes)
250 gms tomatoes (sliced)
125 gms onions (thinly sliced)
1 litre water
1 ½ tsp salt

1 cm cinnamon
5-6 cloves
3 tsp flour (maida)
1 tsp sugar

1. Heat ghee and fry the sliced onions until light brown. 2. Add flour and fry for a minute. 3. Boil the water in a vessel, add the cinnamon pieces and cloves. Simmer it for sometime. Add fried onions, potato pieces and sliced tomatoes, salt and sugar and allow them to cook, stirring all the while, until the Bhaji is ready.

NOTE: If the Bhaji should be pungent add 4 sliced green chillies to it.

19. Ghashhi

250 gms potatoes
700 ml water
1-1 ½ tsp salt
½ tbsp coconut oil
3 tsps coriander seeds*
1 tbsp ghee or coconut oil for seasoning

¾ coconut gratings
½ tsp turmeric powder
1 small ball of tamarind
5-6 red chillies*
1 small bulb of garlic

*Fry in coconut oil

1. Wash, peel and cut the potatoes into 3.5 cms cubes. 2. Boil and cook the cubes with salt in the water. 3. Grind the coconut gratings, turmeric powder, tamarind and fried chillies together. 4. Add the fried coriander seeds and grind the masala fine. 5. Add this to the potato cubes and boil until the masala blends well to form a liquid gravy. Remove the vessel from the flame. 6. Prepare a seasoning with crushed garlic fried in oil until light brown and add it to the dish.

20. Ambat

250 gms potatoes
700 ml water
1-1 ½ tsp salt
1 large onion chopped
1 tbsp ghee or coconut oil for seasoning
¾ coconut gratings
½ tsp turmeric powder
1 small ball of tamarind
5-6 red chillies
¼ tsp fenugreek seeds
½ tbsp groundnut oil

1. Wash, peel and cut the potatoes into large cubes. 2. Boil and cook the cubes with salt in the water. 3. Grind the coconut gratings, turmeric powder, tamarind and fried chillies together. 4. Lastly add the fried fenugreek seeds and grind the masala fine. 5. Add this to the potato cubes and boil until the masala blends well to form a liquid gravy. Remove the vessel from the flame. 6. Prepare a seasoning with chopped onions fried in ghee or oil to a light brown colour and add it to the dish.

21. Kaap

½ kg potatoes
1 tsp salt
1 ½ tsps chilli powder
rice flour or jowar flour
groundnut oil for deep frying

1. Wash, peel and cut the potatoes into rounds, ¾ cm thick. 2. Apply salt and chilli powder and allow it to stand for about 15 minutes. 3. When the water separates, add rice flour or jowar flour enough to mix with the water. 4. Heat the oil in a frying pan and deep fry the potato rounds until reddish brown.

22. Wafers

½ kg potatoes
salt to taste
groundnut oil for deep frying

1. Wash, peel and cut the potatoes into very thin slices. 2. Mix salt in water according to the quantity of potato slices. 3. Heat the

oil in a frying pan, put a few potato slices in it and when they are half fried, add some salt water with a teaspoon. 4. Allow the wafers to fry until they are crisp. 5. When all the wafers are fried allow them to cool and then store them in a glass jar or in an air-tight container to stay crisp.

23. Chips (sali)

½ kg potatoes	½ tsp cumin seeds*
groundnut oil for deep frying	8-10 pepper corns*
salt to taste	

*Powdered together

1. Wash, peel and cut potatoes into 4 cms long and ½ or ¾ cm broad chips. 2. Mix the salt in water according to the quantity of potato chips. 3. Heat oil in a frying pan and put some potato chips. When they are half fried add some salt water with a teaspoon. 4. Allow the chips to fry until golden brown and crisp. Spread them on a flat surface and sprinkle cumin and pepper powder. 5. Allow them to cool and then store in an air-tight container.

24. Fritters

½ kg potatoes	1 handful coriander leaves*
salt to taste	8-10 green chillies*
1 tsp chilli powder	250 gms onions*
groundnut oil for deep frying	1 measure bengal gram flour

*Chopped fine

1. Boil, peel and cut the potatoes into small pieces. 2. Add salt, chilli powder and chopped ingredients and mix well. 3. Add the gram flour and blend thoroughly. 4. Make small balls of the mixture. 5. Heat oil in a frying pan and deep fry the potato balls until reddish brown.

25. Vade

½ kg potatoes	12 green chillies chopped
½ coconut gratings	2 handful coriander leaves chopped
salt to taste	1 handful curry leaves chopped
juice of ½ lemon	1 measure bengal gram flour
water to mix	
groundnut oil to deep fry	

1. Boil, peel and cut potatoes into small pieces. 2. Add the chopped ingredients, coconut gratings, salt and lemon juice to the potato pieces and mix well. 3. Take portions of the mixture and shape

them into small balls. 4. Prepare a thick batter mixing the gram flour with water and some salt. 5. Heat the oil in a frying pan. 6. Dip the potato balls in the gram flour batter and deep fry in oil until they are light brown.

26. Pattice (variety 1)

½ kg potatoes
4 onions chopped fine
1-1½ tsps ghee
salt to taste
ghee for deep frying
8-10 green chillies chopped fine
1 handful coriander leaves chopped fine
1 handful coconut gratings
1 measure coarsely ground rice flour or bread-crumbs.

1. Boil and peel the potatoes. Divide them into two portions; take one portion of potatoes and cut them into small pieces; mash the other portion and add salt to it. 2. Heat 1-1½ tbsps ghee and fry the chopped onions to light brown colour. 3. Add them to the potato pieces along with some salt, coconut gratings, chopped chillies, and coriander leaves, and blend well. 4. Prepare round balls with the mixture (about the size of a lemon). 5. Take a portion of mashed potatoes, flatten it on the palm, stuff it with the potato mixture ball and cover it fully with the mashed potato from all sides. Shape it into a round ball. 6. Roll each ball in rice flour or bread-crumbs. 7. Heat ghee in a frying pan and deep fry the potato pattice until golden brown.

27. Pattice (variety 2)

½ kg potatoes (peeled and cut into small pieces)
250 gms onions chopped fine
juice of ½ lemon
250 grams potatoes washed, boiled, peeled
1 handful flour (maida)
salt to taste
10 chillies green*
1 handful coriander leaves*
8-10 garlic cloves*
1 small piece of ginger*
1 handful coconut gratings*
ghee to fry
1 measure coarsely ground rice flour or bread-crumbs

* Grind to paste

1. Wash, peel and cut the potatoes into small pieces. 2. Heat 1 tbsp ghee in a frying pan and fry chopped onions to light brown colour. 3. Put in the potato pieces and fry them for a few minutes. 4. Add the ground masala paste and lemon juice and cook further until the potato pieces are tender. 5. Allow it to cool, mash slightly and form small balls of the mixture (size of a lemon) and keep aside. 6. Mix the flour and some salt with 250 gms boiled, peeled and mashed potatoes and blend well 7. Take

a small portion and flatten it on the palm. 8. Stuff it with potato mixture ball and cover it fully with mashed potato from all sides. Shape into a ball and flatten slightly. 9. Roll each pattice in rice flour or bread-crumbs. 10. Heat a little ghee on a hot plate and fry the pattice on both sides to a golden brown colour.

NOTE: As a variant, green peas or any other vegetable may be used for stuffing.

28. Cutlet (variety 1)

- 125 gms potatoes (peeled and cut fine)
- 2 kg green peas
- 8-10 garlic cloves chopped
- salt to taste
- a small piece of ginger
- 8-10 green chillies-chopped fine
- 250 gms onions
- 1 handful flour (maida)
- 1 measure coarsely ground rice flour or bread-crumbs
- ghee to fry

1. Steam and cook together the potato pieces, peas, chopped garlic and ginger. 2. Add salt and allow it to cool. 3. Heat ghee in a small frying pan and fry the chopped onions until light brown. 4. Add flour and fry for two minutes. 5. Mix in the vegetables, remove the pan from the fire. 6. When it cools take small portions of the mixture (size of a lemon) and form into a thick flat round. 7. Roll each cutlet in the flour or bread-crumbs and fry them on both sides on a hot plate with a little ghee, on a medium flame.

29. Cutlet (variety 2)

- 125 gms potatoes
- 2 kg green peas
- 250 gms oinions
- ghee to fry
- salt to taste
- 8-10 pepper corns powdered
- 2 tsps sugar
- 1 handful flour (maida)
- 1 measure coarse rice flour or bread-crumbs

1. Steam and cook potatoes and peas. 2. Cut the potatoes into small pieces. 3. Chop onions fine and fry them in ghee until light brown. 4. Add flour and fry slightly. 5. Put in the vegetables and fry for some minutes. 6. Add salt, pepper powder, and sugar. 7. Mash the mixture and prepare small flat rounds to form cutlets. Roll them in rice flour or bread-crumbs. Heat some ghee on a hot plate and fry the cutlets on both sides on a medium flame.

30. Green potatoes

- 1 bunch of Amaranth (Chavali) or any other leafy vegetable
- 1½ tbsp butter
- ½-1 tsp pepper powder
- salt to taste
- 2 large potatoes

1. Sprinkle some salt on the leafy vegetable. Hold the stalks and beat with a whisk to remove little worms, if any. Sort out the leaves from the tough stalks, wash and cut them fine. Cook them in a vessel with 1 tbsp butter until tender. 2. Wash potatoes, peel and grate them. Add salt, pepper powder, flour and remaining butter and mix them together. Prepare small balls of this mixture. 3. Heat about 3-4 measures of water with some salt in a vessel and while it is boiling continuously put in the vegetable balls and allow them to boil. Take them out when they are cooked. Put them in the cooked green vegetable and serve.

NOTE: As a variant finely chopped onions, green chillies and coriander leaves may be used instead of pepper powder.

31. Potato ribbon

½ kg potatoes
ghee or groundnut oil for deep frying
salt and pepper powder to taste

1. Wash potatoes, remove skin and peel them one by one in the form of a continuous ribbon, taking care not to break it as far as possible. 2. Heat ghee or oil in a frying pan and deep fry the potato ribbons, stirring them from time to time, until they are golden brown. 3. Place the ribbons on a plate and sprinkle salt and pepper powder. Serve while hot and crisp with sauce.

Yam

Imp: Yam should not be washed with bare hands. It should be allowed to dry after washing and then cut or grated otherwise hands start itching.

1. Sukke

½ kg yam
½ tsp mustard seeds
a few curry leaves
½ tbsp oil
salt and jaggery to taste
1 ½ measure water
¼ coconut gratings*
¼ tsp turmeric powder*
4-6 red chillies*
1 small ball of tamarind*
1 tsp coriander seeds*
½ tsp blackgram dal*
½ tsp fenugreek seeds*

*Fry in 1 tablespoon oil

1. Skin the yam, wash and cut into 1 cm cubes. 2. Prepare a seasoning of mustard seeds and curry leaves in coconut oil and put in the cubes. 3. Add salt, jaggery and water and allow to cook until soft. 4. Grind the masala with coconut gratings, turmeric powder, chillies and tamarind. 5. When fairly fine, add the fried coriander seeds, blackgram dal and fenugreek seeds, and grind to a paste. 6. Add this masala to the yam cubes and bring it to boil. Remove the dish from the flame.

2. Upkari

½ kg yam
4 tsps coconut oil
½ tsp mustard seeds
salt and jaggery to taste
4-5 green chillies sliced
1 handful coconut gratings

1. Skin the yam, wash and cut it into very fine pieces. 2. Heat oil in a shallow vessel and put in the mustard seeds. Allow them to splutter, then add the yam pieces. Cook them by steaming. 3. When half cooked add salt, jaggery, and sliced chillies and steam further until the yam pieces are tender. 4. When the dish is fairly dry, add the coconut gratings and mix it well.

3. Talasani

½ kg yam
2 tbsps groundnut oil
½ tsp mustard seeds
1 pinch asafoetida
¼ tsp cumin seeds
2 tsps chilli powder
salt to taste

1. Skin the yam, wash and cut it into very small pieces. 2. Heat oil in a frying pan and prepare a seasoning with mustard seeds. Allowing them to splutter, add asafoetida, cumin seeds and chilli powder. 3. Put in the yam pieces and salt and cover the dish with a lid. Cook by steam on a low flame until the yam is tender and the talasani is dry.

4. Koshimbir

½ kg yam
groundnut oil for deep frying
juice of ½ lemon
2 onions
3-4 green chillies
salt to taste
¼ coconut gratings

1. Skin the yam, wash and grate it, or cut it into fine pieces. Apply salt and after a few minutes squeeze out the water content of the

yam. 2. Heat the oil in a frying pan and deep fry the grated yam until reddish brown and crisp. 3. Slice the green chillies and chop the onions fine. 4. Mix them together with fried yam and salt to taste, coconut gratings, and lemon juice just before serving. The addition of onions is optional.

5. Raita

125 gms yam
½ coconut gratings
4-5 green chillies
½ tsp mustard seeds
1-1½ tbsp ghee
salt to taste
½ measure curds

1. Skin the yam, wash and dry. Grate the yam or cut it very fine. 2. Heat a hot plate and using a little ghee, fry the yam until crisp. 3. Likewise fry the green chillies and mustard seeds separately. 4. Grind the coconut gratings, add the fried chillies and mustard seeds, and grind further to a fine mix. 5. Just before serving, mix the ground masala, salt, curds and the fried yam together.

6. Kaap

½ kg yam
salt to taste
½ tsp chilli powder
1 handful coarsly ground rice flour or jowar flour
groundnut oil for deep frying

1. Skin the yam, wash and cut it into 4-5 cms square and ½ cm. thick pieces. 2. Apply salt and chilli powder and keep for about 15-20 minutes. 3. When the water separates, add rice or jowar flour, enough to mix with the water. 4. Heat oil in a frying pan and deep fry the yam pieces until reddish brown and well cooked.

7. Wafers

½ kg yam
½ tsp chilli powder
1 handful coarsely ground rice flour or jowar flour
groundnut oil for deep frying

1. Skin the yam, wash and cut it into very thin 4 cm square slices. Method is same as above for kaap.

NOTE: If the yam gives an itch, apply a little tamarind to the pieces, or when half-cooked strain the water and add fresh water to the yam to cook further.

8. Ghashhi

125 gms yam
½ litre water
salt to taste
1 tbsp coconut oil or ghee for seasoning
1 small garlic bulb
¾ coconut gratings
½ tsp turmeric powder
1 small ball of tamarind
4-5 red chillies
3 tsp coriander seeds
½ tbsp coconut oil to fry

Method is same as for potato ghashhi.

9. Ambat

250 gms yam
½ litre water
1-1 ½ tsp salt
½ tbsp coconut oil to fry
1 large onion chopped
1 tbsp ghee or coconut oil for seasoning
¾ coconut gratings
½ tsp turmeric powder
1 small ball of tamarind
4-5 red chillies
¼ tsp fenugreek seeds
¼ tsp onion seeds

Method is the same as for potato ambat.

10. Koot (Fresh Pickle)

250 gms yam
6 red chillies *
2 tsp. mustard seeds*
½ tsp. fenugreek seeds*
1 pinch asafoetida*
2 tsp grated coconut*
½ tsp turmeric powder*
salt to taste
tamarind (small ball)
½ cup oil for frying

*fry in a little oil

1. Skin the yam. Wash and cut it into very fine pieces. **2.** Apply salt to the pieces, squeeze and deep fry till crisp and spread for a while on a brown paper to drain off the extra oil. **3.** Remove the oil (when cool) in a container and keep aside. **4.** In the same pan fry the other ingredients one by one adding turmeric to the fried coconut last. **5.** Grind together all the fried ingredients, along with the tamarind to a fine paste. **6.** Add salt and a little water and add the masala to the fried yam and blend well. This pickle lasts for two or three days in a fridge.

NOTE : 1. Brinjal and bitter gourd pickle can also be prepared similarly. 2. Instead of frying, put the yam pieces in hot water and strain. Add salt and tamrind and steam cook till soft.

Brinjals

1. Sukke (variety 1)

½ kg tender brinjals
6 drumsticks
½ tbsp groundnut oil or ghee to fry
½ tsp mustard seeds
few curry leaves
1 tbsp oil or ghee for seasoning
salt and jaggery to taste
¼ coconut gratings
¼ tsp turmeric powder
1 small ball of tamarind
½ tsp black gram dal*
¼ tsp fenugreek seeds*
4-6 red chillies*
1 tsp coriander seeds*

* Fry in oil

1. Wash and cut brinjals into 4 cms long and 2 cms broad pieces. Dip them in some water for a few minutes. 2. Scrape a little the outer skin of the drumsticks and cut them into four cms long pieces. 3. Heat the oil or ghee in a vessel, prepare seasoning with mustard seeds and curry leaves. Put in the drumstick pieces and cook them half with the help of some water. 4. Then add the brinjal pieces, salt and jaggery and cook further until the vegetables are tender. 5. Grind coarsely coconut gratings, turmeric powder, chillies and tamarind together; then add the fried spices and grind further to a fairly fine paste. 6. Add this to the cooked vegetables, with some water to form a thick gravy. Mix well and bring it to boil.

2. Sukke (variety 2)

½ kg brinjals
250 gms onions
1 tbsp groundnut oil
1 pinch asafoetida
¼ tsp cumin seeds
salt and jaggery to taste
¼ coconut gratings
1 small ball of tamarind
½ tsp cumin seeds
5-6 green chillies
1 tsp coriander seeds*
4 cloves*
1 cm cinnamon*

*fry in groundnut oil

1. Wash and cut the brinjals into large pieces. 2. Cut the onions fine. 3. Grind coconut gratings, tamarind, cumin seeds, and fried spices. 4. Heat the oil in a vessel and prepare a seasoning with

cumin seeds and asafoetida. 5. Add the cut onions and fry them for a few minutes. 6. Put in brinjal pieces and allow them to cook with the help of some water. 7. Add salt, jaggery and the ground masala, and bring it to boil.

NOTE: As a variety, potatoes, peeled and cut into large cubes can be used with brinjals, in which case, the brinjal pieces should be added after the potatoes are half cooked.

3. Stuffed brinjals, whole (variety 1)

½ kg small brinjals
2 tbsp groundnut oil
1 pinch asafoetida
½ tsp turmeric powder
2 tsps amti masala powder*
1 handful coconut gratings*
pulp of tamarind*
salt and jaggery to taste*
1 large onion chopped fine*

*Mix together

1. Wash and slit the brinjals into four pieces without removing the stems. Dip the brinjals in water for some minutes. 2. Take them out and stuff them with the mixed masala. 3. Heat oil in a shallow vessel or frying pan and prepare a seasoning with asafoetida and turmeric powder. 4. Put in the stuffed brinjals, stir them in the seasoning for a while, cover them with a lid and steam-cook over a low flame until the brinjals are tender.

4. Stuffed brinjals (variety 2)

½ kg small round brinjals
1 tsp salt
groundnut oil for deep frying
bread-crumbs or coarsely ground rice flour
a handful of cooked rice*
salt and pepper powder to taste*
2 tbsp tomato sauce or ketchup*

*Mix together

1. Wash and cut the brinjals breadthwise into two pieces. Apply salt and keep aside for 20 minutes. Press the pieces between the palms and squeeze out the water if any. 2. Heat oil in a frying pan and deep fry the pieces, until half fried. 3. Scrape out the core of the brinjal pieces carefully. 4 Add the cooked core to the mixed masala ingredients and blend well. 5. Stuff small portions of this mixture into the hollow brinjal cups, top up with bread crumbs or rice flour and fry them again until light brown.

5. Bhulbhulavani

½ kg brinjals
2 onions chopped fine
5 tbsps groundnut oil
salt to taste
1 handful chopped
  coriander leaves
3 red chillies
½ tsp coriander seeds
3 cloves
1 small piece of cinnamon
¼ grated coconut
4 garlic cloves

1. Cut brinjals into fine pieces and keep them dipped in sufficient water for some time and drain. 2. Fry chillies, coriander seeds, cloves and cinnamon in a little oil. 3. Grind coconut. Add garlic and fried spices and again grind to a paste. 4. Fry the chopped onions in 4 tbsps oil. 5. Apply salt to the drained brinjal pieces, and add them to the fried onion and fry a little. 6. Add the ground masala, and mix well and fry again till the brinjal pieces are soft. 7. Add chopped coriander, mix well and remove the dish from the fire.

NOTE: As a variant, small whole onions and whole potatoes (peeled) can be used along with brinjals. The dish can also be prepared with vegetables like kovai and ladies fingers.

6. Talasani

750 gms brinjals
1 tsp chilli powder
jaggery and salt to taste
1 tbsp groundnut oil
  or coconut oil
1 tsp mustard seeds
1 tsp black gram dal

1. Cut the brinjals 4 cms long and 2 cms broad. 2. Dip them in water for a few minutes. 3. Take them out and apply chilli powder, salt and jaggery. 4. Heat oil in a shallow vessel and prepare a seasoning with mustard seeds and black gram dal. 5. Put in the brinjal pieces and fry them for 5 minutes. 6. Cover the dish with lid and steam-cook until the pieces are tender and dry.

7. Pachadi

250 gms tender green mangoes
250 gms tender brinjals
salt to taste
jaggery, size of a lemon
a few curry leaves
6 green chillies chopped fine
½ coconut gratings, ground finely
1 tbsp ghee or groundnut oil
½ tsp mustard seeds

1. Wash and peel the tender mangoes and brinjals. 2. Cut them into very fine pieces. 3. Mix them together with salt, jaggery, ground coconut and chopped chillies in a vessel. 4. Heat ghee or

oil in a seasoning ladle and fry the mustard seeds and curry leaves. Add the seasoning to the dish.

8. Koshimbir

½ kg brinjals
salt to taste
groundnut oil or coconut oil to fry
3 green chillies - sliced
2 onions chopped fine
1/8 coconut gratings
juice of ½ lemon

1. Wash and cut the brinjals into very small pieces. 2. Apply salt and keep aside. 3. Squeeze out the water and fry them crisp in oil on a medium flame. 4. Just before serving, mix salt, sliced chillies, chopped onions, coconut gratings, lemon juice together. 5. Add the fried brinjal pieces and blend together.

9. Bhareet (variety 1)

750 gms large brinjals
5 tbsps groundnut oil
½ tsp mustard seeds
a few curry leaves
7-8 green chillies—fried in ghee*
½ coconut gratings*
1 small ball of tamarind*
salt to taste*

*Grind together

1. Wash the brinjals. 2. Apply oil to the outer skin. 3. Roast on a direct low flame, turning them every few minutes until they are cooked. 4. When fairly cool remove the skin and stems, cut or mash the roasted brinjals slightly. 5. Mix in the ground masala and blend well. 6. Heat 1 tbsp oil in the iron ladle and prepare a seasoning with mustard seeds and curry leaves. Add it to the mixture. Instead of tamarind, ½ measure curds can be added.

10. Bhareet (variety 2)

750 gms large brinjals
1-2 onions chopped fine
½-1 measure curds
3-5 red chillies*
½ coconut gratings*
salt to taste*

* Grind together

1. Wash the brinjals. Apply oil to the outer skin. Roast them on a direct flame, turning them every few minutes, until they are well cooked. 2. When cool, remove the skin and stems. 3. Mash the roasted brinjals slightly. Mix the ground masala, chopped onions and curds together and blend with the mashed brinjals.

11. Bhareet (variety 3)

750 gms large brinjals
2-3 tbsp groundnut oil
1 handful coconut gratings
a few chopped coriander leaves
6-7 green chillies
1 small piece of ginger
salt to taste
1 measure curds

1. Wash the brinjals. Apply oil to the outer skin and roast on direct flame, turning them from time to time. 2. When well cooked remove them from the flame and keep aside to cool. 3. Peel off the roasted skin and mash the roasted brinjals slightly. 4. Mix together and crush the finely cut chillies, ginger and salt. 5. Add the mashed brinjals, coconut gratings, coriander leaves and curds. Blend well.

NOTE: Instead of curds, juice of ½ lemon may be added.

12. Kaap

½ kg tender brinjals
salt and chilli powder to taste
coarsely ground rice flour
groundnut oil or ghee for frying.

1. Wash and cut the brinjals into rounds ½ cm thick. 2. Apply salt and chilli powder. 3. After 15 minutes, roll them in the coarse rice flour just enough to coat the brinjal slices. 4. Heat oil or ghee, fry the brinjal slices until light brown. Shallow fry or deep fry as desired.

13. Fritters (Bhaje) (variety 1)

½ kg tender brinjals
1 ½ measures bengal gram flour
salt to taste
1 tsp chilli powder
1 pinch asafoetida
½ tsp turmeric powder
groundnut oil for deep frying

1. Wash and cut the brinjals into rounds ½ cm thick. 2. Apply salt and chilli powder. 3. After 15 minutes, roll them on the coarse rice flour just enough to coat the brinjal slices. 4. Heat oil or ghee, fry the brinjal slices until light brown. Shallow fry or deep fr as desired.

14. Fritters (variety 2)

½ kg tender brinjals
1½ measures bengal gram flour
salt to taste
1 tsp chilli powder
1 pinch asafoetida
½ tsp turmeric powder
groundnut oil for deep frying

1. Wash and cut the brinjals into thin rounds. 2. Mix gram flour, salt, chilli powder, asafoetida and turmeric powder in water enough to make a thick batter. 3. Heat oil in a frying pan, dip the brinjal rounds in the batter to coat them evenly and deep fry, turning them from time to time, until reddish brown.

NOTE: Potato fritters can also be prepared similarly.

15. Sambhare

- 1 measure red gram dal
- 700 ml water to cook dal and brinjals
- 125 gms brinjals, cut into big cubes
- ½ tbsp coconut oil
- 1 small bulb of garlic
- 1 tbsp ghee or oil for seasoning
- ¼ cup coconut gratings
- ½ tsp turmeric powder
- 1 small ball of tamarind
- 4-5 red chillies*
- 3 tsp coriander seeds*

*Fry in coconut oil

1. Wash the dal and cook it in water. 2. When half cooked, add the brinjal pieces and cook further until they are tender and then add salt. 3. Grind the coconut gratings, turmeric powder, tamarind and fried chillies together. Lastly add the fried coriander seeds and grind the masala fine. 4. Add this to the dal and brinjal and bring it to a boil, until the masala blends well to form a liquid gravy. 5. Remove the vessel from flame. 6. Prepare a seasoning with crushed garlic fried in oil until light brown and add it to the dish.

NOTE: Instead of coriander seeds, fenugreek seeds can be fried and used. So also the seasoning can be of fried chopped onions.

16. Ghashhi

- 125 gms brinjals
- ½ litre water
- salt to taste
- 1 tbsp coconut oil or ghee for seasoning
- 1 small bulb of garlic
- ¾ coconut gratings
- ½ tsp turmeric powder
- 1 small ball of tamarind
- 5-6 red chillies
- ½ tbsp coconut oil to fry

Method: Follow the instructions given for potato ghashhi.

Radish

1. Sukke

½ kg radish
250 gms onions
1 ½ tsp salt
jaggery to taste
½ tsp mustard seeds
1 tbsp coconut oil for seasoning

¼ coconut gratings
½ tsp turmeric powder
1 small ball of tamarind
6 red chillies*
2 tsp coriander seeds*

*Fry in groundnut oil

1. Wash and cut radish into small pieces. Cut onions also into cubes. 2. Boil and cook both together in water with some salt until tender. Add jaggery. 3. Grind the masala with coconut gratings, turmeric powder, tamarind and fried chillies. Add the fried coriander seeds and grind further until it is fine. 4. Add the masala to the cooked vegetables and bring it to boil. 5. Heat the oil and prepare seasoning with the mustard seeds and add it to the dish.

NOTE: This dish can be prepared without using onions.

2. Sukki bhaji (variety 1)

½ kg radish
250 gms onions
¼ coconut gratings*
¼ tsp cumin seeds*

pulp of a small ball of tamarind
1-1 ½ tbsps groundnut oil
salt and jaggery to taste
2 tsp amti or garam masala powder

*Grind together

1. Wash and cut the radish into cubes. 2. Chop the onions and fry them in oil. 3. Add the radish pieces and cook them with some water until tender. 4. Put in the tamarind pulp, salt, jaggery, amti or garam masala, and ground coconut and cumin seeds. 5. Stir well and allow to simmer for a few minutes.

3. Sukki bhaji (variety 2)

½ kg radish
1 handful cashewnut pieces
salt and jaggery to taste
½ tbsp ghee

¼ coconut gratings*
3 red chillies*
½ tsp mustard seeds

* Grind together

1. Wash and grate the radish. 2. Boil and cook the radish with cashewnut pieces, salt and jaggery. 3. Add the ground masala, bring it to boil and remove it from the stove. 4. Prepare seasoning with mustard seeds fried in ghee and add it to the bhaji.

4. Koshimbir

½ kg radish
juice of ½ lemon
salt to taste
6 green chillies
2 onions
¼ coconut gratings

1. Wash and grate the radish. Apply salt and keep it aside for a few minutes. Squeeze out the water. 2. Chop the onions fine, slice the chillies and mix chopped onions and chillies with the coconut gratings. 3. Add this to the grated radish and blend well. 4. Lastly add the lemon juice and salt if necessary.

NOTE: Instead of chopped onions, a seasoning of mustard seeds can be added to the koshimbir.

5. Kochholi

½ kg radish
4 green chillies
1 small piece of ginger
1 tbsp ghee or oil
salt to taste
½-1 cup curds
¼ coconut gratings ground
½ tsp mustard seeds
a few curry leaves

1. Wash and cut radish very fine (as if grated). 2. Chop chillies and ginger fine, add salt and crush. Add them to the radish. 3. Add ground coconut gratings and curds. 4. Heat ghee or oil in a ladle and prepare a seasoning with mustard seeds and curry leaves. Add this to the dish.

NOTE: A little ginger may be added to the grated coconut while grinding.

6. Raita

½ kg radish
salt to taste
1 tsp mustard seeds
a few curry leaves
¼ coconut gratings*
3 green chillies*
½ cup curds
1 tbsp ghee or oil for seasoning

*Grind together

1. Wash and cut radish into tiny pieces. 2. Steam-cook them until tender. Remove from the stove. Allow to cool. 3. Add the

ground coconut and chillies, salt and curds, and mix well. 4. Heat the oil and prepare a seasoning with mustard seeds and curry leaves. Add it to the raita.

7. Phodyo

½ kg radish
groundnut oil for deep frying
jaggery and salt to taste*
1 tsp chilli powder*
1 tbsp black gram dal*
2 tbsp rice*
1 small ball of tamarind*

*Grind to thick paste

1. Wash and cut the radish into flat pieces, 4 cm long and 1 cm thick. Press them slightly with a pastel. Dip them in cold water for 15 minutes. 2. Strain and apply the ground masala paste. 3. Heat the oil in a frying pan and deep fry the pieces until they are reddish brown and tender.

8. Ghashhi

½ kg radish
½ litre water
salt to taste
1 tbsp coconut oil or ghee for seasoning
¾ coconut gratings
½ tsp turmeric powder
1 small ball of tamarind
7-8 red chillies*
3 tsps coriander seeds*

* Fry in coconut oil

Method: Follow the instructions given for potato ghashhi.

9. Radish leaf bhaji (variety 1)

½ kg radish leaves
1 tbsp coconut or groundnut oil
1 handful coconut gratings
1 tsp jaggery
½ tsp chilli powder
½ tsp mustard seeds
1 pinch asafoetida
2 handfuls bengal gram dal (soaked in water)
1 tsp salt

1. Wash the radish leaves and cut them fine. 2. Heat oil in a vessel or frying pan and prepare a seasoning with mustard seeds. Allowing them to splutter add asafoetida. 3. Add the washed gram dal and fry for a minute or two. 4. Put in the cut leaves and allow them to cook with the help of some water. 5. When the dal and leaves are well cooked, add salt, jaggery, chilli powder and coconut gratings and cook for 5-10 minutes.

10. Radish leaf bhaji (variety 2)

½ kg radish leaves
½ kg onions
salt and jaggery to taste
1½-2 tbsps groundnut oil
1 pinch asafoetida
¼ tsp cumin seeds

1. Wash the radish leaves and cut fine. 2. Chop the onions. 3. Heat oil in a vessel and prepare a seasoning with asafoetida and cumin seeds. 4. Add the chopped onions, and fry them to golden colour. 5. Put in the leaves, salt and jaggery. Steam-cook till the leaves are tender.

Carrots

---

1. Sukke

½ kg carrots
½ tsp mustard seeds
a few curry leaves
½ tbsp oil
salt and jaggery to taste
1½ measure water
¼ coconut gratings
¼ tsp turmeric powder
1 small ball of tamarind
1½ tsp coriander seeds*
½ tsp blackgram dal*
½ tsp fenugreek seeds*

*Fry with one table spoon oil

Wash and cut the carrots into 1 cm cubes.
Method: Follow the instructions given for yam sukke.

2. Raita

½ kg carrots
salt to taste
½ tsp mustard seeds
a few curry leaves
1 tbsp ghee or oil for seasoning
¼ coconut gratings*
6 green chillies*
½-1 cup curds

*Grind together

1. Wash and cut the carrots into tiny pieces. 2. Steam-cook them until tender. 3. Keep aside and allow them to cool.
Method: Follow the instructions given for radish raita.

3. Phodyo

½ kg carrots
groundnut oil for frying
1 small ball of tamarind*
salt to taste*
1 tsp chilli powder*
1 tbsp black gram dal*
2 tbsp rice*

*Grind to thick paste

1. Wash and cut carrots into flat pieces, 4 cm long and ½cm thick.
2. Press them slightly with a pestle.

Method: Follow the instructions given for phodyo of radish.

4. Koshimbir

½ kg carrots
juice of ½ lemon
salt to taste
6 green chillies
2 onions
¼ coconut gratings

1. Wash and grate the carrots. **2.** Chop the onions fine. **3.** Slice the chillies. **4.** Mix together chillies, salt, chopped onions, coconut gratings and lemon juice in grated carrots and blend well.

Beetroot

---

1. Sukke

½ kg beetroot
½ tsp mustard seeds
a few curry leaves
½ tbsp coconut oil
salt to taste
1 ½ measures water
¼ coconut gratings
¼ tsp turmeric powder
1 small ball of tamarind
1 ½ tsp corriander seeds*
½ tsp black gram dal*
¼ tsp fenugreek seeds*

*Fry in 1 tablespoon coconut oil

Wash, peel off the skin of the beetroot, and cut them into 1 cm cubes.

Method: Follow the instructions given for yam sukke.

2. Raita

½ kg beetroot
salt to taste
¼ tbsp ghee
3-4 green chillies-sliced
½-1 measure curds
½ tsp cumin seeds

1. Wash the beetroot and steam-cook until tender. 2. Peel off the skin and cut the beetroot into small cubes. Keep aside and allow them to cool. 3. Mix salt, chillies and curds. 4. Prepare a seasoning with cumin seeds fried in ghee and add it to raita.

3. Koshimbir (sliced)

½ kg beetroot
250 gms onions
salt to taste
3-4 green chillies-sliced
1 handful coriander leaves chopped
125 gms curds

1. Wash the beetroot and steam-cook until tender. 2. Peel off the skin and cut the beetroot into thin slices about ½ cm thick. 3. Slice the onions and add salt, green chillies and coriander leaves. 4. Mix in the beetroot slices and curds. Lemon juice may be used instead of curds.

NOTE: Thinly sliced ripe tomatoes can also be added to the koshimbir.

4. Beetroot cup-salad

½ kg small sized beetroots
vinegar, salt and pepper powder to taste
1 tbsp salad oil
1 measure curds
a bunch of lettuce leaves
2 small cucumbers
1 handful celery stalks
2 small onions
2 potatoes*
a few french beans*

* Boiled and cooked

1. Wash, steam-cook and peel off the skin of the beetroots. 2. Cut each beetroot into halves breadthwise. 3. Scrape off the inner part of the halves and form cup containers. 4. Apply the mixture of vinegar, salt, pepper powder and salad oil to the cups. 5. Chop all the vegetables and mix them with curds and salt. 6. Fill each cup with this mixture. 7. Take a flat dish, arrange lettuce leaves (dipped in iced water to stay crisp) all round, and place the beetroot cups in the centre before serving.

5. Rainbow salad

1 bunch lettuce leaves
2 hard boiled eggs-sliced
2 carrots, grated
1 beetroot, cooked and sliced thinly
2 cucumbers*
1 turnip*
2 ripe tomatoes*
1 lemon slice
2 tbsps salad oil

*Cut into thin slices

1. Take a flat dish or plate and arrange the finely chopped lettuce leaves (dipped in iced water to stay crisp) all round. 2. Arrange the boiled egg slices in the centre of the dish in a circle. 3. The next layer all around the egg slices should be of sliced cucumber and turnips. 4. Take the grated carrot and arrange it alternately with tomato slices. 5. The last outer circle should be of beetroot. Take care not to cover the lettuce leaves completely. A ring of lettuce leaves should show. Pour salad oil all over the layers of vegetables.

(This salad can also be prepared without using eggs)

Tomatoes

---

1. Koshimbir

½ kg ripe tomatoes
250 gms onions
salt to taste
3-4 green chillies-sliced
1 handful of coriander leaves
125 gms curds

1. Wash the tomatoes and slice them thinly. 2. Cut the onions into thin slices. 3. Add salt and chillies to the onions and mix well. 4. Then mix the tomato slices, coriander leaves, curds and blend together.

2. Raita

½ kg ripe tomatoes
¼ coconut gratings*
½ red chilli*
jaggery and salt to taste
½ tsp mustard seeds
a few curry leaves
¼ tsp ghee or groundnut oil

*Grind together

1. Wash and cut the tomatoes into cubes. 2. Grind grated coconut, chillies and tomato cubes together. Add jaggery and salt to taste. 3. Prepare a seasoning with mustard seeds and curry leaves in ghee or oil, and add it to the raita.

NOTE: As a variant boil tomato cubes, add 2 to 3 green chillies and grind them with grated coconut.

3. Saar

250 gms ripe tomatoes
2 litres water
4 green chillies-sliced
1 tsp salt
2 tsps jaggery or sugar
¼ coconut gratings-extract juice
½ tsp mustard seeds*
10-12 curry leaves*
½ tbsp ghee*
pinch of asafoetida*

*for seasoning

1. Wash and cut the tomatoes into cubes. 2. Add water and chillies to the tomatoes and cook thoroughly. 3. Add salt, jaggery and coconut juice, bring it to boil. 4. Prepare a seasoning with mustard seeds and curry leaves in ghee and add it to the saar.

NOTE: 1. Instead of mustard seeds and curry leaves seasoning, chopped onion fried in ghee can be used. 2. Instead of coconut juice, 1 tbsp coconut gratings, ¼ tsp cummin seeds and the cooked tomatoes should be ground to a paste for making saar. Add enough water and boil. Add the seasoning of mustard seeds and curry leaves.

4. Soup

½ kg ripe tomatoes
4 litres water
2 large onions
2 tbsps ghee
1 tbsp flour (maida)
8 pepper corns powdered
sugar and salt to taste

1. Wash, cut and grind the tomatoes and boil them in water until thoroughly cooked. 2. Chop onions fine. 3. Heat ghee in a small frying pan and fry onions till they are of light golden colour; add flour and fry for 2 minutes. 4. Blend it with cooked tomatoes and boil. 5. Add pepper powder, sugar and salt. 6. Strain the soup before serving.

5. Tomato sheer

½ kg ripe tomatoes cut into small pieces
2 onions chopped
3 green chillies sliced
1 small piece of ginger sliced
½ tsp chilli powder
½ coconut gratings, extract thick and thin juice separately.
2 tbsps ghee or groundnut oil
½ tsp mustard seeds
¼ tsp cumin seeds
a few curry leaves
½ tsp turmeric powder
1 pinch asafoetida
2 tbsps bengal gram flour
salt and sugar to taste
1 handful coriander leaves

1. Heat ghee or oil in a vessel and prepare a seasoning with mustard seeds, cumin seeds and curry leaves. 2. Add chopped onions, chillies and ginger. Fry for a few minutes. 3. Put in the tomato pieces. Cover the vessel with the lid and allow them to cook on a low flame. 4. Mix turmeric and chilli powder, asafoetida and gram flour in the thin coconut juice. 5. Pour it into the tomatoes and bring to boil. 6. While it simmers, add thick coconut juice, salt and sugar. 7. Lastly, put in the chopped coriander leaves. This dish will have a saffron colour when ready.

6. Tomato santosh

½ kg ripe tomatoes
7–8 red chillies
3 large onions
1 handful coconut gratings
salt and jaggery to taste
1 pinch turmeric powder
2 tbsps coconut or groundnut oil

1. Wash and cut the tomatoes into 8 pieces. 2. Chop the onions finely. Heat the oil in a vessel and fry the onions to a reddish brown colour. 3. Add tomato pieces, salt and jaggery. 4. Steam-cook on a low flame until the tomatoes are tender. 5. Grind together red chillies, coconut gratings and turmeric powder and add to the tomatoes. Cook further until the masala comes to boil.

7. Tomato panchamrita

½ kg ripe tomatoes
4-5 green chillies (less pungent)
1 small ball of jaggery
1 handful roasted groundnuts crushed to pieces
1 pinch asafoetida
½ tsp mustard seeds
¼ tsp turmeric powder
1 tbsp ghee or groundnut oil

1. Wash and cut the tomatoes into 8 pieces. Slice the chillies lengthwise. 2. Heat the ghee or oil and prepare a seasoning with mustard seeds, turmeric powder and asafoetida. 3. Add chillies and fry for some minutes. 4. Put in the tomato pieces, salt and jaggery and allow to steam-cook. 5. Lastly, add the crushed groundnut pieces, mix well and remove the vessel from the flame. This dish should be slightly sweet.

8. Tomato vada (stuffed tomatoes)

½ kg tomatotes
¼ cup grated coconut
1 cup sprouted green gram
½ tsp coriander and cumin seed powder
salt, chilli powder and tamarind juice to taste
2 tbsps oil*
1 tbsp mustard*
1 pinch asafoetida*

*For seasoning

1. Slice tomatoes on top and remove the pulp. 2. Mix all the ingredients and fill the tomatoes with the mixture. 3. Prepare seasoning in a pan and arrange the tomatoes in it. Add a little water if necessary, cover it with a lid and cook on a low fire, till the tomatoes are cooked.

Knol-Kol

1. Sukke

½ kg knol-kol
1 tspful salt
water enough to boil and cook knol-khol
1-1½ tsps coconut oil to fry spices
¼ coconut gratings
1 small ball of tamarind
¼ tsp turmeric powder
5 red chillies*
1 tsp coriander seeds*
½ tsp black gram dal*
¼ tsp fenugreek seeds*

*Fry in coconut oil

Wash knol-kol, peel off the skin, and cut into 2.5 cm cubes.
Method: Follow the instructions given for potato sukke.

2. Sukki bhaji

½ kg knol-kol
salt and jaggery to taste
¼-½ tsp chilli powder
1 tbsp ghee or groundnut oil
½ tsp mustard seeds
2 tsp bengal gram dal
1 handful coconut gratings

1. Wash the knol-kol, peel off the skin, and cut into small cubes. **2.** Heat the oil or ghee in a vessel and prepare seasoning with mustard seeds. **3.** Add the gram dal and fry slightly. **4.** Put in the knol-kol pieces, salt, jaggery and chilli powder. **5.** Stir well and steam-cook on a low flame until the pieces are tender. **6.** Add the coconut gratings and mix well.

3. Raita

½ kg knol-kol
salt to taste
½ tsp mustard seeds
a few curry leaves
1 tbsp ghee or oil for seasoning
¼ coconut gratings
6 green chillies
½ measure curds

1. Wash and peel off the skin of the knol-kol. **2.** Cut into small pieces and steam-cook until tender.
Method: Follow the instructions given for radish raita.

4. Ghashhi

250 gms knol-kol
1-1½ tsp salt
½ tbsp coconut oil
¾ coconut gratings
½ tsp turmeric powder
1 small ball of tamarind
7-8 red chillies*
3 tsp coriander seeds*
1 small bulb of garlic
1 tbsp ghee or oil for seasoning

*Fry in coconut oil

Wash, peel off the skin of the knol-kol and cut into 2.5 cm cubes. Steam-cook and mix in salt.
Method: Follow the instructions given for potato ghashhi.

5. Koshimbir

½ kg knol-kol
juice of half lemon
salt to taste
6 green chillies
2 onions
¼ coconut gratings

Method: Follow the instructions given for koshimbirs of other vegetables.

6. Bhaji

½ kg knol-kol
1 tbsp ghee
½ tsp mustard seeds
1 pinch asafoetida
½ tsp pepper powder
salt and sugar to taste

1. Wash and peel off the skin of knol-kol. 2. Cut into small cubes. 3. Heat ghee in a frying pan or a shallow vessel and prepare a seasoning with mustard seeds and asafoetida. 4. Add the knol-kol pieces, salt and sugar and allow the pieces to steam-cook. 5. Lastly add the pepper powder.

Cabbage

1. Sukke

½ kg cabbage
½ tsp mustard seeds
a few curry leaves
½ tbsp coconut oil
salt and jaggery to taste
½ measure water
¼ coconut gratings
¼ tsp turmeric powder
4-6 red chillies
1 small ball of tamarind
1 ½ tsp coriander seeds*
½ tsp black gram dal*
¼ tsp fenugreek seeds*

*Fry in oil

Wash and cut the cabbage into small pieces.
Method: Follow the instructions given for yam sukke.

2. Sukki bhaji (variety 1)

½ kg cabbage
250 gms onions
4 potatoes
½ measure curds
1 tbsp ghee
4 green chillies
a small piece of ginger
5 garlic cloves
1 tsp sugar
salt to taste
½ tsp turmeric powder
1 tsp chilli powder

1. Wash and cut the vegetables into small pieces. 2. Grind green chillies, ginger and garlic together. 3. Heat ghee in a vessel, add vegetables and the ground paste. Mix well and steam-cook. 4. Add salt, sugar, turmeric powder and chilli powder when the vegetables are cooked and tender. 5. Add curds before removing the vessel from the stove.

3. Sukki bhaji (variety 2)

½ kg cabbage
1 tbsp coconut or groundnut oil
1 handful coconut gratings
1 tsp salt
1 tsp jaggery
½ tsp chilli powder
½ tsp mustard seeds
1 pinch asafoetida
2 handful bengal gram dal (soaked in water)

Wash the cabbage and cut into small pieces.
Method: Follow the instructions given for radish-leaf bhaji no.

4. Fritters

½ kg cabbage
½ kg onions
4 tsps salt
4-5 green chillies*
1 handful coriander leaves*
3 measures gram flour
4 tsps chilli powder
½ tsp turmeric powder
1 large pinch asafoetida
groundnut oil for deep frying

*Chopped fine

1. Wash and cut the cabbage, onions, green chillies and coriander leaves fine. 2. Add salt, soda bicarb, chopped chillies, coriander leaves, gram flour, chilli powder, turmeric powder and asafoetida to the vegetable. Mix well with the help of some water. The mixture should be semi-solid. 3. Heat oil in a frying pan, drop small lumps of the mixture (about the size of a small lemon), and deep fry the fritters until reddish brown.

5. Zunaka

250 gms cabbage
250 gms onions
2 tsp chilli powder
2 tsp salt
½ tsp turmeric powder
jaggery to taste
1 large pinch of asafoetida
2-3 tbsp groundnut oil
1 ½ measures gram flour
1 handful coriander leaves

1. Wash and cut the cabbage and onions fine. 2. Heat oil in a pan or vessel and fry the onions to a light golden colour. 3. Add chilli powder, turmeric powder, asafoetida, fry slightly. 4. Put in the cabbage, salt and jaggery. Allow the cabbage to steam-cook on a low flame, stirring from time to time. 5. When the cabbage is well-cooked, add the gram flour gradually. Mix well and cook further until the flour is cooked and the dish is almost dry. 6. Lastly, add the coriander leaves.

NOTE: This dish can be prepared with cauliflower, snake-gourd, ridge-gourd and kovai also.

6. Pithala

Add tamarind pulp to taste, and a little water to the zunaka recipe for pithala with gravy.

7. Koshimbir

½ kg cabbage
juice of ½ lemon
salt to taste
½ tbsp groundnut oil
6 green chillies, sliced
¼ coconut gratings
½ tsp mustard seeds
a few curry leaves

1. Wash and grate the cabbage. 2. Mix and crush together salt and chillies. Add them to the cabbage along with the coconut gratings and lemon juice. 3. Prepare seasoning with mustard seeds and curry leaves and add it to the koshimbir.

NOTE: Instead of seasoning, raw chopped onions can be added.

Onions

1. Sukki bhaji

½ kg onions
3 tbsps groundnut oil
1 pinch asafoetida
½ tsp mustard seeds
¼ tsp turmeric powder
½ tsp chilli powder
salt to taste
1 ½ measures gram flour
1 handful coconut gratings
1 handful chopped coriander leaves

1. Peel the onions and cut them into small pieces. 2. Heat oil in a vessel and prepare a seasoning with asafoetida, mustard seeds, and turmeric powder. 3. Add the onions, cover the vessel with a lid and steam-cook on a low flame. 4. When the onions are tender, add salt and chilli powder. Sprinkle gram flour all over the onions and blend well. 5. Allow it to cook for 5 minutes. 6. Lastly, add the coconut gratings and coriander leaves.

2. Pithale

250 gms onions
1 ½ tbsps groundnut oil
1 measure gram flour
6 green chillies
1 handful coriander leaves
3 measures water
1 tsp chilli powder
½ tsp turmeric powder
¼ tsp asafoetida
2 tbsps salt
1 small ball of tamarind
2 tbsps groundnut oil
½ tsp mustard seeds

1. Wash, peel and cut the onions fine. 2. Heat 1 ½ tbsps oil in a frying pan and fry the onions to a light golden colour. 3. Mix together asafoetida, chilli powder, turmeric powder, salt, tamarind pulp, gram flour, chopped chillies and coriander leaves. Add 3 measures water and blend well. 4. Heat 2 tablespoons oil in a shallow vessel and prepare a seasoning with mustard seeds. Pour the onion mixture into it gradually. Spread it out and steam-cook until it thickens and sets.

NOTE: 1. The above recipe can be prepared without onions. 2. Fenugreek leaves can also be used in the above recipe.

3. Fritters (Bhaje)

½ kg onions
salt to taste
4-5 green chillies*
1 small piece ginger*
2-3 measures gram flour
1-2 tsp chilli powder
1 pinch asafoetida
groundnut oil for deep frying

*Chopped fine

1. Wash and peel the onions. Slice them thinly and separate into shreds. 2. Add salt, chopped chillies and ginger, gram flour, chilli powder, turmeric powder and asafoetida. 3. Mix them well so that all the ingredients are blended with the onions. (Do not add water while mixing.) 4. Heat oil in a frying pan and deep fry the fritters (size of a lemon) until reddish brown and crisp.

4. Ambat

½ kg small sized onions
½ litre water
salt to taste
½ tbsp coconut oil
1 large onion chopped
¾ coconut gratings
½ tsp turmeric powder
1 small ball of tamarind
7-8 red chillies*
¼ tsp fenugreek seeds*

*Fried in oil

Wash, peel and fry the small onions (whole) slightly in 1 tbsp oil. Boil and cook them in water.

Method: Follow the instructions given for potato ambat.

5. Kochholi

5-6 onions
1 green chilli sliced
juice of ½ lemon
salt and sugar to taste
½ tsp mustard seeds
¼ coconut gratings
1 small piece of ginger*
1 handful of coriander leaves*
½ tbsp groundnut oil
1 pinch asafoetida

*Chopped fine

1. Wash, peel and cut the onions very fine. 2. Mix the chillies with lemon juice, salt and sugar and crush slightly. 3. Add them to the onions along with coconut gratings, ginger and coriander leaves. 4. Prepare a seasoning with mustard seeds and asafoetida. Add it to the onions and blend well.

NOTE: This dish can be prepared by using ½ measure curds and salt only.

6. Katla (salad)

5-6 onions
½ to 1 measure firm curds
salt to taste

1. Wash, peel and slice the onions thinly. 2. Mix in salt and add the curds.

Cauliflower

1. Sukke

½ kg cauliflower
250 gms onions
salt and jaggery to taste
1½ tbsps groundnut oil
1 tbsp coconut oil
½ tsp black gram dal*
¼ tsp fenugreek seeds*
¼ coconut gratings
¼ tsp turmeric powder
4-6 red chillies*
1 small ball of tamarind
1½ tsps coriander seeds*

*Fry in coconut oil

1. Cut the cauliflower into large pieces and wash. 2. Peel the onions and cut fine. 3. Heat the groundnut oil in a vessel and fry the onions. 4. Add cauliflower pieces, salt and jaggery, and with the help of a little water steam-cook the pieces. 5. Grind the masala with coconut gratings, turmeric powder, chillies, tamarind and fried ingredients, and add it to the cooked cauliflower. 6. Bring it to boil and remove the vessel from the flame.

NOTE: As a variant, 250 gms peeled potatoes cut into cubes can be added and also the masala of potato sukke (variety 2) can be used in place of the masala indicated in the recipe.

2. Fritters (Bhaje)

½ kg cauliflower
salt to taste
groundnut oil for deep frying
1½ measure gram flour
1 tsp chilli powder
½ tsp turmeric powder
1 pinch asafoetida

Method: Follow the instructions given for brinjal fritters.

3. Patal bhaji

½ kg cauliflower
250 gms onions-chopped
½ litre water
4 kokum rinds (or juice of ½ lemon)
1 tsp salt
1-1½ tbsps ghee or groundnut oil
¼ coconut gratings*
4-5 green chillies*
6 garlic cloves*
1 small piece ginger*
½ tsp turmeric powder*

*Grind to a paste

Wash and cut the cauliflower into large pieces.
Method: Follow the instructions given for potato patal bhaji (variety 1).

4. Ambat

250 gms cauliflower
700 ml water
1-1½ tsps salt
½ tbsp coconut oil
1 large onion chopped
1 tbsp ghee or coconut oil for seasoning
¾ coconut gratings
½ tsp turmeric powder
1 small ball of tamarind
7-8 red chillies fried in oil
¼ tsp fenugreek seeds

Wash and cut the cauliflower into large pieces.
Method: Follow the instructions given for potato ambat.

5. Stew (variety 1)

½ kg cauliflower
5-6 cloves
3-4 cardamoms
3-4 green chillies-sliced
4 onions chopped
1½-2 tbsps ghee
½ coconut gratings*
6-8 cashewnuts*
1 tbsp poppy seeds*
2 ripe tomatoes or 1 tbsp curds
salt to taste

* Grind to a paste

1. Cut the cauliflower into pieces and wash. 2. Heat ghee in a vessel, add cloves and slightly crushed cardamoms (whole). Fry them for a few minutes. 3. Add chopped onions and sliced chillies, and fry until golden brown. 4. Put in the cauliflower pieces and steam-cook until tender. 5. Add the ground paste, tomatoes or curds and salt. Put in some water to form a thick gravy and bring it to boil.

6. Stew (variety 2)

½ kg cauliflower
1-1½ tbsps ghee
salt to taste
¼ tsp pepper powder
½ tbsp mustard seeds

1. Wash and cut cauliflower into thinly sliced pieces. 2. Heat ghee in a vessel and prepare a seasoning with the mustard seeds. 3. Add the cauliflower pieces and salt. Cover the vessel with a lid and steam-cook the cauliflower until tender. 4. Add pepper powder and serve hot. 5. If desired, lemon juice may be added for taste.

7. Soup

½ kg cauliflower
4 cups water
1 tsp butter
2 tsps flour (maida) or cornflour
½ cup milk
salt and pepper powder to taste

1. Wash cauliflower. Cut it into pieces, steam-cook until very tender. 2. Mash the cauliflower pieces, add water, butter, flour or cornflour mixed in cold milk, salt and pepper. 3. Bring it to boil and serve hot.

Lady's Fingers

NOTE: Add kokum rinds or tamarind juice while cooking this vegetable to avoid stickiness.

1. Sukke

½kg tender lady's fingers
1 tbsp groundnut oil
½ tsp mustard seeds
a few curry leaves
salt and jaggery to taste
¼ coconut gratings
¼ tsp turmeric powder
4-6 red chillies
1 small ball of tamarind
1½ tsps coriander seeds*
½ tsp black gram dal*

* Fried in oil

1. Wash lady's fingers. Wipe them dry and cut them into 2.5 cm long pieces. 2. Heat oil in a vessel and prepare a seasoning with mustard seeds and curry leaves. 3. Add the lady's finger pieces and stir them for 1-2 minutes. 4. Put in salt and jaggery and steam-cook until half tender. Grind the masala as given for yam sukke, add it to the lady's fingers and bring it to boil.

2. Huli

250 gms ladies fingers
1 cup grated coconut
3-4 red chillies*
1 tsp mustard seeds*
½ tsp fenugreek seeds*
1 tsp coriander seeds* (optional)
1½ tsp salt
7-8 cloves of garlic
4 tsp oil
1 small ball tamarind

*fried in 2 tsp oil

1. As above. 2. Grind together coconut and fried ingredients to a fine paste. 3. Cook the vegetable in tamarind juice with salt on a low flame. 4. When almost cooked add the masala and enough water to make a thick gravy. Bring to boil. 5. Add seasoning of crushed garlic in oil.

3. Upkari

½ kg lady's fingers
250 gms onions-chopped
6 green chillies-cut fine
salt and jaggery to taste
¼ coconut gratings
1 ½ tbsps groundnut oil

1. Wash and wipe lady's fingers dry. Cut them into 2.5 cm pieces. 2. Heat oil and fry onions and green chillies to a light brown colour. 3. Add the lady's fingers, stir them in the seasoning. Put in salt and jaggery, and steam-cook until tender. 4. Lastly, add coconut gratings.

4. Raita

250 gms tender lady's fingers
salt to taste
a few kokum rinds
¼-½ measure curds
½ coconut gratings*
1-2 green chillies*
½ tsp mustard seeds*
1 tbsp groundnut oil

*Grind to a fine paste

1. Wash, wipe lady's fingers dry and cut them into small pieces. 2. Heat oil and fry the lady's fingers pieces for a few minutes. 3. Add salt and kokum rinds and steam-cook until tender. 4. Cool and mix them in the ground masala and curds.

NOTE: Instead of curds, kokum rinds or tamarind juice can be used to cook lady's finger pieces.

5. Kaap

250 gms lady's fingers
salt to taste
1 tsp chilli powder
1 handful ground rice flour or jawar flour
groundnut oil for deep frying

1. Wash and wipe lady's fingers dry. Cut the stems and tips. Slice the lady's fingers lengthwise into two. 2. Apply salt, chilli powder and flour. 3. Heat oil in a frying pan and fry the lady's fingers until brown and crisp.

6. Fritters

250 gms lady's fingers
1 ½ measures gram flour
salt to taste
1 tsp chilli powder
½ tsp turmeric powder
1 pinch asafoetida
groundnut oil for deep frying

1. Wash and cut lady's fingers as given in recipe No. 5. 2. Follow instructions given for brinjal fritters.

7. Koshimbir

¼ kg lady's fingers
groundnut oil for deep frying
juice of ½ lemon
salt to taste
6 green chillies
2 onions
¼ coconut gratings

1. Wash, wipe-dry and cut lady's fingers into small pieces. 2. Fry them in oil until reddish brown. 3. Follow instructions given for yam koshimbir.

8. Ghashhi

¼ kg lady's fingers
salt to taste
1 ½ tbsps coconut oil
1 pinch asafoetida
½ tsp mustard seeds
a few curry leaves or garlic
¾ coconut gratings
½ tsp turmeric powder
1 small ball of tamarind
7-8 red chillies*
3 tsps coriander seeds*

*Fry in ½ tsp coconut oil

1. Wash, wipe dry and cut lady's fingers into 2 cm pieces. 2. Sprinkle a little salt and steam-cook with tamarind juice. 3. Grind together coconut gratings, turmeric powder, and fried chillies. Lastly, add the fried coriander seeds and grind the masala fine. Add this to the lady's fingers. Add a little water to form a liquid gravy and bring it to boil. Remove the vessel from the flame. 4. Prepare a seasoning of mustard seeds, curry leaves and asafoetida in 1 tbsp oil and add it to the dish. The seasoning can be prepared of garlic also.

9. Buttermilk ambat

½ kg lady's fingers
4 pieces of kokum
salt to taste
water enough to cook lady's fingers
½ tsp mustard seeds
½ coconut gratings
5-6 green chillies*
¼ tsp mustard seeds*
15-20 fenugreek seeds*
¼ cup sour buttermilk
a few curry leaves

*Fried in ghee

1. Wash, wipe-dry and cut lady's fingers into 2 cm pieces. 2. Boil water in a vessel, add salt and kokum. Put in lady's fingers and cook till they are tender. 3. Heat one tbsp ghee and fry mustard seeds. Add green chillies and fenugreek seeds and fry for a minute or two. 4. Grind finely the coconut gratings along with the fried ingredients. 5. Add the masala to the lady's fingers, and bring it to boil. 6. Remove the vessel from the flame and add the sour buttermilk. 7. Heat a tsp ghee, prepare a seasoning with mustard seeds and curry leaves and add it to the dish.

10. Morkholmbo (variety 1)

¼ kg lady's fingers
4 pieces of kokum
salt to taste
water enough to cook lady's fingers
1¼ cup sour buttermilk
1 tbsp ghee/oil
½ coconut gratings fried
5-6 green chillies*
a small piece of ginger*
4-5 pepper corns*
½ tsp turmeric powder*
1 tsp mustard seeds and a few curry leaves for seasoning

* Fried in ghee/oil

Method: Follow instructions given for the above recipe of buttermilk ambat.

11. Morkholmbo (variety 2)

½ kg lady's fingers
salt to taste
4 pieces of kokum
water enough to cook lady's fingers
½ coconut gratings fried
1¼ cups sour buttermilk
2 tbsps ghee/oil
1 tsp bengal gram dal *
8 green chillies*
¼ tsp cumin seeds*
a few fenugreek seeds*
1 tsp roasted rice grains
½ tsp mustard seeds and a few curry leaves for seasoning

*Fry in 1 tbsp ghee/oil

1. Wash, wipe dry and cut lady's fingers into 1.5 cm pieces. Boil and cook them in water, with kokum and a little salt. 2. Grind the masala with coconut gratings, fried ingredients, and roasted rice to a fine paste. 3. Add the masala to the lady's fingers. Pour in the sour buttermilk and add salt to taste. 4. Bring it to boil. Remove the vessel from the flame. 5. Prepare a seasoning of mustard seeds and curry leaves in one tbsp ghee, and add it to the dish.

NOTE: As a variant, boiled potato pieces or ripe tomato pieces may be added. Instead of lady's fingers, vegetables like bottle gourd, cucumber, snake gourd, green tomatoes can also be used.

12. Kodel

¼ kg lady's fingers
salt to taste
water enough to cook lady's fingers
½ coconut gratings
½ tsp turmeric powder
1 small ball of tamarind
7-8 red chillies
5-6 triphala (slightly crushed)

1. Wash, wipe, dry lady's fingers and cut them into 2.5 cm pieces. Boil and cook them in water with some salt until they are tender. 2. Grind the masala with coconut gratings, turmeric powder, tamarind and red chillies. 3. Add triphala to the masala, grinding gently for a minute or so, just to crush the triphala. 4. Mix the masala with the lady's fingers. Add some water, if necessary, to prepare a liquid gravy. Bring it to boil and remove the vessel from the flame.

Raw Banana

1. Sukke

½ kg raw bananas
2 handful bengal gram soaked overnight in water
1 small ball of tamarind
salt and jaggery to taste
½ tbsp coconut oil
¼ coconut gratings
¼ tsp turmeric powder
4-6 red chillies
1½ tsps coriander seeds*
½ tsp black gram dal*
¼ tsp fenugreek seeds*
mustard seeds and a few curry leaves for seasoning

*Fry in 1 tbsp coconut oil

1. Wash bananas, skin and cut them into 2.5 cm long and 1.5 cm broad pieces. Dip them in water to prevent darkening before use. 2. Cook the soaked bengal gram in a vessel, with water enough to cover the gram. 3. When well cooked and soft, add the banana pieces, salt and jaggery to taste. Allow the banana pieces to cook well. 4. Grind the coconut gratings, turmeric powder, chillies and tamarind together. Add the fried ingredients and grind to paste. 5. Add the masala to the cooked bananas and bring it to boil on a low flame. The gravy should be semi-liquid. Remove the vessel from the flame.

2. Upkari

½ kg raw bananas
salt and jaggery to taste
1 tsp chilli powder
1 tbsp groundnut oil
½ tsp mustard seeds
1 tsp black gram dal
1 handful coconut gratings

1. Wash and skin bananas. Cut them into small cubes and dip them in water to prevent darkening. Just before use, remove the cubes from water, apply salt, jaggery and chilli powder. 2. Heat oil in a pan and prepare a seasoning with mustard seeds and black gram dal. 3. When the dal is reddish brown, add the banana cubes and steam-cook them until they are tender. 4. Lastly top it with coconut gratings. Remove the pan from the flame.

3. Koshimbir

¼ kg raw bananas
4 green chillies
2 onions-finely chopped
groundnut oil for deep frying
¼ coconut gratings
salt to taste
½ lemon juice
a handful coriander leaves, chopped finely

1. Wash and skin bananas. 2. Cut them into fine cubes and deep fry in oil until reddish brown. 3. Slice the chillies, chop the onions, and coriander leaves finely. 4. Just before serving, mix together chillies, salt, onions, coriander leaves and coconut gratings. Blend the mixture well with fried banana cubes.

NOTE: This dish can be prepared with banana cubes smeared with salt and fried in a little oil and steam-cooked, instead of deep frying them in oil.

4. Bhareet (bajji)

250 gms raw bananas
2 onions (chopped finely)
pulp of a small ball of tamarind
½ coconut gratings*
3 red chillies*
salt to taste

* Grind finely together

1. Wash bananas. Boil and cook them whole in water enough to cover them. 2. Peel off skin and cut them fine. 3. Mix in the tamarind pulp, salt, chopped onions and finely ground coconut gratings and chillies.

5. Raita

250 gms raw bananas
salt to taste
250 gms curds
2 tbsps ghee or groundnut oil
a few curry leaves for seasoning
¼ coconut gratings*
2-3 green chillies*
¼ tsp mustard seeds
½ tsp mustard seeds for seasoning

* Fry in 1 tbsp ghee

1. Wash bananas. Boil and cook them whole until tender. 2. Peel off skin and cut them fine. 3. Grind coconut gratings coarsely. Add fried chillies and mustard seeds and grind further to a fine paste. 4. Mix the masala with banana pieces, salt and curds. 5. Prepare a seasoning of mustard seeds and curry leaves and add it to the raita.

6. Ghashhi

250 gms raw bananas
700 ml water
salt to taste
1 tbsp groundnut oil
1 small bulb of garlic
¾ coconut gratings
½ tsp turmeric powder
1 small ball of tamarind
7-8 red chillies*
3 tsps coriander seeds*

* Fry in ½ tbsp groundnut oil

1. Wash, peel and cut bananas into 3.5 cm cubes. Boil and cook them with salt in the water. 2. Grind coconut gratings, turmeric powder, tamarind and fried chillies together. 3. Add fried coriander seeds and grind the masala fine. 4. Add this to the banana cubes and boil until the masala blends well to form a liquid gravy. Remove the vessel from the flame. 5. Prepare a seasoning with crushed garlic cloves fried in oil until it is light brown, and add it to the dish.

7. Kaap

½ kg raw bananas
salt and jaggery to taste
1½ tsps chilli powder
rice flour or jowar flour
groundnut oil for deep frying

1. Wash, skin and cut bananas into 2.5 cm long and 0.5 cm broad pieces. 2. Apply salt, jaggery and chilli powder and allow to stand for about 15 minutes. 3. When the water separates, add rice flour or jowar flour enough to mix with the water. 4. Heat oil in a frying pan and deep fry the banana pieces until they are reddish brown.

8. Chutney

2 raw bananas
juice of ½ lemon
1 tbsp groundnut oil
a pinch of asafoetida
½ tsp mustard seeds

½ coconut gratings*
7-8 green chillies*
salt to taste*
¼ tsp cumin seeds*
a handful of coriander leaves*

*Grind coarsely together

1. Wash and steam-cook the whole bananas. Peel off skin, and mash them. 2. Mix the mashed bananas, lemon juice and ground masala well. 3. Heat oil, prepare seasoning with mustard seeds and asafoetida and add it to the chutney.

9. Rajali raw banana wafers

6 unripe rajali bananas
7 cups of water
1 tbsp salt

½ kg coconut oil to deep fry
½ tsp turmeric powder

1. Wash and skin the whole bananas. 2. Mix salt and turmeric powder in 1 cup of water. 3. Cut bananas into thin wafers. Dip them in 6 cups of water until they are used, to prevent discolouration. 4. Heat oil in frying pan. Deep fry the wafers on medium flame. 5. When half fried, pour in a tsp salt water and fry further until crisp and ready.

Banana Flower

1. Sukke

1 banana flower
2 cups thin buttermilk
1 handful dried peas
salt and jaggery to taste
1 tbsp groundnut oil
½ tsp mustard seeds
a few curry leaves

¼ coconut gratings
¼ tsp turmeric powder
4-6 red chillies*
1 small ball of tamarind
1 ½ tsps coriander seeds*
¼ tsp fenugreek seeds*
½ tsp black gram dal*

*Fry in 1 tbsp groundnut oil

1. Wash banana flower. Cut it into very fine pieces. Soak them in buttermilk overnight. 2. Soak peas in water overnight. 3. Grind coconut gratings, turmeric powder, chillies and tamarind together. Add the fried ingredients and grind until it is coarse. 4. Heat oil in a vessel. Prepare a seasoning with mustard seeds and curry leaves and cook the peas and banana flower pieces until they are tender. Add salt and jaggery. 5. Add the ground masala to the cooked peas and banana flower and bring it to boil on a low flame.

2. Upkari

1 banana flower
2 cups thin buttermilk
1 handful dried peas
a handful of coconut gratings
1 tbsp groundnut oil
½ tsp mustard seeds
a few curry leaves
salt and jaggery to taste
optional: ¼ tsp amti powder or garam masala

1. Wash banana flower. Cut it into very very fine pieces. Soak these in buttermilk overnight. 2. Soak peas in water overnight. 3. Heat oil in a pan and prepare a seasoning with mustard seeds and curry leaves. Add the banana flower pieces and peas. Add a little water. Cook them until they are tender. 4. Add salt and jaggery (¼ tsp amti powder or garam masala, if required). 5. Lastly top the dish with coconut gratings.

3. Pithale

1 banana flower
1 measure gram flour
6 green chillies*
1 handful coriander leaves*
3 measures water
2 tbsp groundnut oil
½ tsp mustard seeds
1 tsp chilli powder
½ tsp turmeric powder
¼ tsp asafoetida
salt and jaggery to taste
1 small ball of tamarind

* Cut fine

1. Wash banana flower and cut it into fine pieces and soak them in water overnight. 2. Heat 2 tsp oil in a pan and prepare a seasoning with mustard seeds. 3. Remove the banana flower pieces from water, add them to the seasoning and steam-cook until tender. 4. Mix together asafoetida, chilli powder, turmeric powder, salt, jaggery, tamarind pulp, gram flour, chopped chillies and coriander leaves. Add water and blend well. 5. Pour the mixture into the cooked banana flower and cook further until it thickens to required consistency.

Tender Core of Banana Trunk (Gabbo)

NOTE: Tender core of banana trunk is very heaty. Consumption not advisable specially in pregnancy.

1. Sukke

½ kg tender core of banana trunk
2 cups thin buttermilk
salt and jaggery to taste
1 tbsp groundnut oil
½ tsp mustard seeds
a few curry leaves
¼ coconut gratings
¼ tsp turmeric powder
4-6 red chillies
1 small ball of tamarind
½ tsp coriander seeds*
½ tsp black gram dal*
¼ tsp fenugreek seeds*

*Fry in 1 tbsp groundnut oil

1. Wash the core of banana trunk and cut it into thick rounds, taking care to remove the thread-like parts. 2. Soak them in buttermilk for 2-3 days before use. 3. Cut them into fine pieces. 4. Prepare the dish by following the instructions given for banana flower sukke.

2. Upkari

½ kg tender core of banana trunk
2 cups thin buttermilk
1 handful bengal gram dal
salt and jaggery to taste
1½ tbsps groundnut oil
½ tsp mustard seeds
a few curry leaves
½ tsp chilli powder
1 handful coconut gratings

1. Wash the core of banana trunk and cut it into thick rounds and treat it as given in the above recipe for sukke (steps 2 and 3). 2. Heat oil in a vessel and prepare a seasoning with mustard seeds and curry leaves. 3. Add the finely cut tender core pieces, chilli powder, salt and jaggery to taste. 4. Steam-cook until it is tender and dry. 5. Top the dish with coconut gratings.

3. Kochholi

½ kg tender core of banana trunk
2 green chillies
small piece of ginger
1 tbsp groundnut oil
salt to taste
½-1 measure thick curds
a handful coconut gratings
½ tsp mustard seeds
a few curry leaves

1. Wash and cut the core of banana trunk into rounds and treat it as given in the previous recipes (1 & 2). 2. Cut them into fine pieces. 3. Chop chillies and ginger and add them to the pieces. 4. Mix in salt, coconut gratings and curds. 5. Heat oil in a ladle and prepare a seasoning with mustard seeds and curry leaves. Add this to the dish.

Ripe Rajali Bananas

1. Stuffed bananas (variety 1)

1 doz ripe rajali bananas (good quality)
2–3 tbsps groundnut oil
½ tsp mustard seeds
a pinch of asafoetida
¼ tsp turmeric powder
½ coconut gratings*
4-6 green chillies*
salt and jaggery to taste*
1 handful coriander leaves*
small ball of tamarind*

*Grind to a coarse chutney

1. Wash bananas. Remove the skin. Cut them into 2 or 3 pieces breadthwise. Then make slits on either side of the pieces. 2. Grind chutney coarsely with the above-mentioned ingredients. 3. Stuff the chutney into the banana slits. 4. Heat oil in a shallow frying pan and prepare a seasoning with mustard seeds, asafoetida and turmeric powder. 5. Place the banana pieces in the frying pan, sprinkle a little water, cover the pan with a lid and steamcook them on a low flame until ready.

2. Stuffed bananas (variety 2)

1 doz ripe rajali bananas
2-3 tbsps groundnut oil
½ tsp mustard seeds
a pinch of asafoetida
¼ tsp turmeric powder
½ coconut gratings*
4-6 red chillies*
salt and jaggery to taste*
small ball of tamarind*
1 tsp coriander seeds*
½ tsp cummin seeds*

*Grind to a coarse chutney

Method: Follow instructions given for variety 1.

3. Fritters (variety 1)

1 doz ripe rajali bananas
salt to taste
2 cups water
1-1½ handful rice flour or jowar flour
groundnut oil for deep frying

1. Wash bananas. Peel off skin and cut them breadthwise into 2 or 3 pieces. Slice each piece into two, lengthwise. 2. Dilute salt in water. Dip the banana pieces in the water. 3. Roll them in rice flour or jowar flour. 4. Heat oil in a frying pan and deep fry the fritters until golden brown.

4. Fritters (variety 2)

½ doz ripe rajali bananas
water
salt to taste
¼ tsp chilli powder
⅛ tsp turmeric powder*
1 cup bengal gram flour*
groundnut oil for deep frying

* For batter

1. Wash bananas, cut them into four pieces and slit them into two. Peel off skin. 2. Prepare a thick batter with all ingredients and deep fry in oil until they are golden brown.

5. Ghashhi

4 ripe rajali bananas
small piece of jaggery
salt to taste
1 tbsp groundnut oil
½ tsp mustard seeds
a few curry leaves
½ coconut gratings
¼ tsp turmeric powder
4 red chillies
a small ball of tamarind
1 tsp coriander seeds*
½ tsp black gram dal*
a few fenugreek seeds*

*Fry in groundnut oil

1. Wash and cut the bananas into four pieces. Peel off the skin Slice each piece into two. 2. Steam-cook the banana pieces with salt and jaggery. 3. Grind the coconut gratings, turmeric powder, chillies and tamarind together until coarse. Then add the fried ingredients and grind to paste. Add this to the banana pieces to form a semi-liquid gravy. 4. Heat oil and prepare a seasoning with mustard seeds and curry leaves and add it to the curry.

NOTE: Similary, ghashhi can be prepared with raw green mangoes, wild mango and bitter gourd or wild mango and tender bamboo shoot. If raw green mangoes or wild mangoes are used, tamarind should be omitted and then proportion of jaggery should be more.

Kovai (Tendli)

1. Sukke

¼ kg tender kovai	½ coconut gratings
1 tbsp groundnut oil	½ tsp turmeric powder
½ tsp mustard seeds	4-6 red chillies
a few curry leaves	a small ball of tamarind
1 cup water	1 tsp coriander seeds*
salt and jaggery to taste	½ tsp black gram dal*
	a few fenugreek seeds*

*Fry in one tablespoon groundnut oil

1. Wash kovai and slice off both the ends. Crush the whole kovai slightly with a weight. 2. Heat oil in a vessel and prepare a seasoning with mustard seeds and curry leaves. Add kovai. 3. Boil and cook kovai in 1 cup of water until they are tender. 4. Grind together coarsely coconut gratings, turmeric powder, chillies and tamarind. Add the fried ingredients and grind further to a paste. 5. Add the masala, salt and jaggery to kovai and bring it to boil on a medium flame.

2. Talasani

¼ kg tender kovai	salt and jaggery to taste
1-1½ tbsps groundnut oil	1 tsp chilli powder
6-8 garlic cloves (crushed)	

1. Wash kovai and slice off both the ends. Crush the whole kovai slightly with a little weight. 2. Heat oil in a frying pan and fry garlic until they are reddish brown. 3. Add the crushed kovai to the seasoning and stir well. Cover the pan with a lid and allow kovai to steam-cook in a little water on a low flame. 4. When half-cooked add salt and chilli powder and cook further until they are tender.

3. Upkari (variety 1)

¼ kg kovai	salt and jaggery to taste
½ tsp salt	1 handful coconut gratings
1 tbsp groundnut oil	¼ tsp black gram dal
½ tsp mustard seeds	a few chilli pieces

1. Wash kovai, slice off both the ends and cut them into four pieces lengthwise. Apply ½ tsp salt. 2. Heat oil in a shallow vessel and fry mustard seeds, black gram dal and chilli pieces. 3. Squeeze kovai to remove excess water content. Add them to the seasoning. 4. Add salt and jaggery and stir well. Cover the vessel with a lid and allow kovai to steam-cook in a little water until they are tender.

4. Upkari (variety 2)

¼ kg kovai
½ tsp salt
1½ tbsps groundnut oil
salt to taste
1-2 onions, cut fine
a few red chilli pieces

1. Wash kovai, slice off both the ends and cut them into four pieces lengthwise. Apply ½ teaspoon salt. 2. Heat oil in a shallow vessel and fry onions until they are light brown. Add chilli pieces and fry slightly. 3. Squeeze out excess water content from kovai and add them to the seasoning. 4. Add salt. Stir well and cover the vessel with a lid. Steam-cook kovai in a little water until they are tender.

5. Koshimbir

125 gm tender kovai
1 tsp salt
groundnut oil for deep frying
juice of ½ lemon
salt to taste
4 green chillies, sliced
1 onion, cut fine
a handful coconut gratings

1. Wash kovai, slice off both the ends, cut them into thin rounds. Apply 1 teaspoon salt. 2. Wash kovai pieces in water again. Squeeze out excess water content. 3. Heat oil in a frying pan and deep fry the kovai pieces, until they are light brown. 4. Mix together salt, chillies, onions, lemon juice and coconut gratings. 5. Add the kovai pieces and blend well before serving.

6. Bhutti

¼ kg tender kovai
1 tbsp groundnut oil
½ tsp mustard seeds
a pinch of asafoetida
salt and jaggery to taste
small ball of tamarind
5 red chillies*
1 tsp coriander seeds*
½ tsp black gram dal*
a few fenugreek seeds*
4-5 garlic cloves*
¼ coconut gratings-roasted

*Fry in a little oil

1. Wash kovai, slice off both the ends and cut them into thin rounds or pieces. 2. Heat oil in a vessel and prepare a seasoning with mustard seeds and asafoetida. 3. Add the kovai pieces, salt and jaggery and stir them well. Cover the vessel with a lid and allow them to steam-cook until they are tender. 4. Grind together coconut gratings, chillies, coriander seeds, black gram dal, fenugreek seeds, tamarind and garlic to a paste. 5. Add the masala to the cooked kovai, stir well and bring it to boil until it is almost dry.

NOTE: As variation, chopped onions can be fried for seasoning instead of mustard seeds and asafoetida. And coriander seeds chutney is used as masala. No jaggery.

7. Ambat

125 gms tender kovai
a handful cashew nuts
1 tbsp groundnut oil
1 large onion-chopped
salt to taste
1½ cups water

¼ coconut gratings
¼ tsp turmeric powder
a small ball of tamarind
2-3 red chillies*
¼ tsp fenugreek seeds*

*Fry in ½ tbsp oil

1. Wash kovai, slice off both the ends, and cut them into four pieces lengthwise. 2. Soak cashewnuts in water. Slit them into two pieces. 3. Cook kovai and cashewnut pieces in water until they are tender. Add salt and jaggery. 4. Grind together coconut gratings, turmeric powder, tamarind, chillies and fenugreek seeds to a fine paste. 5. Add the masala to the cooked kovai to form a semi-liquid gravy and bring it to boil. 6. Heat 1 tbsp oil and fry chopped onion to golden brown and add it to the dish.

8. Kaap

125 gms tender kovai
1 tsp salt

Chilli powder and jaggery to taste
½ cup rice flour or jowar flour
groundnut oil for deep frying

1. Wash kovai, slice off both the ends, and cut them lengthwise into two or three thick pieces. 2. Apply salt and keep aside. 3. Squeeze the pieces a little and apply chilli powder and jaggery to taste. 4. Roll them in rice flour. 5. Heat oil in a frying pan and deep fry them until they are reddish brown.

9. Fritters

125 gms tender kovai
groundnut oil for deep frying
a little turmeric powder

1 cup bengal gram flour
salt to taste
¼ tsp chilli powder
a little turmeric powder

1. Wash kovai, slice off both the ends, and cut them lengthwise into 4 thin slices. 2. Mix gram flour, salt, chilli powder, and turmeric powder to form a thick batter adding some water. 3. Heat oil in a frying pan. 4. Dip the kovai pieces in the batter and deep fry them in oil until they are golden brown.

Snake Gourd

1. Sukke

½ kg snake gourd
1 handful bengal gram dal
salt and jaggery to taste
1 tbsp groundnut oil
½ tsp mustard seeds
a few curry leaves
¼ coconut gratings
½ tsp turmeric powder
2-3 red chillies
a small ball of tamarind
1 tsp coriander seeds*
a few fenugreek seeds*

*Fry in ½ tbsp groundnut oil

1. Wash snake gourd scrape off skin thinly. Remove seeds and core. Cut the gourd into 2.5 cm pieces. 2. Soak bengal gram dal in water for an hour. 3. Cook the dal in ½ cup water until it is soft. Add the gourd pieces, salt and jaggery and cook until the gourd is tender. 4. Grind together coconut gratings, turmeric powder, chillies, tamarind and the fried ingredients to a paste. 5. Add the masala to the cooked gourd and bring it to boil. 6. Heat oil in a ladle, prepare a seasoning with mustard seeds and curry leaves and add it to the dish.

2. Sukki bhaji

½ kg snake gourd
¾ cup fresh green peas
or ¾ cup field beans soaked overnight and skinned
1 tbsp groundnut oil
½ tsp mustard seeds
6 green chillies, sliced
a handful coriander leaves, chopped
salt and jaggery to taste
a handful coconut gratings
¼ tsp turmeric powder
a pinch of asafoetida

1. Wash snake gourd, scrape off skin thinly. Remove seeds and core. Cut the gourd into 2.5 cm pieces. 2. Heat oil in a vessel and prepare a seasoning with mustard seeds, turmeric powder and asafoetida. 3. Cook peas or beans in the seasoning with as much

water as needed until they are soft. 4. Add gourd pieces, chillies, coriander leaves, salt and jaggery and cook until they are tender on a low flame. 5. When the dish is almost dry add coconut gratings and remove the vessel from the fire.

3. Upkari

½ kg snake gourd
1 tbsp groundnut oil
½ tsp mustard seeds
a pinch of asafoetida
3-4 green chillies, sliced
a handful coconut gratings
salt and jaggery to taste

1. Wash gourd and scrape off skin thinly. Remove seeds and core. Cut the gourd into 2.5 cm pieces. 2. Heat oil in a vessel and prepare a seasoning with mustard seeds and asafoetida. 3. Add chillies and stir well. 4. Add the gourd pieces, salt and jaggery and cover the vessel with a lid. Steam-cook on a low flame. 5. When the gourd is tender add coconut gratings and remove the vessel from the flame.

4. Patal bhaji

½ kg snake gourd
1 tbsp groundnut oil
½ tsp mustard seeds
a pinch of asafoetida
¼ tsp cumin seeds
5-6 green chillies-sliced
¼ cup green gram dal (soaked for 2 hours)
1 handful coriander leaves
salt to taste
a little jaggery

1. Wash gourd, scrape off skin thinly, remove seeds and core. Cut the gourd into small pieces. 2. Heat oil in a vessel and prepare seasoning with mustard seeds, asafoetida and cumin seeds. 3. Add chillies and stir well. 4. Add green gram dal to the gourd pieces, salt and jaggery. Allow it to cook on a low flame adding a little water. 5. When the gourd pieces are soft and well-cooked add chopped coriander leaves and remove the vessel from the fire.

5. Stuffed snake gourd

½ kg snake gourd
½ cup bengal gram flour
¼ tsp turmeric powder
salt and jaggery to taste
1 tsp garam masala or amti powder
1½ tbsp groundnut oil
1 onion*
3 green chillies*
1 handful coriander leaves*
4 garlic cloves*

*Chopped fine

1. Wash gourd, scrape off skin thinly, and remove seeds and core. Cut the whole gourd into 7 to 8 cms long pieces. 2. Heat 1½ tbsp oil and fry the chopped onion for 2-3 minutes. Add gram flour and fry for some more minutes. Remove the pan from the flame. 3. Mix together all the chopped ingredients, gram flour, turmeric powder, salt, jaggery and garam masala. 4. Stuff the gourd pieces with the filling. 5. Heat 2-3 tablespoons oil in a shallow vessel and prepare a seasoning with mustard seeds. 6. Arrange the gourd pieces in the vessel and sprinkle a little water. Cover it with a lid and steam-cook on a low flame, turning the gourd pieces from time to time until they are well cooked.

6. Kochholi

¼ kg snake gourd
1 handful green gram dal
salt to taste
a small ball of tamarind
a pinch of asafoetida
¼ coconut gratings
2-3 green chillies
1 tbsp groundnut oil
½ tsp mustard seeds

1. Wash gourd, scrape off skin thinly, remove seeds and core. Chop or grate the gourd. 2. Apply a little salt to the gourd pieces. 3. Grind together coarsely coconut gratings, chillies, tamarind, salt and jaggery. 4. Mix the gourd pieces in the ground masala. Add soaked green gram dal. 5. Heat oil in a ladle and prepare a seasoning with mustard seeds and asafoetida and add it to the kochholi.

7. Zunaka

½ kg snake gourd
3 onions, chopped
1½ tbsp groundnut oil
½ tsp mustard seeds
¼ tsp turmeric powder
1 tsp garam masala
a pinch of asafoetida
½ tsp chilli powder
salt and jaggery (optional) to taste
1 cup bengal gram flour
a handful of coriander leaves, chopped

1. Wash gourd, scrape off skin thinly, and remove seeds and core. Cut the gourd into fine pieces. 2. Heat oil in a vessel and prepare a seasoning with mustard seeds, turmeric powder and asafoetida. 3. Add chopped onions and fry slightly. 4. Add the gourd pieces, chilli powder, garam masala, salt and jaggery. Sprinkle some water. Cover the vessel with a lid and allow the gourd pieces to cook on a low flame until they are tender. 5. Sprinkle gram flour and stir well until it blends well with the vegetable. Allow it to cook for a few minutes. 6. Add coriander leaves and remove the vessel from the flame.

8. Fritters

¼ kg snake gourd
1-1½ cups bengal gram flour
¼ tsp turmeric powder
1 tsp chilli powder
salt to taste
water enough to form a thick batter
groundnut oil for deep frying
1 pinch of asafoetida

1. Wash gourd, scrape off skin thinly, and remove seeds, cut the whole gourd into .5 cm thick rings. 2. Mix gram flour, turmeric powder, chilli powder, asafoetida, and salt to form a batter, adding enough water. 3. Heat oil in a frying pan. Dip the gourd rings in the batter so as to cover them with the batter evenly. Deep fry them until they are golden brown and crisp.

9. Fritters (stuffed)

½ kg snake gourd
3-4 onions, chopped
salt to taste
1-1½ tsp chilli powder
½ tsp mustard seeds
a pinch of asafoetida
1-1½ cups bengal gram flour
¼ cup groundnut oil
¼ tsp turmeric powder
a little turmeric powder

1. Wash gourd, scrape off skin thinly and remove seeds and core. Cut the whole gourd into 6 cm long pieces. 2. Mix together the chopped onions, salt, chilli powder, turmeric powder, asafoetida and bengal gram flour. 3. Add a little water to form a dough. 4. Stuff the mixture into the gourd pieces and steam-cook. 5. Heat oil in a shallow vessel and prepare a seasoning with mustard seeds, asafoetida and turmeric powder. 6. Arrange the gourd pieces in the vessel and fry them turning the pieces from time to time.

NOTE: 1. The stuffed gourd pieces can be half steam-cooked and fried like potato pattice. 2. Add the core or seeds, cut fine, to the filling.

10. Chutney

½ cup snake gourd seeds
3-4 green chillies
1 tbsp ghee
a pinch of asafoetida
1 small ball of tamarind
¼ coconut gratings
salt to taste

1. Heat the ghee in a ladle or a small frying pan and fry gourd seeds and green chillies until they are light brown. Add asafoetida and remove the ladle from the flame. 2. Grind together coconut gratings, tamarind, salt and the fried ingredients to a paste. Serve it with chapatis.

11. Tambli

½ cup snake gourd seeds
5-6 green chillies
a pinch of asafoetida
1 tsp ghee
½ coconut gratings
a little tamarind
salt to taste
1-1½ cups buttermilk

1. Heat ghee in a small frying pan and fry gourd seeds, green chillies and lastly add asafoetida. 2. Grind together coconut gratings, tamarind, salt and the fried ingredients to a very fine paste. 3. Use a little water, make it slightly liquid. 4. Add buttermilk to form a liquid cold curry. Serve with rice.

Bitter Gourd

1. Pickles (variety 1)

250 gms tender bitter gourd
1 tbsp salt
½ cup groundnut oil
1 big ball of jaggery and tamarind
8-10 red chillies*
1 tsp mustard seeds*
¼ tsp fenugreek seeds*
salt to taste

*Fry in oil

1. Wash bitter gourd, wipe them dry and cut them into small cubes. 2. Apply 1 tbsp salt and keep aside for 30 minutes. 3. Squeeze out all juice from the gourd. 4. Heat oil in a frying pan and deep fry the gourd pieces. 5. Grind together the fried ingredients into a fine paste. 6. Prepare a thick liquid by boiling together, jaggery, tamarind and salt to taste in some water. 7. Add the ground masala and gourd pieces and cook them for a few more minutes.
This pickle can be preserved for 4 or 5 days.

2. Pickle (variety 2)

1. Use the same proportion of ingredients as in variety 1. 2. Cut gourd into thin round slices, squeeze out juice and instead of deep frying the slices, steam-cook them. 3. Follow the same method as for variety 1.

3. Koshimbir

½ kg tender bitter gourd
1 tbsp salt
a few tbsps ghee or groundnut oil
¼ coconut gratings
2 small onions, finely chopped
juice of ½ lemon

1. Wash gourd and cut them into fine pieces. 2. Apply salt and keep them aside for 30 minutes. 3. Squeeze out all juice from the gourd pieces, and dry them in the sun, or over a warm metal plate. 4. Heat ghee or oil in a frying pan and stir the gourd pieces until they are reddish brown. 5. Mix coconut gratings, onions, salt and lemon juice together, and lastly add the gourd pieces and serve.

4. Kaap

½ kg tender bitter gourd
1 tbsp salt
1 cup groundnut oil for deep frying
a small ball of tamarind
1 tsp chilli powder
salt and jaggery to taste
¼ cup rice flour or jawar flour

1. Wash and cut gourd into thick slices, 8 cm long. 2. Apply salt and keep aside. Squeeze out juice from the slices after about 20 minutes. 3. Apply salt and jaggery to taste, tamarind and chilli powder, allow it to marinate. 4. Sprinkle rice flour or jawar flour. 5. Heat oil in a frying pan and deep fry the gourd slices until they are reddish brown.

5. Raita

250 gms tender bitter gourd
1 tbsp salt
a few tablespoons groundnut oil
½ cup curds
¼ coconut gratings
8 green chillies-fried in a little ghee or oil
salt to taste
a handful coriander leaves

1. Wash and cut gourd into small cubes. Apply salt and keep aside for ½ hour. 2. Squeeze out juice from the gourd. 3. Heat oil in a frying pan and deep fry the gourd cubes until they are reddish brown. 4. Grind together coconut gratings and fried chillies to a paste. 5. Mix the gourd cubes in the masala, add salt to taste, curds and chopped coriander leaves.

6. Sukke

½ kg tender bitter gourd
1 tbsp salt
½ tsp mustard seeds
a few curry leaves
1 ½ tsp groundnut oil
salt and jaggery to taste

¼ coconut gratings
¼ tsp turmeric powder
4-5 red chillies
a small ball of tamarind
1 tsp coriander seeds*
1 tsp black gram dal*
¼ tsp fenugreek seeds*

*Fry in 1 tbsp groundnut oil

1. Wash and cut gourd into small pieces. Apply salt and keep aside for a few minutes. 2. Squeeze out juice from the gourd pieces. 3. Grind together finely coconut gratings, turmeric powder, red chillies, tamarind and the fried ingredients. 4. Heat oil and prepare a seasoning with mustard seeds and curry leaves. 5. Steam the gourd pieces until they are tender. 6. Add the ground masala, salt and jaggery to taste, and cook for a few more minutes.

7. Ghashhi

250 gms tender bitter gourd
salt and jaggery to taste
1 ½ tbsp groundnut oil
½ tsp mustard seeds
a few curry leaves

½ coconut gratings
¼ tsp turmeric powder
a small ball of tamarind
4-6 red chillies*
1 tsp black gram dal*
1 ½ tsps coriander seeds*
¼ tsp fenugreek seeds*

*Fried in oil

1. Wash and cut gourd into thin rounds. 2. Apply salt and jaggery to taste and steam-cook them without adding water. 3. Grind together finely coconut gratings, turmeric powder, tamarind and the fried ingredients. 4. Mix together the cooked gourd pieces and the masala in a vessel. Add a little water and bring it to boil. 5. Heat oil in a frying ladle and prepare a seasoning with mustard seeds and curry leaves. 6. Add the seasoning to the dish.

NOTE : *For variation*, instead of tamarind, raw green mango pieces or wild mango (ambade) can be used. Tender bamboo shoots may be used with bitter gourd.

8. Valvale (sweet and sour bhaji)

¼ kg tender bitter gourd
¼ kg raw green mangoes
1 tbsp salt
1 ½ tbsp groundnut oil
5-6 garlic cloves
jaggery, size of onion
¼ coconut gratings
¼ tsp turmeric powder
5-6 red chillies*
1 tsp black gram dal*
1 tsp coriander seeds*
4-5 garlic cloves*
salt to taste

*Fried in oil

1. Wash and cut gourd into thin rounds. Apply salt and keep aside for a few minutes. 2. Squeeze out juice from the gourd pieces. 3. Cut green mango into thick slices. 4. Grind together finely coconut gratings, turmeric powder, garlic and the fried ingredients into a paste. 5. Heat oil in a vessel, fry the crushed garlic cloves. 6. Add the gourd pieces and mango slices, salt and jaggery, and steam-cook until they are tender. 7. Add the ground paste and cook for a few minutes.

White Gourd (Bottle Gourd)

1. Bhareet

½ kg white gourd
2 green chillies
1 cup grated coconut
curry leaves
¾ tbsp tamarind juice
1 ½ tsps salt
1 tsp mustard seeds

1. Skin and remove seeds from white gourd and cut into small pieces. Cook with green chillies. 2. Grind grated coconut fine. Add the cooked gourd and chillies and lime juice. Grind again. Add salt to taste. 3. Prepare a seasoning with mustard seeds and curry leaves in ghee and add it to the dish.

NOTE: 1. Finely chopped onions can be added instead of seasoning. 2. This bhareet is of semi-solid consistency.

2. Upkari (of white gourd peel)

Follow instructions for cluster beans upkari.

Ripe Mango

1. Andurli (kuval)

5-6 medium-sized ripe wild mangoes
1 tbsp jaggery
1 tsp soaked rice
salt to taste
1 green chilli slit
2 red chillies (broken)*
½ tsp mustard seeds*
a few curry leaves*
1 tbsp oil*
¼ tsp pepper powder
1 cup water

*For seasoning

1. Peel the mangoes and keep them aside, whole. Add a little water to the skins of the mangoes, squeeze well and add this extract to the whole mangoes. 2. Add salt to taste, jaggery, pepper powder, slit green chilli and the paste of the soaked rice blended with water. Simmer for 10 minutes. 3. Add the seasoning of mustard seeds broken red chillies and curry leaves prepared in oil.

NOTE: Instead of soaked rice paste, 1 tspful of rice flour or wheat flour or maida or corn flour diluted in water can be used for the thickening.

2. Sukke

2 Totapuri or Rajapuri mangoes (nearly ripe and firm)
¼ coconut grated
1 tsp jaggery
salt to taste
⅛ tsp turmeric
very little tamarind
2 small red chillies*
½ tsp coriander seeds*
⅛ tsp fenugreek seeds*
½ tsp black gram dal*
½ tsp mustard seeds and a few curry leaves for seasoning
1 tbsp oil for seasoning

*Fry in oil

1. Peel the mangoes and cut into medium sized cubes. Add jaggery and salt. 2. Grind the masala with coconut gratings, turmeric, tamarind and the fried ingredients. Add it to the mango cubes. 3. In a broad vessel prepare a seasoning with a tbsp oil, mustard seeds and curry leaves. Add the mango cubes and masala mixture to the seasoning and simmer for a few minutes.

Raw Green Mango

1. Pachadi

¼ kg tender green mangoes
salt and jaggery to taste
¼ tsp mustard seeds
a few curry leaves

¼ coconut gratings*
2 green chillies*
2 tsp groundnut oil

*Grind together

1. Wash green mangoes. Peel off the skin and cut them into fine pieces. **2.** Apply salt and jaggery to the mango pieces. **3.** Mix in the ground semi-solid masala. **4.** Heat oil in a frying ladle and prepare a seasoning with mustard seeds and curry leaves, and add it to the dish.

2. Ghashhi

100 gms tender green mangoes
salt to taste
jaggery, size of a big lemon
1½ tbsps groundnut oil
½ tsp mustard seeds
a few curry leaves

½ coconut gratings
¼ tsp turmeric powder
4-6 red chillies*
1 tsp black gram dal*
1½ tsp coriander seeds*
¼ tsp fenugreek seeds*

*Fried in oil

1. Wash and cut green mangoes into big cubes. 2. Apply salt and jaggery and steam-cook them. **3.** Grind together finely coconut gratings, turmeric powder and the fried ingredients. **4.** Mix together the cooked mango pieces and the masala in a vessel; add a few cups of water to form a semi-liquid gravy and bring it to boil. **5.** Heat oil in a frying ladle, prepare a seasoning with mustard seeds and curry leaves and add it to the dish.

NOTE: For a variation, seasoning of 5-6 garlic cloves may be used instead of mustard seeds and curry leaves.

3. Chutney

1 raw green mango
salt and jaggery to taste

½ coconut gratings
2 green chillies
3 garlic cloves or a pinch of asafoetida

1. Wash raw mango, peel off the skin and cut it into small pieces. **2.** Grind together mango pieces, coconut gratings, chillies, garlic or asafoetida, salt and jaggery to a coarse paste.

Tender Bamboo Shoots

Bamboo shoots should be cut into three separate parts. The outer layer of the skin is removed, then the tough part and the tender part are separated, and lastly the inner core is cut. These pieces are soaked in water for 48 hours before use, changing water every 12 hours.

1. The tough part is cut into big squares and used for ghashhi. Follow instructions as given for potato or bitter gourd ghashhi. 2. The tender part is cut fine. Follow instructions as given for yam sukke. 3. The inner core is cut into small flat pieces and used for kaap. Follow instructions as given for yam kaap.

Cluster Beans

1. Sukke

¼ kg tender cluster beans
2-3 onions, chopped
salt and jaggery to taste
1½ tbsps groundnut oil
¼ coconut gratings
¼ tsp turmeric powder

1 green chilli
2-3 red chillies
1 tsp coriander seeds*
a small piece of cinnamon*
2 cloves*
¼ tsp cumin seeds*
a little tamarind

*Fry in ½ tbsp groundnut oil

1. Wash and trim both the ends of beans and cut them into 2-3 pieces. 2. Heat oil and fry the chopped onions until they are light brown. 3. Add the cut beans, salt and jaggery and cook them with a little water until they are tender. 4. Grind together coconut gratings, turmeric powder, green chilli, tamarind, and the fried ingredients to a paste. 5. Add the masala to the beans and cook for a few more minutes on medium flame.

2. Upkari (variety 1)

250 gm tender cluster beans
salt and jaggery to taste
1 tbsp groundnut oil
½ tbsp mustard seeds
½ tbsp black gram dal
¼ tbsp chilli powder/2 green or red chillies
a handful coconut gratings

1. Wash a trim both the ends of beans and cut them into small pieces. 2. Heat oil in a vessel, and prepare a seasoning with mustard seeds and black gram dal. (Do not allow the dal to turn too brown.) 3. Add chilli powder, cut-beans, salt, jaggery and a little water and allow it to cook until they are tender. 4. Lastly add coconut gratings when the water is absorbed and remove the vessel from the fire.

NOTE : Same method for any vegetable like Lady's Fingers etc.

3. Upkari (variety 2)

¼ kg tender cluster beans
1 handful sprouted fenugreek seeds
salt and jaggery to taste
2 tbsps groundnut oil
½ tsp mustard seeds
1 pinch asafoetida
¼ tsp turmeric powder

1. Wash and cut both the ends of beans; cut them into small pieces. 2. Heat oil in a vessel and prepare a seasoning with mustard seeds and asafoetida. 3. Add turmeric powder, cut beans, sprouted fenugreek seeds, salt and jaggery, and steam-cook on a low flame until they are tender. 4. Lastly add coconut gratings.

4. Talasani

¼ kg tender cluster beans
salt and jaggery to taste
3 tsps groundnut oil
½ tsp mustard seeds
a pinch of asafoetida
½ tsp turmeric powder
½ tsp chilli powder
6 pepper corns*
¼ tsp cumin seeds*

*Fry in oil and pound together

1.. Wash beans and par-boil them in water. Strain them on a sieve. 2. Heat oil and prepare a seasoning with mustard seeds and asafoetida. 3. Add turmeric and chilli powder, cooked whole beans, salt and jaggery. 4. Allow the beans to cook on low flame until they are tender. 5. Lastly, add the pounded pepper and cumin seeds.

5. Phodi

125 gms tender cluster beans
groundnut oil for deep frying
1 tbsp black gram dal*
2 tbsps rice*
1 small ball of tamarind*
jaggery and salt to taste*
½ tsp chilli powder

*Grind to a thick paste

1. Wash and press slightly the whole cluster beans with a pestle. 2. Apply the ground masala paste and keep aside for a few minutes. 3. Heat oil in a frying pan and deep fry the whole cluster beans until they are reddish brown. Serve while they are hot.

6. Raita

125 gms tender cluster beans
salt to taste
¼ teaspoon mustard seeds
a few curry leaves
1 tbsp oil for seasoning
¼ coconut gratings*
3 green chillies*
½ cup curds

*Grind together coarsely

1. Wash, trim and cut cluster beans into small pieces. 2. Steam-cook them until they are tender.

Method: Follow instructions for other raitas.

French Beans

1. Sukke

250 gms french beans
¼ tsp mustard seeds
a few curry leaves
½ tbsp groundnut oil for seasoning
salt and jaggery to taste
½ coconut gratings
¼ tsp turmeric powder
4 red chillies
a small ball of tamarind
1 tbsp coriander seeds*
½ tbsp black gram dal*
¼ tsp fenugreek seeds*

*Fry in a tbsp oil

1. Wash, trim both the ends, and cut french beans into large pieces. 2. Steam-cook the beans with salt and jaggery to taste. 3. Follow instructions for yam sukke.

2. Upkari

250 gms tender french beans
salt and jaggery to taste
1 tbsp groundnut oil
½ tsp mustard seeds
½ tsp black gram dal
¼ tsp chilli powder
a handful of coconut gratings

Method: Wash, trim both the ends and cut french beans into small pieces. Follow instructions as for cluster beans upkari variety 1.

3. Talasani

250 gms tender french beans
1 tbsp groundnut or coconut oil
½ tsp mustard seeds and a pinch of asafoetida.
salt and jaggery to taste
4-5 pepper corns-powdered

For method follow instructions as for cluster beans talasani.

4. Koshimbir

250 gms french beans washed and cut fine
1 onion, chopped fine
2 tsps groundnut oil to fry
2 green chillies
¼ coconut gratings
salt to taste
¼ lemon juice
a handful coriander leaves, chopped fine

1. Heat oil in a pan and toss the finely cut beans until they are fried and soft. 2. Slice chillies, mix them with the chopped onion, coriander leaves, lemon juice, salt and coconut gratings. 3. Add the fried beans to the mixture. Serve cold.

NOTE: For variation, the cut beans may be partly steam-cooked with a pinch of salt instead of frying. Chillies can be cut very fine, crushed with salt and added.

Fritters

125 gms french beans
¾ cup bengal gram powder
salt to taste
¼ tsp chilli powder
a pinch of asafoetida and a little water to mix
groundnut oil for deep frying

1. Wash and trim both the ends of beans. 2. Prepare a thick batter of bengal gram powder, salt, chilli powder, asafoetida with a little water. 3. Heat oil in a frying pan on medium flame. 4. Dip the whole beans in the batter and deep fry until they are reddish brown. Serve hot.

Ridge Gourd

1. Sukke

¼ kg tender ridge gourd
1 tbsp groundnut oil
½ tsp mustard seeds
a handful of bengal gram dal
salt and jaggery to taste

¼ coconut gratings
⅛ tsp turmeric powder
4 red chillies
a small ball of tamarind
1 tsp coriander seeds*
½ tsp black gram dal*
¼ tsp fenugreek seeds*

*Fry in 1 tbsp oil

1. Wash and peel off thick ridges of gourd. Cut gourd into fairly big pieces. 2. Heat oil in a vessel, prepare seasoning with mustard seeds and fry gram dal for a minute or two. 3. Add gourd pieces, salt and jaggery to taste. Cook on a low flame until the gourd pieces and dal are tender. 4. Grind the masala with coconut gratings, turmeric powder, chillies, tamarind, and the fried ingredients. 5. Add the masala to the gourd and simmer on a low flame for a few minutes.

2. Sukki bhaji

¼ kg tender ridge gourd
1 tbsp groundnut oil
½ tsp mustard seeds
a handful bengal gram dal
salt and jaggery to taste

¼ coconut gratings*
2-3 green chillies*

*Grind together

1. Wash and peel off thick ridges of the gourd. Cut gourd into fairly large pieces. 2. Heat oil in a vessel, prepare a seasoning with mustard seeds, and fry dal for a minute or two on a low flame. 3. Add the gourd pieces, salt and jaggery. Cook until the gourd pieces and dal are tender. 4. Add ground coconut and chillies and allow to simmer for a minute.

3. Raita

125 gms tender ridge gourd
salt to taste
1 tbsp groundnut oil
½ tsp mustard seeds
a few curry leaves
¼ coconut gratings
2 green chillies
a small ball of tamarind or ½ cup sour curds

1. Wash and peel off thick ridges of gourd. Cut gourd into pieces. 2. Steam-cook the gourd pieces and chillies. 3. Grind coconut gratings, tamarind, and salt together. Add cooked gourd pieces and chillies and grind further to semi-solid consistency. 4. Heat oil in an iron ladle, prepare seasoning with mustard seeds and curry leaves and add it to the raita.

NOTE: If curds are to be added, do not use tamarind.

4. Fritters

¼ kg ridge gourd
¾ cup bengal gram flour
salt to taste
½ tsp coriander and fenugreek powder
⅛ tsp turmeric powder
½ tsp chilli powder
a pinch asafoetida
a little water to mix
groundnut oil for deep frying

1. Wash gourd, peel off thick ridges. Cut gourd into fairly thin rounds. 2. Mix gram flour, salt, chilli and turmeric powder, coriander and fenugreek seeds powder, asafoetida, with water to form a thick batter. 3. Heat oil in a frying pan. 4. Dip the gourd pieces in the batter and deep fry them until they are reddish brown.

Green Peas

1. Sukke

1 kg green peas (with pods)
1 tbsp groundnut oil
½ tsp mustard seeds
a few curry leaves
salt and jaggery to taste
turmeric powder
¼ coconut gratings
4 red chillies
a small ball of tamarind
1 tsp coriander seeds*
½ tsp black gram dal*
¼ tsp fenugreek seeds*

*Fry in 1 tablespoon oil

1. Shell green peas and wash them. 2. Prepare a seasoning of mustard seeds and curry leaves in a vessel. 3. Add peas and steam-cook them until they are tender. 4. Grind coarsely coconut gratings, turmeric powder, chillies, tamarind and the fried ingredients. 5. Add the masala, salt and jaggery to taste to the cooked peas and simmer for a few minutes.

2. Sukki bhaji

1½ kg green peas
3-4 tbsp groundnut oil
3 onions, chopped finely
4 green chillies-sliced
½ tsp mustard seeds
a pinch asafoetida
¼ tsp cummin seeds
salt and jaggery to taste

1. Shell green peas and wash them. 2. Heat oil in a vessel, prepare a seasoning with mustard seeds, asafoetida and cummin seeds. 3. Add chopped onions and chillies and fry until they are golden brown. 4. Mix in the peas, salt and jaggery. Steam-cook the peas until they are tender.

3. Usal

1½ kg green peas
4 green chillies, sliced
a small piece of ginger, chopped
salt and jaggery to taste
¼ coconut gratings*
¼ tsp turmeric powder*
1½ tbsp groundnut oil
a handful coriander leaves-chopped

*Grind together coarsely

1. Shell green peas and wash them. Steam-cook the peas. 2. Heat oil in a vessel and toss the chopped ginger and sliced chillies for a few minutes. 3. Add the cooked peas, ground masala paste, salt and jaggery. Allow it to simmer on a low flame. 4. Lastly add chopped coriander leaves.

4. Ambat

1½ kg green peas
salt to taste
2 small onions, chopped
2 tbsp groundnut oil
¾ coconut gratings
¼ tsp turmeric powder
a small ball of tamarind
3 red chillies*
¼ tsp fenugreek seeds*

*Fry together in ½ tbsp oil

1. Shell green peas and wash them. Steam-cook the peas. 2. Grind coconut grating, turmeric powder, tamarind, chillies and fenugreek seeds together finely. 3. Mix the cooked peas, ground masala and salt in a vessel. Add a little water to form a liquid gravy. Bring it to boil. 4. Prepare a seasoning with chopped onions in oil and add it to the dish.

5. Samosas (karanjis)

1½ kg green peas
salt to taste
1 tbsp groundnut oil
½ tsp mustard seeds
3-4 green chillies
2 handful chopped coriander leaves
a little jaggery (optional)
1½ cups flour (maida)*
a pinch of salt*
2 tsps hot fat*
a little water to mix*
groundnut oil for deep frying

*Knead into a stiff dough

1. Shell green peas, wash and steam-cook them until they are tender. 2. Prepare a seasoning with mustard seeds in oil. 3. Add the cooked peas, salt and ground coriander leaves and chillies. Allow it to simmer until it is dry. Allow to cool and use it for filling. 4. Knead a stiff dough of flour and using small portions roll it into small thin rounds. 5. Take a spoonful of the filling and place it on each round piece and fold one part of the round over the filling. With the help of a drop of water seal the edges of the samosas. Trim the edges with a samosa trimmer. 6. Heat oil in a frying pan and deep fry the samosas to golden brown colour.

6. Cutlets

1 kg green peas
2 slices of bread
salt and pepper to taste
1 mashed potato
½ cup wheat rava
or rice flour
fat for deep frying

1. Shell green peas, wash and steam-cook them until they are tender. 2. Cut bread slices into tiny crumbs. 3. Mix the mashed potato, bread crumbs, salt and pepper and add the peas into the mixture. 4. Form oval shaped cutlets of the mixture and roll them into wheat rava or rice flour. 5. Heat fat in a frying pan and deep fry the cutlets to reddish brown colour.

Capsicums

---

1. Sukke

4-5 capsicums
4 brinjals
2-3 drumsticks
1 tbsp groundnut oil
½ tbsp mustard seeds
a few curry leaves
salt and jaggery to taste
½ coconut gratings
¼ tsp turmeric powder
4 red chillies
a small ball of tamarind
1 tsp coriander seeds*
½ tsp black gram dal*
¼ tsp fenugreek seeds*

*Fry in ½ tbsp oil

1. Wash all vegetables. Cut capsicums and brinjals into large pieces. Remove the outer skin of drumsticks and cut them into 4 cm long pieces. 2. Heat oil in a vessel and prepare a seasoning with mustard seeds and curry leaves. 3. Add drumsticks to the seasoning and half-cook with a little water. 4. Add the capsicum and brinjal pieces, salt and jaggery and cover the vessel with a lid. Steam-cook until they are tender. 5. Grind coconut gratings, turmeric powder, chillies, tamarind and fried ingredients. 6. Add the masala and allow to simmer for a few minutes on a low flame.

2. Stuffed capsicums (variety 1)

25 capsicums
6 tbsp groundnut oil
½ tsp mustard seeds
a pinch of asafoetida
½ tsp turmeric powder
1 measure bengal gram flour
salt and jaggery to taste
½ tsp chilli powder
a handful coconut gratings
1 large onion-chopped
½ tsp garam masala

1. Wash capsicums with the stems. Slit each whole capsicum from the lower end into 4 sections. 2. Dip capsicums in warm water for 15 minutes. Remove them and drain off the water. 3. Heat 2 tbsp oil, fry onion until it is light golden. Add chilli powder, garam masala, gram flour, coconut gratings, salt and jaggery. Fry for a few minutes and remove the vessel from fire. Use this as stuffing. 4. Heat 4 tbsps oil in a shallow vessel, prepare a seasoning with mustard seeds, asafoetida and turmeric powder. 5. Place the stuffed capsicums carefully in the vessel and cover it with a lid and steam-cook until the capsicums are ready.

3. Stuffed capsicums (variety 2)

25 capsicums
4 tbsp groundnut oil
½ tsp mustard seeds
a pinch of asafoetida
½ tsp turmeric powder
1 measure roasted bengal gram dal (coarsely crushed)
salt and sugar to taste
juice of ½ lemon
a handful coconut gratings
a handful coriander leaves, chopped

1. Wash capsicums with the stems. Slit each whole capsicum from the lower end into 4 sections. 2. Dip them in warm water for 15 minutes. Remove them and drain off the water. 3. Mix together crushed dal, salt and sugar, lemon juice, coconut gratings and coriander leaves. 4. Stuff the capsicums with the mixed ingredients. 5. Heat oil, prepare a seasoning with mustard seeds, asafoetida and turmeric powder. 6. Place the stuffed capsicums carefully in the vessel and cover it with a lid and steam-cook on a low flame until the capsicums are tender.

4. Stuffed capsicums (variety 3)

25 capsicums
4 tbsps groundnut oil
½ tsp mustard seeds
a pinch of asafoetida
½ tsp turmeric powder
1 measure roasted groundnuts, crushed coarsely
a handful roasted sesame seeds, pounded
salt and sugar to taste
juice of ½ lemon
a handful coconut gratings
a handful coriander leaves, chopped

Method: Follow instructions given for recipe for variety 2 to stuff and cook the capsicums.
For variation: Potato Sukki bhaji variety 5 may be used for stuffing the capsicums.

5. Kayaras

5-6 capsicums
1 ½ tbsp groundnut oil
½ tsp mustard seeds
a pinch of asafoetida
a few fenugreek seeds
salt to taste
jaggery, size of a lemon
a handful sesame seeds*
a handful coconut gratings*
a small ball of tamarind
a handful raw groundnuts (soaked and cooked)

*Roast and grind together

1. Wash and cut capsicums into 8 pieces. 2. Soak tamarind in a cup of hot water and extract pulp. 3. Heat oil in a vessel and prepare a seasoning with mustard seeds, asafoetida and fenugreek seeds. 4. Add the capsicums pieces, groundnuts, tamarind pulp, salt and jaggery. Cook on a low flame for a few minutes. 5. Add the ground paste of coconut and sesame seeds and simmer for some more minutes.

NOTE: This dish should be semi-solid and slightly sweet

For variation: Raw green mango may be used instead of tamarind pulp. While grinding coconut and sesame seeds, 1 tsp coriander seeds, 2 tsps bengal gram dal, ½ tsp mustard seeds, 4-5 pepper corns and ¼ tsp fenugreek seeds fried in a tbsp of groundnut oil may be added.

6. Ros

12 capsicums
1 ½ cups bengal gram flour
½ cup chopped onions
½ tsp turmeric powder
salt to taste
a small ball of tamarind pulp
1 small bunch of coriander leaves chopped finely
½ coconut gratings*
½ onion*
6 pepper corns*
salt and tamarind to taste

*Grind together and extract juice

1. Wash and cut capsicums lengthwise into two pieces. Remove the seeds. 2. Mix together gram flour, onions, turmeric powder, salt,

tamarind pulp, coriander leaves with a little water. **3.** Stuff the capsicum halves with the mixture and steam-cook them. **4.** Use the left-over mixture for gravy by adding some more water, salt and tamarind pulp if necesary. **5.** Heat it in a vessel and as it comes to boil pour in the extracted juice and remove the vessel from the fire. **6.** Add the steam-cooked stuffed capsicums to the gravy.

7. Ambat

2 pungent capsicums
1 tbsps groundnut or coconut oil
salt and jaggery to taste
tamarind pulp to taste
¼ tsp mustard seeds and a few curry leaves
½ coconut gratings
½ tsp turmeric powder
¼ tsp fenugreek seeds fried in a little oil

1. Wash and cut capsicums into 8 pieces. **2.** Heat oil in a vessel. Prepare seasoning of mustard seeds and curry leaves, add and toss the capsicum pieces for 5-10 minutes. **3.** Add salt, jaggery and tamarind pulp. **4.** Grind coconut, turmeric powder and fenugreek seeds together finely. **5.** Add the masala and some water to the capsicum pieces to form a gravy. Bring it to boil.

Cucumber

1. Sukke

½ kg cucumber
¼ tsp mustard seeds
a few curry leaves
½ tsp groundnut oil
salt and jaggery to taste
½ coconut gratings
¼ tsp turmeric powder
4 red chillies
a small ball of tamarind
1 tsp coriander seeds*
½ tsp black gram dal*
¼ tsp fenugreek seeds*

*Fry in 1 tbsp oil

1. Wash cucumber and cut into large pieces. 2. Steam-cook with salt and jaggery to taste. 3. Grind coarsely coconut gratings, turmeric powder, chillies, tamarind and the fried ingredients. 4. Add the masala to the cooked cucumber and allow to simmer for a few minutes. 5. Lastly prepare a seasoning with mustard seeds and curry leaves in oil and add it to the dish.

2.Sukki bhaji

½ kg cucumber
1 tbsp groundnut oil
½ tsp mustard seeds
¼ tsp cumin seeds
a pinch asafoetida
a handful gram dal (soaked in water for 1 hour)
salt to taste
¼ tsp turmeric powder
2 green chillies, sliced
1tbsp grated coconut (optional)

1. Wash cucumber and cut into small pieces. 2. Heat oil in a vessel, prepare a seasoning with mustard seeds, cumin seeds, turmeric powder, asafoetida. 3. Add the sliced chillies, toss for a few minutes. 4. Add the dal and allow to cook with a little water. 5. Put in the cucumber pieces and salt and steam-cook until they are tender. Add coconut.

3. Kochholi

¼kg cucumber
½tbsp groundnut oil
½tsp mustard seeds
a few curry leaves
¼coconut gratings*
2 green chillies*
salt to taste
½ cup curds or ½ lemon juice

*Grind together

1. Wash cucumber, peel off the skin and cut very fine. 2. Mix cucumber, ground coconut and chillies, salt and curds/lemon together. 3. Heat oil in an iron ladle, prepare a seasoning with mustard seeds and curry leaves. 4. Add the seasoning to the dish.

NOTE : 2 tbsp soaked green gram dal can be added.

4. Koshimbir

¼ cucumber
½ cup green gram dal (soaked in water for 1 hour)
½ tbsp groundnut oil
¼ tsp mustard seeds
a few curry leaves
a pinch of asafoetida
¼ coconut gratings
4 green chillies sliced
salt and sugar to taste
juice of ½ lemon
a few coriander leaves, chopped

1. Wash cucumber, peel off the skin and cut very fine. 2. Mix together soaked dal, coconut gratings, chillies, salt, sugar, cucumber, lemon juice and coriander leaves. 3. Prepare a seasoning of mustard seeds, curry leaves and asafoetida in oil. 4. Add the seasoning to the dish.

NOTE: For variation grated raw cabbage *or* cut raw tomatoes may be added.

5. Kayaras

½ kg cucumber	a handful coconut gratings*
½ cup tamarind pulp	2 green chillies*
salt to taste	½ tsp mustard seeds*
jaggery-size of a lemon	½ tbsp groundnut oil
1 tsp methakoot	½ tsp mustard seeds for seasoning
¼ tsp turmeric powder	a pinch of asafoetida

*Grind together into a paste

1. Wash cucumber and peel off the skin. Cut cucumber into small pieces. 2. Mix together tamarind pulp, salt, jaggery, methakoot, ground coconut paste and cucumber. 3. Prepare a seasoning with mustard seeds, turmeric powder and asafoetida. 4. Add the seasoning to the mixture.

6. Khamang kakdi

¼ kg cucumber	3-4 green chillies*
salt and sugar to taste	½ cup roasted groundnuts*
a handful coconut gratings	a handful coriander leaves*
juice of ½ lemon	

*Chopped fine

1. Wash cucumber and peel off the skin and chop cucumber into small pieces. 2. Apply a little salt to the chopped cucumber. After a few minutes squeeze out the excess water content. 3. Crush groundnut into fine pieces. 4. Mix together cucumber, crushed groundnuts, chillies, coriander leaves, coconut gratings, lemon juice, salt and sugar.

7. Ghashhi

Follow instructions given for potato ghashhi.

8. Ambat

Follow instructions given for potato ambat.

9. Sambaren

Follow instructions given for brinjal sambaren.

10. Cucumber baskets

12 small cucumbers
salt and sugar to taste
juice of ½ lemon
6 tooth-picks
¼ kg cabbage*
2 carrots*
a handful coconut gratings

*Grate and mix together

1. Wash cucumber and peel off the skin. Slit each cucumber lengthwise into two parts. Apply a little salt. 2. Remove all the core of the cucumbers carefully. 3. Mix together grated raw cabbage, the core, carrots, coconut, salt, sugar and lemon juice. 4. Fill the mixture into each half of the cucumber. 5. Use the peeled off skin of cucumber as handles for the cucumber baskets, fixing them with toothpick pieces.

Koshimbirs

---

1. Bengal gram dal koshimbir

¼ kg bengal gram dal
salt to taste
juice of ½ lemon
1 tbsp groundnut oil
a pinch of asafoetida
a few curry leaves
¼ coconut gratings*
3 green chillies*
a handful coriander leaves*
½ tsp mustard seeds
¼ teaspoon turmeric powder

*Grind coarsely

1. Wash dal and soak in water for about 2-3 hours. Drain off the water. 2. Grind dal coarsely and mix salt and lemon juice and ground coconut mixture. 3. Heat oil and prepare a seasoning with mustard seeds, asafoetida, turmeric powder and curry leaves. Add it to the koshimbir.

NOTE : Koshimbir can be prepared with green gram dal similarly. Raw mango or cauliflower finely chopped or grated raw cabbage and cut raw tomatoes can be mixed with koshimbir.

Tender Raw Jackfruit

1. Sukke

½ kg raw jackfruit
½ tbsp groundnut oil
½ tsp mustard seeds
a few curry leaves
salt and jaggery to taste
½ coconut gratings
4 red chillies
a small ball of tamarind
1 tsp coriander seeds*
½ tsp black gram dal*
¼ tsp fenugreek seeds*

*Fry in 1 tbsp oil

1. Apply a tablespoon of oil to the palms and to the knife. Remove the thick skin of the jackfruit deep enough, and also the centre core. 2. Cut the jackfruit into large pieces. Steam-cook them. 3. Heat oil, prepare a seasoning with mustard seeds, and curry leaves. 4. Grind together coconut gratings, chillies, tamarind, and the fried ingredients. 5. Add the masala, salt and jaggery and the cooked jackfruit to the seasoning. 6. Simmer on a low flame until it comes to boil.

For variation: ½ cup pre-soaked bengal gram may be cooked and added to the jackfruit.

2. Sukki bhaji

250 gms raw jack fruit
1 tsp cumin seeds
1 onion
1 cm ginger
1 cup grated coconut
a small ball of tamarind
1 tbsp coriander seeds
4 dry chillies
6 cloves of garlic
chopped coriander leaves for garnishing

1. Cut the jackfruit into 2 cm cubes, removing the skin and the cen tral stem. 2. Grind all the other ingredients with a little water. 3. Apply salt to the jackfruit cubes and fry them a little. 4. Fry the masala in the remaining oil and boil without adding water. Simmer it on a low fire. 5. Add the fried jackfruit cubes and salt to taste. 6. When cooked, add chopped coriander leaves and serve.

NOTE: The jackfruit cubes can be pounded a little and fried in a little oil before adding the masala.

3. Fritters (variety 1)

½ kg tender raw jackfruit
salt and jaggery to taste
½-1 tsp chilli powder
pulp of a small ball of tamarind
groundnut oil for deep frying
a handful of jawar flour

1. Apply oil to the palms and knife. Remove the thick skin and the core of the jackfruit. 2. Cut jackfruit into large thick sections. 3. Apply salt, jaggery, tamarind pulp, chilli powder and jawar flour. 4. Heat oil in a frying pan. 5. Deep fry the jackfruit pieces until they are crisp and reddish brown.

4. Fritters (variety 2)

½ kg almost ripe jackfruit
groundnut oil or coconut oil for deep frying
table salt and chilli powder to taste

1. Apply oil to the palms and knife. Remove the thick skin and the core of the jackfruit. 2. Use only the inner sections, after removing the seeds, and cut the sections into long shreds. (The seeds and the remaining part of the jackfruit can be used for some savoury dish like sukke.) 3. Heat oil in a frying pan and deep fry the jackfruit shreds until they are crisp like chips. 4. Sprinkle salt and chilli powder while the fritters are hot and toss lightly.

Red Pumpkin

---

1. Bendi

¼ kg red pumpkin
salt and jaggery to taste
6 triphal
¼ coconut gratings*
6-8 red chillies fried in oil*
¼ teaspoon turmeric powder*
a small ball of tamarind

*Grind together

1. Wash pumpkin and remove the thick skin and cut it into large pieces. 2. Steam-cook the pumpkin pieces with salt and jaggery. 3. Add the ground masala to the cooked pumpkin. Bring it to boil. 4. Crush triphals and add them to the dish. Simmer for a few more minutes.

NOTE: Garlic seasoning can be added.

2. Khotkhoten

¼ kg red pumpkin
salt and jaggery to taste
1 tbsp groundnut oil
6 garlic cloves (for seasoning)
6-7 triphals

¼ coconut gratings*
3-4 red chillies*
1 tsp coriander seeds*
3-4 garlic cloves (optional)*
a small ball of tamarind*

*Grind together

1. Wash pumpkin and cut it along with the skin into large pieces. 2. Steam-cook the pumpkin pieces, add salt and jaggery. 3. Add the ground masala and add crushed triphal. Allow to simmer on a low flame until it comes to boil. 4. Heat oil in an iron ladle, crush garlic slightly and fry them until they are reddish brown. Add the seasoning to the dish (seasoning optional).

NOTE: Tender leaves of pumpkin creeper cut fine and stalks cut into 2 cm pieces, cooked together earlier before adding pumpkin pieces makes this dish tastier.

3. Raita

¼ kg pumpkin
3 green chillies, sliced
salt and jaggery to taste
1 tbsp groundnut oil
a few curry leaves

¼ coconut gratings*
a small ball of tamarind*
a small piece of ginger
½ tbsp mustard seeds

*Grind together

Wash pumpkin. Remove the skin, cut and steam-cook pumpkin with chillies. Follow instructions for brinjal bhareet variety 1 and 3.

4. Kaap

¼ kg pumpkin
salt and jaggery to taste
a handful of rice or jawar flour

groundnut oil for deep frying
¼ tsp chilli powder

1. Wash and cut pumpkin into thick slices along with the skin. 2. Apply salt, jaggery and chilli powder and keep aside for ½ hour. 3. Roll pumpkin slices in rice or jawar flour. 4. Heat oil

in frying pan and deep fry or shallow fry the slices until they are reddish brown. Serve hot.

5. Fritters

¼ kg pumpkin
groundnut oil for deep frying
¼ tsp turmeric powder
a pinch of asafoetida
1 cup bengal gram flour
½ tsp chilli powder
salt to taste

1. Wash and cut pumpkin into thin slices along with the skin. 2. Prepare a thick batter with gram flour, chilli powder, turmeric powder, salt and asafoetida with some water. 3. Heat oil in a frying pan. 4. Dip the pumpkin slices in the batter, deep fry them until they are light brown. Serve hot.

Semi Liquid Chutneys

---

1. Coriander leaves chutney

¼ coconut gratings
2-3 green chillies
1 bunch of coriander leaves
salt and sugar to taste
a small ball of tamarind

1. Sort out coriander leaves. Wash them clean and chop. 2. Grind together all the ingredients along with coriander leaves coarsely. Serve cold.

For variation: (1) instead of tamarind, raw green mango, peeled and cut, may be used. (2) a small piece of ginger and ¼ teaspoon cumin seeds may be added. (3) 2-3 garlic cloves, a small piece of ginger, ½ onion and instead of tamarind lemon juice may be used.

2. Bitter gourd chutney

¼ kg bitter gourd
groundnut oil for deep frying or shallow frying
¼ coconut gratings
2-3 green chillies
salt to taste
a small ball of tamarind

1. Wash gourd. Wipe and cut into small pieces. 2. Apply a little salt to the pieces, allow to stand for some minutes. Squeeze out the excess water content. 3. Heat oil and deep fry or shallow fry the gourd pieces until they are crisp. 4. Grind together coconut gratings, chillies, salt, tamarind and fried gourd into a semi-liquid chutney.

3. Dried brinjal chutney

2 medium size brinjals
salt
1½ tbsp groundnut oil
½ tsp mustard seeds
a large pinch of asafoetida
¼ dried coconut, grated
3-4 red chillies
2 tsps black gram dal
¼ tsp fenugreek seeds
a ball of tamarind

1. Wash brinjals and cut them into small pieces. 2. Apply salt to the pieces, keep aside. After a few minutes squeeze out the water content. 3. Heat oil in a frying pan, prepare a seasoning with mustard seeds and asafoetida. 4. Add gram and fry for a few minutes. Add fenugreek seeds, chillies and fry again. 5. Put the brinjal pieces and grated coconut and stir until they are also fried. 6. Remove from the flame. 7. Grind all the ingredients, including salt and tamarind, to a thick paste, without using water.

NOTE: This chutney lasts for 4-5 days. Dried coconut may be omitted, if not desired.

4. Bengal gram dal chutney

¼ cup bengal gram dal
1 tbsp groundnut or coconut oil
salt to taste
¼ coconut gratings
4-5 red chillies
a small ball of tamarind

1. Heat oil in a frying pan and roast gram dal until it is light brown. Remove it from the oil. 2. Fry chillies similarly. 3. Mix all the ingredients and grind together into a chutney.

NOTE: Peeled off skin of knol-kol or ridge gourd can be fried in oil and used similarly to prepare a chutney.

5. Sesame seed chutney

Follow instructions given for the above recipe.

6. Green chilli chutney

Follow instructions given for No. 4 recipe, but do not use red chillies.

7. Garlic chutney

6 garlic cloves (skinned)
salt to taste
a small ball of tamarind
½ coconut gratings
3-4 red chillies

Mix all the ingredients and grind to a semi-solid chutney.

NOTE: Less proportion of coconut may be used if the chutney is to be hot.

8. Cumin-coriander seed chutney

1 tsp cumin seeds
1 tsp coriander seeds
1 onion, chopped fine
salt to taste
½ coconut gratings
3-4 red chillies
a small ball of tamarind

1. Mix together all the ingredien'ts except onion. 2. Grind to a semi-solid chutney. 3. While serving mix in the chopped onion and salt.

9. Sweet and sour chutney

1 bunch coriander leaves
3-4 green chillies
salt to taste
a small ball of tamarind
or lemon juice
jaggery size of a small lemon

1. Sort the coriander leaves. Wash them clean and chop coarsely.
2. Mix all the ingredients together and grind coarsely into a semi-liquid chutney.

Pounded Dry Chutneys

---

1. Bengal gram dal chutney

½ cup bengal gram dal
a handful curry leaves
1 tbsp coconut oil
½ dried coconut-grated
5-6 red chillies
a small ball of tamarind
1½ tsp salt

1. Roast the gram dal, dried coconut gratings and salt separately on a dry hot plate until light brown. 2. Heat oil and fry the curry leaves. 3. Mix all the ingredients and pound them together or dry-

grind in the mixer until the consistency is fine. Store in a glass jar.

NOTE: White sesame seeds, black gram dal *or* horse gram dal can be used for this chutney instead of bengal gram dal.

2. Roasted bengal gram chutney (variety 1)

1 cup roasted bengal gram
1 bulb garlic
salt to taste
1 tbsp groundnut oil
½ dried coconut, grated
8-10 red chillies
a small ball of tamarind
¼ tsp asafoetida

1. Roast the gram and salt separate on a dry hot plate. 2. Fry the chillies in oil until crisp. 3. Mix all the ingredients and pound them together or dry-grind until fine. Store in a glass jar.

3. Roasted bengal gram dal chutney (variety 2)

1 kg roasted bengal gram dal
a small ball of tamarind
2 handfuls curry leaves
10 gms asafoetida
½ kg dried coconut, grated
125 gms red chillies
125 gms salt
1 tbsp coconut oil

1. Roast the coconut gratings and salt separately on a dry hot plate. 2. Heat oil in a frying pan, fry the asafoetida. 3. Similarly, fry the red chillies and curry leaves in oil. 4. Grind the dal in a dry grinder or pound along with the other ingredients. Store the chutney in a glass jar.

4. Sesame seed chutney

½ kg sesame seeds (sorted and cleaned)
250 gms dried coconut (grated)
125 gms red chillies (fried in a little groundnut oil)
60 gms salt
a small ball of tamarind

1. Roast the sesame seeds, grated coconut, and salt separately on a dry hot plate. 2. Pound or dry-grind all the ingredients separately at first, then mix together and pound or grind further to blend well. Store in a glass jar.

5. Curry leaves chutney

½ kg dried coconut-grated
50 gms red chillies*
50 gms curry leaves*
25 gms salt
a small ball of tamarind

*Fried in a little groundnut oil

1. Roast the grated coconut and salt separately on a dry hot plate. 2. Mix all the ingredients together and dry-grind or pound them to a fine consistency. Store in a glass jar.

6. Garlic chutney

50 gms garlic (skinned)
½ kg dried coconut (grated)
25 gms tamarind
250 gms red chillies, fried in a little groundnut oil
50 gms salt

1. Roast the grated coconut and salt separately on a dry hot plate. 2. Mix all the garlic roasted coconut, salt, fried red chillies and tamarind together. 3. Pound or dry-grind them together until the ingredients are well blended. Store in a glass jar.

NOTE: The above mentioned four forms of dry chutneys can be stored for a month or so.

Leafy Vegetables

Fenugreek leaves

1. Sukki bhaji (variety 1)

2 bunches fenugreek leaves
1 tbsp groundnut oil
½ tsp mustard seeds
1 pinch of asafoetida
2 handfuls bengal gram dal (soaked in water)
salt and jaggery to taste
½ tsp chilli powder
a handful coconut gratings

1. Sort and clean the tender stalks of fenugreek leaves. Wash thoroughly and drain off the water. 2. Cut the leaves fine, apply salt and rub it well. After a few minutes squeeze out the water content. 3. Heat oil in a vessel or frying pan and prepare a seasoning with mustard seeds and asafoetida. 4. Add the dal to the seasoning, fry for a minute or so. 5. Put in the fenugreek leaves and cover with a lid. Steam-cook until the dal is tender. 6. Add salt, jaggery, chilli powder and coconut gratings. Allow it to cook for a few more minutes.

2. Sukki bhaji (variety 2)

2 bunches fenugreek leaves
salt and jaggery to taste
2-3 potatoes (peeled and cut into small pieces)
2-3 tbsps groundnut oil
2 onions, chopped
2-3 green chillies, sliced

1. Sort out and clean the tender stalks of leaves. Treat them as given in recipe No.1. 2. Heat oil in a frying pan. Fry the onions until light golden. 3. Add the chillies and fry for a few minutes. 4. Put in the potato pieces, stir for a few minutes, and add the fenugreek leaves. 5. Add salt and jaggery. Stir well. Cover with a lid and allow to steam-cook on a low flame until the potato and leaves are ready.

3. Sukki bhaji (variety 3)

3 bunches fenugreek leaves
salt and jaggery to taste
2 large onions, chopped
250 gm brinjals, cut into small pieces
2 tbsps groundnut oil
5-6 garlic cloves crushed
¼ grated dried coconut*
4 green chillies*
5 garlic cloves
6 pepper corns*
¼ tsp turmeric powder

*Grind together

1. Sort out the tender stalks of leaves, wash them thoroughly and cut fine. Treat them as given in recipe No.1. 2. Heat oil in a vessel, prepare a seasoning with crushed garlic. 3. Add the fenugreek leaves, onions, brinjals, salt and jaggery. Steam-cook them until tender. 4. Put in the ground masala and allow it to simmer until the gravy comes to the boil.

4. Muthias

4 bunches fenugreek leaves
1 cup bengal gram flour
4 onions, chopped fine
groundnut oil for shallow frying
jaggery to taste
1 tsp chilli powder
¼ tsp turmeric powder
1 pinch asafoetida
Salt to taste

1. Sort out and clean the tender stalks of leaves. Wash and drain off the water. Cut the leaves fine. 2. Measure the cut leaves. 3. Mix the leaves, salt, jaggery, chilli powder, turmeric powder, gram flour, asafoetida and chopped onions. Blend well and form oval-shaped balls. 4. Place the balls on a lid and steam-cook them in the cooker. Allow them to cool. 5. Heat the oil in a frying pan and carefully shallow fry the muthias until light brown.

5. Zunaka

2 bunches fenugreek leaves
2-3 tbsps groundnut oil
3 medium onions (chopped)
¼ tsp turmeric powder
½ tsp garam masala
1 tsp chilli powder
salt to taste
jaggery (size of a lemon)
½ cup gram flour
a handful coconut gratings
a handful chopped coriander leaves

1. Sort out and clean the tender stalks of leaves. Treat them as given in recipe No.1. 2. Heat oil and prepare a seasoning with onions. 3. Add turmeric powder, chilli powder, and garam masala. 4. Add the leaves, salt and jaggery and cover with a lid. Steam-cook until the leaves are cooked. 5. Sprinkle the gram flour gradually, stirring all the time. Cook for a few minutes. 6. Add coconut gratings and coriander leaves.

6. Koshimbir

12 bunches tender shoots of fenugreek leaves
½ cup green gram dal (soaked in water)
1 tbsp groundnut oil
½ tsp mustard seeds
2 green chillies (chopped)
salt and sugar to taste
½ cup curds or juice of ½ lemon
a few curry leaves

1. Sort out the bunches and wash thoroughly, remove the sand. Drain off the water from the leaves. 2. Cut the leaves fine. 3. Mix together the chopped leaves, dal, chillies, salt, sugar and curds. 4. Heat the oil, prepare a seasoning with mustard seeds and curry leaves and add it to the koshimbir.

Colocasia Leaves (Aalu)

---

1. Patal bhaji (variety 1)

6 colocasia leaves with stalks
salt and jaggery to taste
2 cups water
¼ coconut gratings*
3-4 green chillies*

*Grind together

1. Wash the colocasia leaves and stalks. Cut off the stalks, remove their thin outer skin and cut them into thin rounds. Cut the leaves fine. 2. Boil and cook the cut leaves and stalks in 2 cups water with salt and jaggery. 3. When the leaves and stalks are tender, add the ground paste and bring it to boil.

2. Patal bhaji (variety 2)

6-8 colocasia leaves with stalks
1 handful bengal gram dal*
1 handful raw groundnuts*
salt to taste
jaggery (size of a lemon)
1 tsp chilli powder
1 tsp amti or garam masala
pulp of a small ball of tamarind
2 tsps bengal gram flour
5-6 garlic cloves or ½ tsp mustard seeds and a few curry leaves
1 tbsp groundnut oil

*Soaked in water

1. Wash the leaves and stalks. Remove the thin skin of the stalks, cut them into small pieces. Cut the leaves fine. 2. Boil and cook the dal and groundnuts until tender. 3. Add the cut leaves and stalks and cook further until they are soft. 4. Add the salt, jaggery, chilli powder, amti masala, pulp of tamarind. 5. Mix the gram flour in a little water, and pour it into the cooked vegetables stirring briskly. Allow it to cook for 5-10 minutes. 6. Heat oil in an iron ladle, prepare a seasoning with either garlic or with mustard seeds and curry leaves. Add it to the bhaji.

3. Saar

6-8 colocasia stalks
4-5 cups water
6 kokum rinds or a small ball of tamarind
1 tbsp groundnut oil or ghee
5-6 garlic pods (crushed)
salt to taste
jaggery (size of a lemon)
½ tsp cumin seeds*
5-6 garlic cloves (crushed)
5 pepper corns*

*Roasted dry and powdered

1. Wash the stalks, remove the skin and cut the stalks into small pieces. 2. Boil and cook them in water until soft. 3. Add salt, jaggery, tamarind or kokum rinds, powdered cumin seeds and pepper. Boil for 5 more minutes. 4. Heat oil in an iron ladle, prepare a seasoning with garlic and add it to the saar.

NOTE: This recipe can be prepared with fenugreek leaf stalks, negro coffee leaf stalks, red amaranths leaf stalks.

4. Patrodo/Patrel (variety 1)

1 cup red gram dal*
½ cup rice*
10 red chillies
¼ tsp asafoetida
a small ball of tamarind
jaggery (size of a lemon)
9-10 medium-sized colocasia leaves
salt to taste

*Soaked in water overnight

1. Wash the colocasia leaves, remove the stalks and slice off the centre stem of the leaves carefully. 2. Grind together all the ingredients to a coarse paste. 3. Place a leaf on a flat surface and apply a layer of the masala. Place another leaf on top and repeat the procedure until three leaves are used for each roll. 4. Fold the sides of the leaves inwards, and roll the leaves together tightly to form a medium-sized roll. Tie each roll securely from all sides with a piece of string. 5. Heat the cooker and place the rolls in a shallow vessel. Steam-cook them until the patrel is well-cooked. 6. Allow the rolls to cool. Remove the strings, and cut rolls into thick round slices.

NOTE: These slices can be served as they are, or they can be deep-fried in oil. The slices can also be shallow fried in a seasoning of ½ tsp mustard seeds. If desired the patrel can be served with a curry (ghashhi) prepared with ½ coconut gratings, 3-4 red chillies, a small ball of tamarind, ½ tsp turmeric powder and ½ tsp cumin seeds ground together. Add a seasoning with mustard seeds and a few curry leaves.

5. Patrodo (variety 2)

5-6 large onions*
2 handfuls coriander leaves*
6-8 green chillies*
pulp of a small ball of tamarind
  or juice of a lemon
3 cups bengal gram flour
3 tsps salt
3 tsps chilli powder
½ tsp turmeric powder
¼ tsp asafoetida
9-10 colocasia leaves

*Chopped fine

1. Treat the colocasia leaves as given in recipe No.4. 2. Mix all the ingredients together, blend them well to form a thick paste. Add a little water if necessary. 3. Apply the mixture to the leaves as instructed in recipe No. 4 and steam-cook the rolls in a double boiler or cooker until ready. Allow to cool before serving.

6. Patrodo (variety 3)

¼ kg green gram (soaked in
  water and sprouted)
½ coconut gratings
½ tsp turmeric powder
salt to taste
jaggery (size of a lemon)
1 tsp coriander seeds
½ tsp cumin seeds
a small ball of tamarind
4-5 red chillies
9-10 colocasia leaves

1. Treat the leaves as given in recipe No.4. 2. Grind together all the ingredients to a coarse paste. 3. Apply the mixture to the leaves as instructed in recipe No.4, steam-cook the rolls. Allow to cool before serving.

7. Patrodo (variety 4)

10 colocasia leaves
1 cup wheat flour
2 cups bengal gram flour
1 cup rice flour
1 onion grated fine
2 tbsps chilli powder
salt to taste
1 tbsp jaggery
1 tbsp tamarind juice
2 tsps coriander and cumin seed powder
1 tbsp oil

1. Wash the leaves, wipe them dry and keep aside. 2. Mix all the flours, onion, chilli powder, salt, jaggery, tamarind juice and coriander and cumin seed powder. Make a thick paste adding enough water. 3. Apply the mixture or paste as in recipe 4 . Steam-cook the rolls for 20 minutes. 4. Cut into thick slices and deep fry or season with mustard seeds, fenugreek and asafoetida.

8. Sukke

6-8 tender colocasia leaves
½ cup green gram or bengal gram (soaked in water overnight)
salt and jaggery to taste
1 tbsp groundnut oil
½ tsp mustard seeds
a few curry leaves
½ coconut gratings
½ tsp turmeric powder
a small ball of tamarind
4-5 red chillies*
1 tsp coriander seeds*
½ tsp black gram dal*
¼ tsp fenugreek seeds*

* Fried in ½ tbsp oil.

1. Wash the leaves and wipe them dry. Cut each leaf into two, lengthwise. Roll each piece and form a knot. Steam-cook the knots. 2. Steam-cook the green gram or bengal gram in a cooker until soft. 3. Grind together finely the coconut gratings, turmeric powder, tamarind and all the fried ingredients. 4. Heat oil in a vessel, prepare a seasoning with mustard seeds and curry leaves. 5. Add the cooked colocasia leaf knots and gram to the seasoning. 6. Add the ground masala, salt and jaggery and simmer until it boils.

9. Sukki bhaji

10-12 tender colocasia leaves
3-4 green chillies (sliced)
salt and jaggery to taste
pulp of a small ball of tamarind
1½ tbsps groundnut oil
10-12 garlic cloves (crushed)

1. Treat the leaves as given in recipe No. 7 and form knots. Steam-cook them in a cooker. 2. Heat oil in a vessel, prepare a seasoning with garlic cloves. 3. Add the chillies and fry for a few minutes. 4. Put in the cooked leaf knots, salt, jaggery, and tamarind pulp and allow it to cook for a few minutes.

10. Chutney

4 medium-sized colocasia leaves
salt and jaggery to taste
a small ball of tamarind
4 garlic cloves
2-3 green chillies

1. Wash and cook the colocasia leaves. Cut them fine. 2. Grind all the ingredients including the cut leaves to a fine paste.

Negro Coffee Leaves or Takla

---

1. Sukki bhaji

2 bunches tender negro coffee leaves
4 medium onions (chopped)
1 ½ tbsps groundnut oil
2 potatoes, peeled and cut into small pieces
salt and jaggery to taste
½ tsp chilli powder

1. Sort out the tender stalks of leaves. Wash them thoroughly and cut fine. 2. Heat oil in a vessel and fry the onions until light golden. 3. Add the cut leaves, potato pieces, salt, jaggery and chilli powder. Steam-cook until the leaves are soft.

2. Vade (negro coffee leaves vade)

1 cup bengal gram dal or red gram dal (soaked in water 3-4 hours)
2 bunches negro coffee leaves (chopped fine)
3 onions
groundnut oil for deep frying
6-8 red chillies*
1 pinch asafoetida*
a small ball of tamarind*
salt to taste*
jaggery (size of a lemon)
two handfuls rice or jawar flour

* Grind together to a paste and keep overnight.

1. Prepare the masala overnight. 2. Sort out the leaves, wash and chop them fine along with onions. 3. Mix the masala, cut leaves and onions. Form small balls, press them lightly. 4. Roll the balls, in the flour. 5. Heat oil in a frying pan and deep-fry or shallow-fry the balls until reddish brown.

NOTE: Fenugreek leaves, radish leaves, knol-kol leaves, cauliflower leaves, onions, cabbage, snake gourd seeds or fresh onion leaves can be used in place of negro coffee leaves for this recipe.

1. Leafy vegetable upkari

2-3 bunches leafy vegetable
2 tsps salt
a small piece of ginger (chopped)
2-3 red or green chillies
2 tbsps groundnut oil
2 large onions (chopped)
4-5 garlic cloves (crushed)
salt to taste
jaggery (size of a small lemon)

1. Sort out the bunches of leaves. Sprinkle salt on the leaves and beat the bunches to remove worms, if any. 2. Wash the leaves in water thoroughly, drain off the water, and cut the leaves fine. 3. Heat the oil in a vessel, add the garlic, fry for a few minutes. Add the onions and fry until soft. 4. Put in the chopped ginger, pieces of chillies, and the cut leaves. Allow to steam-cook for a few minutes. 5. Add salt and jaggery and cook further until the leaves are soft.

NOTE: Any kind of leafy vegetable can be used.

For variations: Seasoning of mustard seeds, asafoetida and turmeric powder may be used. A handful of coconut gratings and bengal gram flour can be added.

1. Indian spinach (vaali) sukki bhaji

½ cup green gram (soaked in water overnight)
2-3 bunches spinach (use stalks only)
salt and jaggery to taste
1 tbsp groundnut oil
½ tsp mustard seeds
a few curry leaves
½ coconut gratings
¼ tsp turmeric powder
a small ball of tamarind
4-5 red chillies*
1 tsp coriander seeds*
½ tsp black gram dal*
¼ tsp fenugreek seeds*

*Fry in a little oil

1. Wash and cut the spinach-stalks into 5 cm long pieces. 2. Steam-cook with green gram in cooker. 3. Grind together finely the coconut gratings, turmeric powder, tamarind and all the fried ingredients. 4. Heat oil in a vessel and prepare a seasoning with mustard seeds and curry leaves. 5. Add the cooked spinach, gram, ground masala, salt and jaggery. Bring it to boil.

2. Spinach leaf fritters

1 bunch spinach
salt to taste
1 tsp coriander and cumin seed powder
groundnut oil for deep frying
1 cup bengal gram flour
½ tsp chilli powder
½ tsp turmeric powder
1 pinch asafoetida

1. Wash the spinach leaves, drain off the water. 2. Mix all the ingredients together (except oil and spinach). Prepare a thick batter by adding water. 3. Heat the oil in a frying pan. 4. Dip each leaf in the batter and deep fry until the fritters are light brown.

Raitas

1. Leafy vegetable raita

2 small bunches of leaves (any kind of leafy vegetable)
salt to taste
½ cup curds or a little tamarind
½ coconut gratings*
2-3 green chillies fried in oil*
½ tsp mustard seeds*

*Grind together

1. Sort out the tender stalks of leaves. Sprinkle a little salt and beat the stalks to remove worms, if any. 2. Wash the stalks and cut them fine. Steam-cook them. 3. Mix the cold ground masəla paste with the vegetable. 4. Add salt and curds. This dish should be semi-solid and is served cold.

NOTE: Instead of leafy vegetable, steam-cooked tender cluster beans, french beans, cucumber, magge, or ladies fingers may be used to prepare the raita. Steam cooked colocasia stalks can also be used for this type of raita.

2. Machola raita

2 bunches of machola stalks (remove roots and use stalks only)
½ cup curds or a little tamarind
½ coconut gratings*
2-3 green chillies* (fried in oil)
½ tsp mustard seed*

*Grind to a paste

1. Wash the stalks of leaves and boil and cook in water. Allow it to cool. 2. Scrape the stalks and use only the cooked leaves. Throw away the stalks. 3. Cut the leaves fine and mix with the ground masala paste and curds.

NOTE: Do not use salt as this vegetable is inherently saline to taste.

3. Fresh ginger raita

½ tbsp groundnut oil
½ tsp mustard seeds
½ coconut gratings
salt to taste
2-3 green chillies*
a few curry leaves
2½ cms ginger (cut fine)*
½ cup curds

*Fry in ghee

1. Grind together coconut gratings, salt, fried chillies and ginger to a thick paste. 2. Mix in curds and blend lightly. 3. Heat oil in an iron ladle, prepare a seasoning with mustard seeds and curry leaves, and add it to the raita.

NOTE: Instead of the seasoning, dried raisins soaked in water previously, can be added to the raita.

4. Wild mango sasam (sweet)

8-10 ripe wild mangoes
salt and jaggery to taste
½ coconut gratings*
2 red chillies*
¼ tsp mustard seeds*

*Grind to a paste

1. Wash the mangoes. Peel off the skin. 2. Extract juice from the skin by dipping the skin in a little water. 3. Mix together the mangoes, salt and jaggery. 4. Add the ground paste and the extracted juice. Blend well. Serve cold.

For variation: Fruits like ripe bananas, pineapple, grapes, oranges or tomatoes can also be used.

Golyan sambare (Ball sambare)

1 cup bengal gram flour
2 onions chopped fine
4 green chillies chopped fine
a handful coriander leaves chopped fine
½ coconut gratings (extract juice)
groundnut oil for deep frying
salt to taste
¼ coconut gratings*
1 onion*
1 tsp coriander seeds*
4 pepper corns*
1 pinch asafoetida*
¼ tsp turmeric powder*
2 red chillies*
2-3 cloves*
tamarind pulp to taste

*Fry in oil and grind to a paste

1. Mix together bengal gram flour, chopped ingredients and salt with a little water. Form small balls. 2. Heat oil in a frying pan and fry the balls to light brown colour. 3. Mix the ground masala, add the tamarind pulp and salt to taste. Add a little water and bring it to boil. 4. Pour in the extracted juice, allow it to simmer for 2-3 minutes. Remove from fire. 5. Add the fried balls.

NOTE: The balls can be dipped in boiling water and allowed to cook for 5-10 minutes (instead of deep frying), and then added to the curry.

Avial (mixed vegetables)

Yam
raw banana
ladies fingers
red pumpkin
potato
salt and jaggery to taste

½ coconut gratings*
4-5 green chillies*
¼ tsp cumin seeds*
¾ cup sour buttermilk mixed with a little salt

*Grind to paste

1. Wash all the vegetables, cut into 2½ cms. pieces and steam-cook them. 2. Add the ground masala, salt and jaggery to the cooked vegetables. Simmer on a low flame. 3. Pour in the buttermilk and remove the vessel from the flame after 1-2 minutes.

Coconut Curries

The curries are of two types, hot or cold. They are usually of seven to eight variations. The hot preparations are called kadis, whereas the cold ones are called tambalis. Kadis are preferably used in cold seasons, and the tambalis in hot seasons.

Warm kadis are prepared in eight variations: 1. Cumin seed and pepper corns, 6 garlic cloves crushed, all fried in groundnut oil. 2. **Aval kaati:** 6-8 pieces soaked in hot water, 6 garlic cloves fried in a little oil. 3. **Mango stone:** Stone of a pickled mango should be roasted on live coals. The shell should be broken open. The inner core to be fried in ghee with cumin seed and pepper corns. 4. **Tender shoots or leaves:** Pomegranate, radish, cauliflower, pumpkin,

kovai or negro coffee steam-cooked, and fried cumin seed, pepper corns and garlic cloves (crushed). If the skin of ridge gourd is used, fry it with the other ingredients (do not steam-cook). 5. **Shirkaal:** 1 tbsp fried in a little oil or ghee (do not use cumin seed, pepper corns or garlic). 6. ***Asafoetida:** A large pinch. 7. ***Ajawan:** 1 teaspoon. 8. ***Triphala:** 10 triphals.
*To be fried in oil and used in the same way as shirkaal.

Other common ingredients for the above mentioned kadis are:

- ¾ coconut gratings
- 4-5 red chillies
- a small ball of tamarind
- salt to taste
- 3-4 cups water
- 1 tsp ghee
- 6-8 garlic cloves-crushed

1. Grind together coconut gratings, chillies, tamarind and salt to a coarse paste. 2. Add any one of the variations mentioned above, as desired. Grind further to a fine paste. 3. Put the masala in a vessel, add water to form liquid gravy. Bring it to boil, remove the vessel from the fire immediately. 4. Heat oil or ghee in an iron ladle and fry the garlic to reddish brown colour. Add the seasoning to the kadi. Serve with rice.

Cold tamblis are prepared in eight variations: 1. **Asafoetida:** 1 teaspoon asafoetida fried in a little ghee. 2. **Tender shoots or leaves of pomegranate, radish, cauliflower, pumpkin, kovai or negro coffee (steam-cooked) and fried asafoetida. If the skin of ridge gourd is used, fry it with asafoetida (do not steam-cook).** 3. **Mango stone:** Treat the mango stone as for kadi No. 3 and add 1 tsp fried cumin seed. 4. **Shirkaal:** 1 tbsp shirkaal fried in a little ghee. 5. **Ginger-onion:** A piece of raw ginger to be ground with other ingredients, finely chopped onion mixed later in the ready tambli. 6. **Green chillies:** 3-4 chillies fried in 1 tbsp. ghee along with a pinch of asafoetida (no red chillies to be added). 7. **Garlic:** 8-10 raw garlic cloves. 8. **Triphala:** 10 pieces fried in a little ghee.
Other common ingredients for the above-mentioned tambalis are:

- ¾ coconut gratings
- 4-5 red chillies
- 1-1½ cups sour buttermilk
- salt to taste

1. Grind together coconut gratings, chillies and salt to a coarse paste. 2. Add any one of the variations mentioned above as desired. Grind further to a fine paste. 3. Put the masala in a vessel, add a little water and the sour buttermilk to form a liquid gravy. Serve cold with rice.

Saar or Rasam (Liquid dal curries)

1. Red gram dal (Toor dal) saar (variety 1)

½ cup red gram dal
tamarind, size of a lemon
jaggery, size of a lemon
salt to taste
6-8 curry leaves
1½ litres water

1½ tbsps groundnut oil
½ tsp mustard seeds
pieces of 3 red chillies
1 pinch asafoetida
a few curry leaves

1. Wash the dal and cook it with 3 cups water in a cooker until very soft. Beat it well. 2. Extract pulp from the tamarind, add it to the cooked dal. 3. Add salt, jaggery, curry leaves and water. Cook the dal again on a direct flame until it boils. 4. Heat oil in an iron ladle, prepare a seasoning with mustard seeds, chillies, curry leaves and asafoetida. 5. Add the seasoning to the dal.

2. Saar (variety 2)

All the ingredients mentioned in recipe No. 1. In addition:

2 tsps coriander seeds
½ tsp fenugreek seeds
¼ tsp cumin seeds

1 tsp mustard seeds
½ tsp turmeric powder
8 pepper corns

1. Fry in 2 tbsps groundnut oil and pound or grind together. Add this to the cooked dal. 2. Follow instructions given for Recipe No. 1.

NOTE: Use less proportion of jaggery.

3. Saar (variety 3)

½ cup red gram dal
pulp of a small ball of tamarind
2 green chillies-sliced or
½ tsp chilli powder

1½ tbsps coconut oil or ghee
6-8 garlic cloves-crushed
pieces of 2 red chillies
salt to taste

1. Cook dal as in recipe No. 4. Beat well. 2. Add tamarind pulp, chillies, salt to the dal and cook until it boils. 3. Heat oil in an iron ladle, prepare a seasoning with garlic and chillies. Add it to the dal.

4. Ambat-varan

½ cup red gram dal
salt and jaggery to taste
½ tsp turmeric powder
1½ litres water
tamarind pulp to taste
3-4 green chillies sliced or
½ tsp chilli powder
a handful coriander leaves, chopped
1 tbsp groundnut oil
½ tsp mustard seeds
½ tsp cumin seeds
1 pinch asafoetida
a few curry leaves

1. Wash and cook dal in the cooker until very soft. Beat it well. 2. Add salt, jaggery, turmeric powder, chillies and water to bring it to the required liquid consistency. Cook until the dal comes to boil. 3. Heat oil, and prepare a seasoning with mustard seeds, cumin seeds, asafoetida and curry leaves. Add it to the dal. **4.** Lastly add the coriander leaves.

NOTE: This **varan** should be sweet and sour to taste.

5. Dal kadi

½ cup red gram dal
salt to taste
1 tbsp groundnut oil
6 garlic cloves, crushed
4 pepper corns*
a handful coconut gratings*
6 red chillies*
a small ball of tamarind*
5-6 garlic cloves*

*Grind to paste

1. Cook dal as given in recipe No. 4. Beat well. **2.** Grind the masala and add it to the dal along with salt. Bring the dal to boil. 3. Heat oil in an iron ladle, prepare a seasoning with garlic and add it to the dal.

6. Tamil saar

½ cup red gram dal
1-1½ tsps tamili rasam masala
tamarind pulp, salt and jaggery to taste
1 tbsp groundnut oil
½ tsp mustard seeds
a few curry leaves

1. Cook dal in the pressure cooker until very soft as given in recipe No. 4. Beat well. **2.** Add water to make it to the required liquid consistency. **3.** Add tamarind pulp, salt and the ready **Tamili masala**. Bring it to boil. **4.** Prepare a seasoning of mustard seeds and curry leaves in oil and add it to the saar.

7 Rasam (variety 1)

1½ cups red gram dal
tamarind pulp, salt and jaggery to taste
1 tbsp groundnut oil
6 garlic cloves-crushed
½ tsp coriander seeds*
½ tsp cumin seeds*
4-5 pepper corns*

*Roasted on a hot plate and pounded

1. Wash the dal, cook it in the pressure cooker with extra quantity of water, until it is very soft. Strain the water and use it for rasam. The thick cooked dal can be used for **parapu** (recipe No. 9 given below). 2. Add the pounded ingredients, tamarind pulp, salt and jaggery. Bring it to boil. 3. Heat oil in an iron ladle, prepare a seasoning with garlic and add it to the rasam.

8. Rasam (variety 2)

½ cup red gram dal
½ tsp coriander seeds*
½ tsp cumin seeds*
¼ tsp fenugreek seeds*
5-6 red chillies*
a few curry leaves*
tamarind pulp
salt and jaggery to taste
1 tbsp groundnut oil
½ tsp mustard seeds
a few curry leaves
1 pinch asafoetida

*Fry in a little oil and pound together

1. Wash and cook the dal in a pressure cooker until very soft. Beat it well. 2. Add water to bring the dal to the required liquid consistency. 3. Add tamarind pulp, salt, jaggery and 2 teaspoons of pounded mixture. Bring the dal to boil. 4. Prepare a seasoning with mustard seeds, curry leaves and asafoetida in oil, and add it to the dal.

NOTE: The pounded masala, if prepared in a larger proportion, can be stored in a glass jar, and used whenever needed.

9. Parapu

1½ cups red gram dal (cooked for recipe No. 8)
250 gm ladies-fingers (sliced)
3-4 green chillies (sliced)
tamarind pulp and salt to taste
1-1½ cups water
1 tbsp groundnut oil
½ tsp mustard seeds
½ tsp black gram dal
¼ tsp fenugreek seeds

1. Cooked dal should be mixed with sliced ladies fingers and green chillies, tamarind pulp and salt. 2. Add water enough to bring to a thick consistency. Heat the dal on a low flame until the vegetable cooks. 3. Heat oil and prepare seasoning with mustard seeds, black gram dal and fenugreek seeds. Add it to the dal.

NOTE: Chopped brinjals or radish can be used instead of ladies fingers.

10. Coriander leaves saar

4-6 cups water
½ bunch coriander leaves
tamarind, salt and jaggery to taste
a few curry leaves
1 handful coconut gratings*
1 green chilli*
1 tbsp groundnut oil
½ tsp mustard seeds

*Grind to a paste

1. Wash the coriander leaf-stalks and chop them fine. 2. Mix chopped leaves, water, tamarind, salt and jaggery in a vessel. Bring it to boil. 3. Add the ground coconut paste and simmer for 5-6 minutes. 4. Heat oil and prepare a seasoning with mustard seeds and curry leaves. Add it to the saar.

11. Kokum saar

4-6 cups water
12 kokum rinds (wash before use)
4-5 pepper corns*
1 tsp cumin seeds*
1 pinch asafoetida
salt and jaggery to taste
¼ coconut gratings—grind and extract juice
1 tbsp groundnut oil
½ tsp mustard seeds

*Fried in a little ghee and pounded

1. Boil water in a vessel, add the kokum rinds and remove the vessel from the flame. Allow it to stand for a few minutes. 2. Remove the rinds from the water and throw them away. 3. Add the pounded ingredients (fried pepper corns and cumin seeds), salt and jaggery to the water and heat again. 4. Heat oil, prepare a seasoning with mustard seeds and asafoetida. Add it to the saar.
5. Lastly pour the extracted juice of coconut into the kokum saar.

12. Kokum kadi

4-6 cups water
12 kokum rinds (wash before use)
salt and jaggery to taste
4-5 garlic cloves-crushed
¼ coconut gratings*
3-4 garlic cloves*
4 pepper corns*
1 tbsp groundnut oil

*Grind finely

1. Boil water in a vessel, add the kokum rinds and remove the vessel from the flame. Allow it to stand for a few minutes. 2. Remove the rinds from the water and throw them away. 3. Add the ground ingredients to the water and bring it to boil. 4. Heat oil, prepare a seasoning with garlic cloves and add it to the kadi.

Preparations using Red Gram Dal (Toor Dal)

1. Dali saar

1 cup toor dal
4 cups water
1 pinch asafoetida
salt to taste
2-3 red chillies – broken*
1/4 tsp mustard seeds*
a few curry leaves*
1/4 tsp turmeric powder*
1 tbsp ghee or oil*

*For seasoning

1. Cook the dal in the pressure cooker with 2 cups water and a little turmeric. 2. Add salt, blend well and simmer again adding 2 more cups of the remaining water. 3. Add the seasoning.

NOTE: The consistency of saar is thinner than that of tauy

2. Dali tauy

1 cup toor dal
3 cups water
2-3 green chillies
a small piece ginger
salt to taste
1/4 tsp mustard seeds
1 pinch asafoetida
1/4 tsp turmeric powder
a few curry leaves
1 tbsp ghee or oil for seasoning

1. Cook the dal with 2 cups water, crushed ginger and slit green chillies in the pressure cooker. 2. Add salt to taste, half of the turmeric powder, remaining 1 cup water. Blend well and simmer again. 3. Prepare a seasoning with ghee or oil, mustard seeds, the rest of the turmeric powder, asafoetida and curry leaves. Add to the dal and serve.

3. Dali tauykadi

1/2 cup toor dal
1 cup water
tamarind – 1 small marble size
or
3-4 kokum rinds
or
green mango cubes
(of 1/2 mango)
1 tbsp grated coconut*
3 red chillies*
6-8 cloves garlic*
6-7 pepper corns*
1/4 tsp cumin seeds*
turmeric powder 1/4 tsp
salt to taste

*Fry in oil

1. Cook the dal in the pressure cooker with water and turmeric powder. 2. Blend the dal well. Add salt to taste, tamarind juice or

kokum rinds or green mango cubes and simmer. 3. Grind the fried ingredients together to a paste, add to the dal and boil.

NOTE: seasoning of garlic is optional.

4. Dali varan

¾ cup red gram dal
salt to taste
1 tbsp groundnut oil
½ tsp mustard seeds
a few curry leaves

½ coconut gratings*
3-4 red chillies*
½ tsp turmeric powder*
¼ tsp cumin seeds*
4 pepper corns*
a small ball of tamarind*

*Grind finely

1. Wash the dal and cook it in a cooker with enough water (about 2½ cups), until very soft. 2. Beat the cooked dal, add salt and the ground masala. 3. Add some water to bring it to a required thick consistency. 4. Heat in a medium flame until the dal comes to boil. 5. Prepare a seasoning of mustard seeds and curry leaves in oil and add it to the varan.

5. Dali ambat

¾ cup red gram dal
salt to taste
1 tbsp coconut or groundnut oil
1 onion, chopped fine

½ coconut gratings*
4-6 red chillies*
½ tsp turmeric powder*
½ tsp cumin seeds*
or ¼ tsp fenugreek seeds fried in oil*

*Grind finely

1. Wash the dal and cook it in a cooker with 2-3 cups water until very soft. 2. Beat the dal slightly, add salt and the ground masala. 3. Add some water to bring it to the required liquid consistency. 4. Heat on a medium flame until the dal comes to boil. 5. Prepare a seasoning of onion in oil and add it to the ambat.

6. Dali sambare

¾ cup red gram dal
2-3 brinjals (cut into big pieces)
salt to taste
1 tbsp groundnut oil or coconut oil
5-6 garlic cloves (crushed)

½ coconut gratings
a small ball of tamarind
½ tsp turmeric powder
5-6 red chillies*
1½ teaspoon coriander seeds*

*Fry in a little oil

1. Wash the dal. Cook the dal in a cooker in enough water until soft. 2. Add brinjal pieces and salt and cook. 3. Grind together

the coconut gratings, tamarind, turmeric powder and fried ingredients until fine. 4. Add the ground masala to the dal and bring it to boil. 5. Heat oil and prepare a seasoning with garlic and add it to the sambare.

For variation: Instead of brinjals, cut potatoes, yam, cucumber, drumsticks, Indian spinach (vaali) or spinach may be used for ambat and sambare.

7. Sweet varan

1 cup red gram dal
½ tsp turmeric powder
⅛ tsp asafoetida
salt to taste
¼ tsp sugar (optional)
¼ tsp cumin seed powder

1. Wash the dal. Add turmeric powder, asafoetida and cuminseed powder to the dal and cook it with enough water in a cooker until very soft. 2. Beat the dal well. Add extra water to bring it to a thick liquid consistency. 3. Add salt and sugar, and heat the dal until it comes to boil.

8. Seasoned varan

¾ cup red gram dal
1½ tsps amti powder
1 tsp chilli powder
salt and tamarind pulp to taste
a large pinch asafoetida
1 tbsp coconut gratings
1 tbsp groundnut oil
½ tsp mustard seeds
¼ tsp turmeric powder

1. Wash the dal. Cook it with 2-3 cups water in a cooker until very soft. 2. Add amti powder, chilli powder, salt, tamarind pulp and some water to bring it to a required liquid consistency. 3. Heat the dal until it boils, sprinkle the coconut gratings into the dal. 4. Prepare a seasoning with mustard seeds, turmeric powder and asafoetida in oil and add it to the dal.

9. Amti

¾-1 cup red gram dal
2-3 potatoes boiled and cut into big cubes
2-2½ tsp amti powder
salt and tamarind pulp to taste
3-4 green chillies-sliced
a handful coconut gratings
coriander leaves chopped fine
1 tbsp groundnut oil
1 onion-chopped fine

1. Wash the dal and cook it in a cooker with enough water (2-3 cups), until very soft. Beat well. 2. Add the cut potatoes, and chillies and cook. Add amti powder, salt, tamarind pulp to the dal

and some water to bring it to the required liquid consistency. Bring the dal to boil. **3.** Sprinkle the chopped coconut gratings and coriander leaves into the dal. **4.** Heat oil, prepare a seasoning with onion and add it to the amti.

For variation: Instead of potatoes, vegetables like brinjals, yam or radish may be used.

10. Kholamba

3/4 cup red gram dal
3-4 brinjals (cut into big pieces)
salt and tamarind pulp to taste
2-3 tsps kholamba powder
1 tbsp groundnut oil
1/2 tsp mustard seeds
a pinch of asafoetida
a few curry leaves
pieces of 2-3 red chillies

1. Wash the dal. Cook the dal and cut brinjals separately with enough water until very soft. **2.** Add salt, tamarind pulp and kholamba powder to the dal, and enough water to bring it to the required liquid consistency. Bring it to boil. **3.** Heat oil and prepare a seasoning with mustard seeds, chillies, curry leaves and asafoetida. Add the seasoning to the dal.

11. Dal curry

1 cup red gram dal
2 green chillies (sliced)
3-4 tomatoes (cut into big cubes)
4 garlic cloves*
1/4 tsp turmeric powder
1-1 1/2 tsps chilli powder
salt to taste
a handful coriander leaves*

*Chopped fine

1. Wash the dal. Cook it with enough water in a cooker until very soft. **2.** Add the chillies, cut tomatoes, chopped coriander leaves and garlic, turmeric powder, chilli powder and salt to the dal. **3.** Add some water to bring it to the required liquid consistency and boil the dal until it simmers.

Preparations using Pulses

Pulses like bengal gram, dried green peas, lentils, kidney beans, cow peas, green gram etc. should be soaked in water overnight before use.

To sprout the pulses, soak them in water for 12 hours. Strain them from water the next morning. Tie the pulses in a piece of cloth. Keep the bundle in a container covered with a lid for 12 hours, to sprout.

The sprouted pulses should be dipped in water for 4-6 hours before use to remove the outer skin or covering of the pulses. These sprouted pulses (green gram, lentils or kidney peas) can be used to prepare saar, usal sambare etc.

Horse Gram

1. Saar

1½ cups horse gram (kulith soaked overnight in water – optional)
salt and jaggery (optional) to taste
6 garlic cloves (crushed)
4 garlic cloves*
1 tbsp groundnut oil
2-3 red chillies*
a small ball of tamarind*
1 tsp coriander seeds*
a handful cooked horse gram*

*Grind together

1. Wash the horse gram, and add 4-5 cups water. Cook in a pressure cooker until the gram is soft (20 minutes). 2. Strain the water and use it to prepare saar. (The cooked gram may be used for usal, recipe given below). 3. Add salt, jaggery and the ground ingredients to the strained water. Bring it to boil. 4. Heat oil, prepare a seasoning with garlic and add it to the saar.

NOTE: 1. If desired, consistency can be made thick by using extra quantity of cooked gram in the masala. This is called kadi. 2. South Indian cucumber (muggen) cut and boiled can be added to the saar.

2. Usal

1 cup cooked horse gram
salt to taste
jaggery (size of a lemon)
a few curry leaves
a handful coconut gratings
1 tbsp groundnut oil
½ tsp mustard seeds
2-3 red chillies (cut)

1. Heat oil in a pan and prepare a seasoning with mustard seeds, curry leaves and chillies. 2. Add the cooked gram, salt and jaggery. Cook on a low flame for 5-10 minutes. 3. Sprinkle the coconut gratings and remove the pan from the flame.

3. Kodel

1 cup cooked horse gram
salt to taste
1 handful cooked horse gram*
½ coconut gratings*
8 red chillies*
tamarind (size of a lemon)*
10 triphal (add last, crushed slightly)

1. Mix together horse gram, salt and the ground masala. 2. Add enough water to form a thick gravy and bring it to boil.

NOTE: This preparation will be spicy and hot. Muggen, tender bamboo shoots or raw jackfruit pieces can be added to this kodel.

Green Gram

Amti (Variety 1)

1 cup sprouted green gram
2 onions chopped
1½ tbsps groundnut oil
salt and tamarind pulp to taste
a handful chopped coriander
½ coconut gratings-roasted slightly
5 cloves*
1 piece of cinnamon*
¼ tsp black cumin seed*
½ tsp coriander seeds*
½ tsp chilli powder*
1 pinch asafoetida*

*Fry in a little oil

1. Boil and cook the sprouted pulse (do not cook in the pressure cooker) until tender. 2. Fry the chopped onions in oil until light

brown. 3. Grind together coconut gratings, fried ingredients including fried onions to a fine paste. 4. Add the ground masala, salt and tamarind pulp to the cooked gram. 5. Add enough water to form a liquid gravy. Bring it to boil. 6. Lastly sprinkle the chopped coriander leaves, and remove the vessel from the flame.

NOTE: This type of preparation can be made by using any sprouted pulses.

2. Amti (Variety 2)

1-1½ cups sprouted green gram (or any sprouted pulses)
salt and tamarind pulp to taste
1 tsp amti powder
a handful chopped coriander leaves
a handful coconut gratings*
2 onions chopped*
½ coconut gratings (grind and extract juice)
1 tbsp groundnut oil
1 onion (chopped)

*Fry in oil

1. Boil and cook the sprouted gram (do not cook in a pressure cooker) until tender. 2. Grind the fried ingredients to a paste. Add it to the cooked gram. 3. Add salt, tamarind pulp and amti powder. 4. Keep the vessel on the flame and bring the mixture to boil. 5. Add the coconut juice and coriander leaves and remove the vessel from the flame. 6. Heat oil, prepare a seasoning with onion and add it to the amti.

3. Saar

½ cup cooked sprouted green gram (bengal gram or dried peas)
a small ball of tamarind
2 red chillies
4-5 cups water
salt to taste
jaggery (size of a lemon)
1 tbsp groundnut oil
½ tsp mustard seeds
a few curry leaves

1. Grind together cooked gram, tamarind and chillies to a fine paste. 2. Add water to the ground ingredients to form a thin liquid consistency. 3. Add salt and jaggery, and bring it to boil. 4. Heat oil, prepare a seasoning with mustard seeds and curry leaves. Add it to the saar.

4. Usal (variety 1)

2 cups sprouted green gram
1 tbsp groundnut oil
½ tsp mustard seeds
a few curry leaves
salt and jaggery to taste
1 tsp chilli powder
a handful coconut grating

1. Heat oil in a pan and prepare seasoning with mustard seeds and curry leaves. 2. Add the gram and cook on a low flame with a lit-

tle water until tender. **3.** Add salt and jaggery, and simmer for a few minutes. **4.** Lastly add coconut gratings and remove the pan from the flame.

5. Usal (variety 2)

2 cups sprouted green gram
2 onions chopped
1½ tbsps groundnut oil
1 tsp amti or garam masala powder
salt and jaggery to taste
a handful chopped coriander leaves

1. Heat oil in a pan and fry the onions until light brown. **2.** Add the sprouted gram and a little water. Cook the gram on a low flame until tender. **3.** Add salt, jaggery and amti powder. Simmer for a few minutes. **4.** Lastly add the chopped coriander leaves.

NOTE: This is a dry preparation.

Field Beans (Vaal)

1. Bendi (spicy and hot)

1 cup field beans (soaked in water overnight)
10-15 red chillies
tamarind, size of a lemon
salt to taste
1 tbsp coconut or groundnut oil
6 garlic cloves (crushed)
3-4 garlic cloves

1. Cook the beans in a pressure cooker for 10 minutes until soft. **2.** Grind chillies, tamarind, garlic, and a handful cooked beans to a fine paste. **3.** Add the ground paste to the cooked beans, and a little water to form a thick gravy. **4.** Add salt and bring the mixture to boil. **5.** Heat oil, prepare a seasoning with garlic, and add it to the bendi.

NOTE: To prepare Saar, ghashhi, kodel or bendi of any pulses, follow the above mentioned instructions given for those recipes.

2. Ambat (of sprouted green gram or field beans)

1½ cups sprouted pulses (remove skin)
salt to taste
1½ tbsps groundnut oil
1 large onion-chopped
½ coconut gratings
½ tsp turmeric powder
a small ball of tamarind
4-5 red chillies*
¼ tsp fenugreek seeds*

* Fry in a little oil

1. Boil and cook the sprouted pulses in water until soft. 2. Grind the masala with coconut gratings, turmeric powder, tamarind, fried ingredients and a handful cooked pulses. 3. Add the masala, a little water to form a thick gravy, and salt to the cooked pulses. Bring it to boil. 4. Heat oil in an iron ladle, prepare a seasoning with onions and add it to the ambat.

NOTE: Instead of onion seasoning, seasoning with mustard seeds and curry leaves can be used (specially for religious occasions).

3. Usal

1½ cups sprouted field beans
1½ tbsps groundnut oil
¼ tsp cumin seeds
¼ tsp turmeric powder
1 pinch asafoetida
¼ coconut gratings*
1-2 green chillies*
½ tsp poppy seeds*
a handful coriander leaves, chopped
salt and jaggery to taste

*Grind finely

1. Remove the skin of the sprouted beans. 2. Heat oil in a pan and prepare a seasoning with cumin seeds, turmeric powder and asafoetida. 3. Add the beans to the seasoning, and with the help of a little water cook the beans until soft. 4. Add salt, jaggery and the ground paste. Simmer on a low flame for a few minutes. 5. Lastly sprinkle the chopped coriander leaves, and remove the pan from the flame.

Maize

1. Usal (variety 1)

6 corn cobs
3 onions, chopped
3-4 green chillies, sliced
salt to taste
1½ tbsps ghee
a handful coconut gratings

1. Wash the corn cobs and grate them on a grater. 2. Heat ghee in a pan and fry the chillies for a few minutes. 3. Add onions and fry until golden brown. 4. Add the grated corn and steam cook on a low flame until ready. 5. Add salt and coconut gratings. Remove the pan from the flame.

2. Usal (variety 2)

6 corn cobs
1 tbsp ghee or groundnut oil
salt and sugar to taste
a handful coconut gratings
½ tsp mustard seeds
2 red chillies (cut into pieces)
a few curry leaves

1. Wash the corn cobs and grate them on a grater. 2. Heat ghee or oil and prepare a seasoning with mustard seeds, chillies and curry leaves. 3. Add grated corn and steam-cook on a low flame until ready. 4. Add salt and sugar and sprinkle the coconut gratings, stir for a few minutes. Remove the pan from the flame.

Sweet and Savoury Dishes

---

1. Idlis (black gram dal)

1¼ cups coarse rice (wash, dry, and grind coarsely)
salt to taste
1 cup black gram dal (wash and soak in water for 2-3 hours)
2-3 tsps groundnut oil

1. Use the water in which the washed dal is soaked for grinding. 2. Grind the dal by adding a little water from time to time, until it is very fine and frothy. 3. Mix the ground rice with ground dal. Add salt and blend well. Add a little water, if necessary to bring it to a thick semi-liquid consistency. 4. Cover the vessel with a lid and allow it to ferment overnight. 5. Apply oil to the small metal containers in which the idlis are to be steam-cooked. 6. Beat the dough well, take portions of dough and fill ½ of each of the containers. 7. Steam-cook idlis in an ordinary cooker or pressure cooker, without using the weight, for 7 minutes until the idlis are cooked. 8. Remove the containers from the cooker. Allow the idlis to cool slightly, and turn them out carefully with a knife. Serve the idlis with hot chutney.

NOTE: 1. Idlis can be made with roasted wheat rava (coarsely ground wheat) by using the proportion of 1 cup wheat rava to 1 cup black gram dal. 2. Wheat rava can be steam-cooked in the cooker (by tieing it in a piece of cloth) separated and cooled immediately, and then mixed with the idli dough. 3. Roasted or steam-cooked wheat rava should be added to the fermented batter just a few minutes before steam-cooking the idlis. Vari rice can also be used instead of rice or wheat rava. Soak vari in water, grind it coarsely and mix in the dough. Add a few chopped green chillies and a piece of chopped ginger along with ½ tsp cumin seeds

2. Khotte

1½ cups black gram dal
1½ cups roasted wheat rawa or rice rawa
salt to taste
containers made out of jackfruit leaves

1. Follow instructions given for recipe No. 1 to grind the dough. 2. Instead of using metal containers, the dough should be distributed in the jackfruit leaf-containers. 3. Steamcook the khotte in a cooker until they are ready. (The leaves should appear discoloured).

3. Sweet idlis

1½ cup black gram dal
1½ cup rice rava or roasted wheat rava
salt to taste
½ coconut gratings*
½ cup grated jaggery*
3-4 cardamoms pounded*

*Mix together

1. Follow instructions given for recipe No. 1 to grind the dough. 2. Mix the wheat or rice rava. Blend well. 3. Fill the containers with a little dough. Spread a layer of sweetened coconut, and over it another layer of dough. 4. Steam-cook them until ready (instructions given in recipe No. 1).

4. Dudhi sandan (idlis)

1 cup beaten rice (poha)
½ coconut gratings
1½ cups coarse rice (ground coarsely)
2 cups jaggery grated
5-6 cardamoms (pounded)
½ cup milk
½ cup buttermilk

1. Wash the beaten rice. Mix it with all the other ingredients. Blend well. 2. Allow it to ferment overnight in a vessel covered with lid. 3. Steam-cook the sweet idlis in a cooker.

5. Hot and spicy sandan (idlis) variety 1

1 cup rice
¼ coconut gratings*
3 red chillies*
½ tsp turmeric powder*
1 pinch asafoetida*
a small ball of tamarind*
jaggery, size of a lemon*
¼ cup red gram dal (washed and soaked in water for 2-3 hours)*

*Grind finely

1. Wash, dry and grind the rice coarsely. Mix together the ground ingredients, the coarsely ground rice and salt. 2. Allow it to fer-

ment overnight in a vessel covered with a lid. 3. Add a little warm water to the dough and blend well. 4. Steam-cook the idlis in metal containers or jackfruit leaf-containers.

NOTE: Idlis made with ground rice require more time to get steam-cooked.

6. Hot and spicy sandan (idlis) (variety 2)

1 cup wheat rava
1 cup buttermilk
1 cup water
salt to taste
3 chopped green chillies
a handful coriander leaves
1 ½ tbsps ghee
jaggery to taste

1. Roast the wheat rava with the help of a little ghee. 2. Follow instructions given for recipe No. 7.

7. Jaggery-rava idlis

1 cup wheat rava (coarsely ground wheat)
1 cup buttermilk
1 cup water
¾ cup jaggery
salt to taste
2-3 cardamoms (pounded)
a handful cashewnut pieces
1 ½ tbsps ghee

1. Roast the wheat rava with the help of a little ghee. 2. Mix together buttermilk, water, jaggery, salt and cardamoms. Heat the mixture on a low flame. Bring it to boil. 3. Add the cashewnut pieces and the wheat rava. 4. When the mixture thickens, remove the vessel from the flame. 5. Steam-cook the mixture in idli containers as given in recipe No. 1.

8. Dudholi

2 cups rice (soak in water overnight)
2 cups jaggery (grated)
a handful cashewnut pieces
1 coconut gratings
6-8 cardamoms (pounded)

1. Grind the coconut gratings and extract thick and thin juice separately. 2. Grind the soaked rice in thin juice until fine. 3. Mix the jaggery, cardamoms and cashew-nut pieces with the ground rice along with thick coconut juice. This will be a liquid mixture. 4. Apply ghee to the metal containers, pour portions of the liquid mixture in the containers. 5. Steam-cook the idlis in a cooker until ready.

NOTE: These idlis should be thinner in thickness than ordinary idlis.

9. Pumpkin kadamb

1 cup rice (wash dry and grind coarsely)
2 cups grated pumpkin
¼ coconut gratings
salt to taste
a handful grated jaggery
3-4 banana leaves or turmeric leaves

1. Mix together all the ingredients. 2. Divide the mixture into small handful portions. 3. Bind each portion with the pieces of banana leaves securely. 4. Steam-cook in a cooker until ready.

NOTE: For variation vegetables like cucumber or maggen can be used instead of pumpkin.

10. Rice sevayo and rassu

4 cups rice (soak in water for 4-5 hours)
1 coconut gratings
salt to taste
hot water to mix the dough
1 ½ coconut gratings (grind and extract juice)
1 cup grated jaggery
4-5 pounded cardamoms

1. Grind the rice very fine. Add water and allow it to ferment overnight. 2. Grind the coconut gratings until very fine. 3. Mix the salt, coconut gratings and finely ground rice. 4. Add hot water, stirring the mixture all the time, until the mixture is of semi-liquid consistency. 5. Steam-cook portions of the mixture in oil-greased metal containers. 6. While the cooked mixture is hot, pass each portion through a sevaya-press. 7. Place them carefully in a damp cloth until use. 8. Mix together coconut juice, jaggery and cardamom powder. Use this juice to serve with the sevayas.

11. Rice undiyo

1 ½ cup rice (wash, dry and grind coarsely)
¼ coconut gratings (grind coarsely)
3 tsps ghee or coconut oil
a few curry leaves
2 cups water
1 ½ tsp salt
a small ball of jaggery
½ tsp mustard seeds

1. Heat ghee or oil in a vessel and prepare a seasoning with mustard seeds and curry leaves. 2. Add water, salt, jaggery, ground coconut and ground coarse rice, stirring all the time. 3. Bring it to boil on a low flame until it thickens. 4. Allow the rice grains to cook until soft. 5. When the mixture comes to the consistency of a soft dough, spread it in a thali (a flat plate). 6. Allow the dough to cool slightly. Form long-shaped balls by pressing portions of

dough with the hand. Press each ball in the centre to form a depression. 7. Steam the balls in a cooker again before serving. 8. Serve with sweetened coconut juice (see recipe No. 10).

12. Patholyo (vari)

1½ cups vari rice (wash and soak in water)
water to mix
salt to taste
¼ coconut gratings (grind coarsely)
1 tbsp ghee
a few turmeric leaves or banana leaves (wash and cut into broad pieces)

1. Mix the vari rice, ground coconut, salt, ghee and a little water to bring to a semi-solid consistency. (It should be easy to spread on the leaves.) 2. Take portions of the mixture and spread evenly on the leaves. Fold the leaves. 3. Arrange the leaves in a pressure cooker and steam cook for 10-15 minutes (without the weights on).

NOTE : If desired a sweet filling of coconut gratings, jaggery and cardamom powder mixed together may be used. (This preparation is usually done for Gouri puja.) Instead of vari rice, coarsely ground rice/flour/maida may be used.

13. Jackfruit patholyo

2 cups jackfruit sections (seeds removed)
½ coconut gratings
a small ball of jaggery
1 cup rice (washed)
salt to taste
a few turmeric leaves or broad pieces of banana leaves

1. Cut jackfruit sections into small pieces. 2. Mix together jackfruit, rice, coconut gratings, salt and jaggery and grind to a fine paste. 3. Mix a little water to bring the ground paste to consistency of idli (semi-liquid). 4. Spread portions of dough evenly on the leaves, fold the leaves. 5. Heat the pressure cooker, arrange the leaves and steam-cook for 10-15 minutes (without the weights on).

14. Chunachyo nevaryo

1¼ cups rice flour
salt to taste
½ coconut gratings*
a few cardamoms (pounded)*
½ coconut gratings (grind and extract 1 cup juice)
¼ cup jaggery-grated*

* Mix together for filling

1. Mix together rice flour, coconut juice and salt. 2. Bring it to boil on a low flame. Cook until it forms a thick dough. 3. Allow

it to cool slightly. Take portions of dough and spread on the palm. **4.** Spread the filling on half the portion. Cover with dough from all sides to form a semi circular shape. **5.** Steam-cook them in a pressure cooker for 5-8 minutes (without the weights on).

15. Jackfruit muluk

2 cups finely cut jackfruit sections (good quality)
½ tsp salt
6 cardamoms, pounded
a little milk to mix or coconut water
2 cups rice flour
a handful jaggery
½ coconut gratings
cooking fat to deep fry

1. Mix together cut jackfruit, rice flour, salt, jaggery, cardamom powder, coconut gratings and milk to form a soft dough. **2.** Heat fat in a frying pan. **3.** Take portions of dough (size of a lemon) and deep fry until reddish brown. Can be preserved for 2-3 days.

16. Green gram sukrunde

2 cups green gram (soak in water overnight)
2 cups jaggery grated
2 cups flour (maida)
2 measures water
6 cups water (to boil and cook the green gram)
6 cardamoms pounded
1 tsp turmeric powder
cooking fat to deep fry

1. Boil and cook the green gram in water until soft. Drain off the water. **2.** Mix the cooked gram, jaggery and cardamoms. **3.** Cook the mixture again on a low flame until the water is absorbed, and a soft dough is formed. **4.** Allow it to cool and form small balls of the mixture. **5.** Heat fat in a frying pan. Mix together maida, turmeric powder and water to form a semi-liquid batter. Dip each ball in the semi-liquid batter to cover it evenly. **6.** Deep fry in fat until light brown.

NOTE: Bengal gram dal or green gram dal may be used instead of whole green gram for the above-mentioned recipe. For the outer covering, batter of rice flour may be used.

17. Puranpoli

1½ cups bengal gram dal (soak for 2-3 hours in water)
4-5 cardamoms and a small piece of nutmeg pound together
½ cup water
5-6 tsp groundnut oil
1½ cups grated jaggery
1½ cup flour (maida)
1 tsp turmeric powder

1. Wash the dal, add enough water to cover the dal. 2. Cook dal in a pressure cooker until very soft. Drain off the water. 3. Add jaggery to the dal and simmer it on a low flame, stirring all the time. Cook until the water absorbs and the mixture is a soft ball. 4. Allow it to cool slightly and grind to a fine paste. (Do not use water.) 5. Divide the mixture into small balls. 6. Prepare a very soft dough with flour, water, turmeric powder. Knead it well with the help of groundnut oil. 7. Apply a little groundnut oil to the palm, take a portion of dough, flatten it on the palm. 8. Place a ball of ground dal in the centre, cover it up from all sides evenly with the dough. 9. Dip each ball in flour, flatten it slightly. Roll each into a flat puranpoli (pancake). 10. Roast the puranpolis on a dry hot tava until little light brown spots appear on both sides. 11. Serve with ghee.

18. Naral (coconut) poli

1 coconut grated (grind finely without using water)
10 cardamoms, pounded
½ cup water
5-6 tsps groundnut oil
grated jaggery (¾ cup jaggery to 1 cup ground coconut)
1½ cups of flour (maida)
1 tsp turmeric powder

1. Mix together ground coconut and grated jaggery. 2. Heat on a low flame until the water content is absorbed, and the mixture becomes a soft ball. Add cardamom powder. 3. Mix together flour, water, turmeric powder and groundnut oil to form a very soft dough. Follow instructions given in recipe No. 17 (above) from step No. 6 to prepare the **naralpoli.**

19. Sanjiryo

1 cup wheat rava (coarsely ground wheat)
1½ cups sugar
10 cardamoms, pounded
¼ tsp turmeric powder (optional)
1½ cup water
3-4 tsps ghee
1½ cups flour (maida)
½ cup water
5-6 tsps groundnut oil

1. Heat ghee in a vessel and roast the wheat rava for 5-6 minutes on a low flame. 2. Add water and sugar, stirring all the time, until it blends well. 3. Allow it to cook until the water absorbs and the mixture is a soft ball. Cook for a few more minutes. 4. Remove the vessel from the flame. Allow the mixture to cool slightly. Add cardamom powder and mix. 5. Divide it into small balls. 6. Prepare a very soft dough with flour, water and groundnut oil. Knead it well. Follow instructions given in the above mentioned No. 17 recipe from step No. 6 to prepare the sanjiryo.

Pole (Pan Cakes)

1. Black gram dal and rice pole

1 cup black gram dal*
2 cups coarse rice*
a few tbsps groundnut oil
2-2½ tsps salt
a little water to mix

*Soak in water for 2-3 hours separately

1. Wash the dal and rice thoroughly. 2. First grind the dal by adding water from time to time until it is very fine and frothy. 3. Grind the rice separately similarly until very fine. 4. Mix the ground dal, rice and salt, and add a little water to form a semi-liquid consistency. The batter should be left for 2-3 hours to ferment and rise. 5. Heat the iron hot plate on a medium flame. Apply a little groundnut oil all over the surface. 6. Beat the dough well; take a ladleful of dough, spread it evenly on the hot plate to form a flat pancake. 7. Cover it with a lid. After two minutes when the pancake is reddish brown on the lower side turn it carefully and roast the other side similarly. Serve with hot chutney or butter.

For variation: vari, wheat rava, flour (maida), wheat flour or jowar flour can also be used with black gram dal instead of coarse rice.

Vari should be used as rice. Other substitutes like wheat rava, flour, wheat flour or jowar flour should be mixed in a little water to avoid lump-formation, and blended with ground dal **just before use.**

2. Pole (mixed dals)

½ cup black gram dal
½ cup green gram dal
salt to taste
½ cup bengal gram dal
2-3 green chillies*
a handful coriander leaves*

*Chopped finely

1. Soak the dals together in water for 4-5 hours. Wash the soaked dals thoroughly. 2. Grind them to a fine consistency adding a little water from time to time. 3. Add salt, chopped ingredients and a little water to bring the dough to a semi-liquid consistency. 4. For making pole follow the instructions as for the first variety.

3. Masala dosa (variety 1)

½ cup black gram dal
¼ tsp fenugreek seeds
1 ½ cups coarse rice
salt to taste

NOTE: Soak in water for 2-3 hours. Wash and grind to fine paste and allow to ferment.

For filling

Chutney

½ coconut gratings*
salt and tamarind to taste*
½ tsp mustard seeds and
a few curry leaves for seasoning
4 red chillies*
1 tbsp groundnut oil

* Grind to a fine paste with a little water.

Prepare seasoning and add it to the chutney.

Bhaji

5-6 potatoes, boiled, peeled and cut into small pieces
¼ tsp cumin seeds
½ tsp turmeric powder
3-4 onions, chopped
2 tbsps groundnut oil
1 pinch asafoetida
5-6 green chillies, sliced

After seasoning fry onions and green chillies in it, add cut-potatoes and salt. Remove from fire after 5 minutes.

1. Before use beat the dough well. 2. Heat an iron hot plate, apply one tbsp groundnut oil evenly on the surface. 3. Take a ladleful of dough and spread it evenly into a very thin pancake. 4. Roast the pancake until it is crisp and brown. Do not turn over. (The pancake should be roasted only on one side.) 5. Place the pancake on a flat plate, spread the chutney on one half and bhaji on the other half of the non-roasted side of the dosa. Fold and serve.

4. Masala dosa (variety 2)

1 cup fine wheat rava (coarsely ground wheat)
salt to taste
1 cup flour
½ cup rice flour
buttermilk to blend the flour into a semi-liquid dough.

For filling

Chutney and bhaji: 1. Follow instructions given for recipe No. 3 above. 2. Mix together wheat rava, flour, rice flour and salt. Blend with the help of water to form a semi-liquid consistency. 3. For pancakes follow the instructions as for masala dosa-variety 1.

5. Panpole

3 cups coarse rice (soak in water for 2 hours)
a few tbsps groundnut oil or coconut oil
½ coconut gratings
salt to taste

1. Wash the soaked rice thoroughly. 2. Mix together rice and coconut gratings. 3. Add salt and grind to a very fine thin consistency with the help of water. (The dough should be of buttermilk consistency.) 4. For pancake follow instructions for masala dosa. 5. Fold the panpole into four folds. Remove it from the hot plate.

6. Rassa-pole

1 ½ coconut gratings (grind and extract juice)*
3 cups coarse rice (soak in water for 2 hours)
jaggery enough to sweeten the juice*
12 cardamoms (pounded)*
½ coconut gratings
salt to taste

* Mix together and keep aside

1. Follow the instructions given for the above-mentioned recipe No. 5 to prepare panpole. 2. When the panpoles are hot, soak them in the sweetened coconut juice. 3. Serve when the rassa-poles become slightly cool.

7. Pan cake pudding

3 cups rice flour*
water enough to mix*
fruit jam or shredded jaggery with cardamom powder
1 tsp salt*
a few tbsps groundnut oil

*Mix together to form a thin batter.

1. Heat a hot plate and apply a little oil evenly. 2. Spread a ladleful of batter to form a thin pancake. 3. Allow it to become crisp and light brown. 4. While the pancakes are hot, spread a tbsp of jam or jaggery on the pancakes, roll them and serve.

8. Suranoly (honey comb pancake)

3 cups rice
½ coconut gratings
2 cups shredded jaggery
½ cup milk
groundnut oil to grease the hot plate
1 ½ cups beaten rice washed or 1 cup puffed rice
2 tsps turmeric powder
salt to taste
butter milk to soak the rice

1. Wash and soak rice in buttermilk (enough to cover) for 5 to 6 hours, **2.** Grind soaked rice and coconut gratings together. **3.** When fine, add beaten or puffed rice, turmeric powder, jaggery, salt and grind further. **4.** If necessary, add remaining buttermilk. Cover the vessel with a lid and allow the dough to ferment overnight. **5.** Heat a tava, apply a little oil. **6.** Spread a ladleful of dough to form a thick pancake. **7.** Cover the pancake with a lid and allow it to fry, **on one side only**, on a low flame. When the "honeycomb" forms, the pancake is ready.

9. Suranoly (variety 2)

3 cups rice, soak in water for 5-6 hours
½ coconut gratings
jaggery and salt to taste.

1. "Maggen" cucumber, or white part of the water-melon can be grated and soaked with the rice and ground, or ground with the soaked rice (proportion, 1 measure of grated vegetable to 1 measure of rice) and coconut gratings. 2. Add jaggery and salt to taste and allow to ferment 1-2 hours. 3. Follow instructions given for recipe No. 8.

10. Suranoly (variety 3)

All ingredients mentioned in recipe No. 8 (except turmeric powder)
½ tsp fenugreek seeds
2 tsps black gram dal (soaked in water)

Follow instructions given for recipe No. 8 but use ½ cup pounded sugar instead of jaggery.
For variation: 8 green chillies and a handful coriander leaves chopped fine, and ¼ cup pounded sugar instead of jaggery may be mixed into the dough.

11. Dhodak (Thalipith)

3 cups rice (coarsely ground)
½ coconut gratings
salt and jaggery to taste
2 cups grated maggen, cucumber or white part of the water melon
groundnut oil to grease the hot plate

1. Mix together the ingredients and keep for ½ hour. Heat the tava, apply a little oil on the surface. **2.** Take a portion of mixture and spread it evenly into a thick pancake. **3.** Cover and fry on a low flame until the pancake is reddish brown. **4.** Turn over carefully and fry the other side.

12. Dhodak (variety 2)

1 cup wheat rava (coarsely ground wheat)
2-3 green chillies (chopped)
butter milk (enough to mix into a semi-solid dough)
salt and jaggery to taste
a small ball of butter or ghee
a handful coconut gratings
groundnut oil to grease the hot plate

1. Mix the wheat rava, salt, jaggery, chopped chillies and coconut gratings together. 2. Add buttermilk to blend the ingredients into a semisolid dough. 3. Heat a tava, grease it with 2 tsps of oil. 4. Take a big lump of the dough and spread it evenly to form a thick pancake. 5. Cover and fry on a low flame until the pancake is reddish brown. 6. Turn over carefully and fry the other side.

Appe

There are four different varieties of Appe: 1. **Coconut appe**: The dough is to be prepared as given for panpole (recipe No. 5) but the consistency should be thicker. 2. **Jaggery appe**: The dough is to be prepared as given for suranolyo (recipe No. 8) but the consistency should be thicker. 3. **Black gram dal appe**: The dough is to be prepared as given for black gram dal pole (recipe No. 1), but the consistency should be thicker. 4. **Taavar appe**: Coarse parboiled rice (ukade tandul), bengal gram dal, black gram dal, green gram dal, and red gram dal, to be taken in equal proportion.

Wash well and soak in water for 4 hours. Grind to a fine paste, adding a little water from time to time. The consistency should be like the idli dough. Mix 1 pinch asafoetida, a handful chopped coriander leaves, 5 chopped green chillies, and finely cut 2.5 cm ginger in the dough.

Appes are roasted on a special appe hot plate which has small depressions. The hot plate should be greased with a little oil and heated on a low flame. Pour in 2 tspful of dough in each container and cover the hot plate with a lid. Roast the appes on both sides until they are light brown and well-cooked.

1. Eriyappe

3 cups rice
½ coconut gratings
2 tsps turmeric powder
salt to taste
cooking fat or ghee for deep frying
1 ½ cups washed beaten rice or 1 cup puffed rice
2 cups shredded jaggery
½ cup milk

1. Wash the rice and soak it in water for 4 to 5 hours. 2. Grind together rice, beaten or puffed rice, coconut gratings and turmeric powder to a fine dough. 3. Add jaggery, salt and milk and whip the dough well. (The consistency should be like beaten curds.) 4. Heat the fat in a small frying pan, pour a ladleful of dough and deep fry until the eriyappe are light brown and crisp.

2. Pakode

1 cup bengal gram flour
1 cup rice flour
1 cup cashewnuts (cut fine)
salt to taste
½ tsp turmeric powder
½ tsp soda bicarb
10 green chillies*
4 onions*
1 small piece of ginger*
a handful coriander leaves*
1 tbsp groundnut oil for dough
groundnut oil for deep frying

* Chopped fine

1. Mix gram flour, rice flour, cashewnuts, salt, turmeric powder, soda bicarb, chopped ingredients and heated 1 tbsp oil together to form a semi-solid dough. 2. Heat oil in a frying pan, drop small portions of the dough in the oil and fry them to a golden brown colour.

3. Palervade

2 cups bengal gram dal (wash and soak in water for 2-3 hours)
½ tsp turmeric powder
½ coconut gratings
groundnut oil for deep frying
2 tsps salt
3 tsps chilli powder
¼ tsp asafoetida
5 onions-chopped fine

1. Grind the gram dal until very fine. 2. Add salt, chilli powder, turmeric powder, asafoetida, coconut gratings and chopped onions to the dough. 3. Grease a shallow container with oil, pour in the dough about 4 cm thick, spread it evenly. 4. Steam-cook the dough in a double-boiler or cooker until it is ready. Remove from the cooker. 5. When slightly cool, cut the cooked dough into squares. 6. Heat oil in a frying pan and deep fry the palervade until reddish brown.

Vade

1. Black gram dal vade (variety 1)

3 cups rice (wash, dry and grind finely into rava)
½ tsp fenugreek seeds
1 ½-2 tsps salt
1 banana leaf
¾ cup blackgram dal
½ coconut gratings
a small ball of jaggery
coconut or groundnut oil for deep frying

1. Soak the gram dal and fenugreek seeds in water for 2-3 hours and grind them together with water until fine. 2. Mix in the ground rice rava, coconut gratings, salt and jaggery and prepare a stiff dough. Keep it overnight to ferment. 3. Grease a banana leaf with oil, take a small ball of the dough and pat it with the palm to form a thick round shape. 4. Heat oil in a frying pan, and on a very low flame, deep fry the vadas until they are reddish brown on both sides.

2. Black gram dal vade (variety 2)

4 cups rice
½ coconut gratings
groundnut oil for deep frying
¼ cup black gram dal
2 tsps salt

1. Wash rice, gram dal and gratings and soak in water for 3-4 hours. Grind the rice and black gram dal together until very fine. 2. Add the coconut gratings and salt to the dough. (The consistency should be semi-solid.) 3. Heat the oil in a frying pan. Dip small balls of dough into the oil and fry until the vadas are crisp and reddish brown.

3. Jowar vade

4 cups jowar flour
salt to taste
½ coconut gratings
groundnut oil for deep frying
¼ cup black gram dal (wash, soak in water for 3-4 hours, and grind fine)

1. Mix all the ingredients, except oil, with a little water to form a semi-solid dough. Keep it aside for 10-15 minutes. 2. Heat oil in a frying pan. Drop small portions of dough and deep fry the vadas until crisp and reddish brown.

4. Banana vade

3 cups rice flour
salt to taste
groundnut oil for deep frying
8-10 ripe bananas
jaggery (a handful)

1. Mash the peeled bananas. Add salt and jaggery and blend well. 2. Steam-cook the mashed mixture. 3. Remove the mixture from the cooker while it is hot. 4. Blend the rice flour with the banana mixture gradually while it is hot. 5. Heat oil in a frying pan. Prepare small flat rounds of the dough and deep fry in oil until they are crisp and reddish brown.

For variation: Papaya or red pumpkin may be used instead of bananas.

5. Kaay vade

½ coconut gratings (grind and extract 1¼ cup juice)
groundnut oil for deep-frying
salt to taste
3 cups rice flour

1. Mix salt in the coconut juice. 2. Add the rice flour gradually and blend well to form a soft dough. 3. Apply a little oil on the palm and prepare small flat rounds of the dough. 4. Heat oil in frying pan and deep fry until they are reddish brown.

6. Anaras (variety 1)

3 cups rice (wash, dry and grind finely)
3 cups jaggery
groundnut oil for deep frying
½ coconut gratings (grind and extract juice)
8 cardamoms*
16 pepper corns*

*Pounded

1. Mix together rice flour, coconut juice, jaggery and the pounded cardamoms and pepper. 2. Steam-cook the dough in the cooker for 5 minutes. 3. Apply a little oil on the palm and prepare small flat rounds. 4. Heat oil in a frying pan and fry the vadas until they are reddish brown.

7. Anaras (variety 2)

3 cups rice
a little milk (to soften the dough)
cooking fat to deep fry the anaras
2 cups jaggery
25 gm khuskhus (poppy seeds)

1. Soak the rice in water for a week, washing it every day and adding fresh water to soak. Drain off all the water and allow it to dry on a piece of cloth. Do not keep it in direct sunshine. 2. Grind the rice finely and sieve it on a fine sieve. 3. Mix together the rice flour according to the following proportion—3 cups flour to 2 cups jaggery—into a dry mixture. Knead it well and preserve in a porcelain jar with an air-tight lid. 4. When the anarase are to be prepared use a portion of the dough mixture from the jar as required. 5. Mix in a little milk to soften the dough. Knead it well and make into soft balls, press each ball slightly to half centimetre thickness. 6. Coat each anarase with khuskhus on one side only. 7. Heat the cooking fat in a deep frying pan and deep fry the anarase (with khuskhus layer side up) on a medium flame until they are reddish brown.

8. Ras vade

3 cups rice (soak it in water for 2 hours before use)
6-8 cardamoms (powdered)
milk extract of ½ coconut
3 cups jaggery
cooking fat to deep fry

1. Wash the rice and dry it on a piece of cloth in shade (not in direct sunshine). 2. Grind the rice finely into dry powder. Sieve it in a fine sieve. 3. Mix the milk extract of coconut and jaggery thoroughly. Add the cardamom powder. 4. Add the rice flour to the milk and jaggery blending it carefully. 5. Steam the mixture in a cooker until the mixture is cooked. 6. Take small portions of the mixture and press them into flat rounds. 7. Heat the cooking fat in a deep frying pan and fry the vade on a medium flame until they are reddish brown.

9. Sardali vade

1½ cups black gram dal
6-8 green chillies (chopped fine)
salt to taste
cooking fat to deep fry
1½ cups bengal gram dal
a few curry leaves (cut fine)
½ coconut gratings
a bowlful of warm water to soak the fried vade.

1. Wash the black gram dal and bengal gram dal and soak in water together for 3 to 4 hours at noon. 2. Drain off the water thoroughly over a strainer. 3. Grind the dals coarsely into a dry mixture. 4. Add salt, chopped green chillies, cut curry leaves and coconut gratings to the dal mixture. 5. Keep the mixture overnight and use it the next morning to prepare vade. 6. Knead the mixture slightly before use, take portions of the mixture and press into small rounds. 7. Heat the cooking fat in a deep frying pan and deep fry the vade on medium flame until ready.

10. Taira vade (Dahi vade)

1 cup black gram dal
a pinch of asafoetida
1 litre milk to be prepared into curds overnight
a small piece of ginger (chopped fine)
¼ cup bengal gram dal
1 tsp salt (or to taste)
a handful chopped coriander leaves
3-4 green chillies (chopped fine)

Seasoning:
2 tsps ghee or cooking fat, ½ tsp mustard seeds, 3 red chillies cut into pieces, a few curry leaves (chopped).

1. Soak the dals together in water for 3 to 4 hours. 2. Wash the dal well. Drain off the water over a strainer. 3. Grind the dals into a dry coarse mixture, adding the asafoetida and salt to it. 4. Take small portions of the dal dough and make small flat rounds by pressing on the palm. 5. Heat the cooking fat in a deep frying pan and deep fry the vade to a medium brown colour. 6. Dip the fried vade in a bowlful of warm water for sometime. 7. Beat the curds well—add salt, chopped coriander leaves, ginger and green chillies. 8. Prepare the seasoning with ingredients given above and add it to the curds. 9. Press the vade to drain off the warm water, and soak them in the curds for some minutes before serving.

11. Dried green-peas dal ambode

1 cup green-peas dal
salt to taste
a few coriander leaves-chopped
½ tsp red chilli powder
½ tsp sugar
groundnut oil to deep fry

1. Wash and soak the dal in water for 1½ hours. 2. Drain off the water and grind it dry to a coarse mixture. 3. Add chilli powder, sugar and chopped coriander leaves to the dal mixture. 4. Take portions of the mixture and press them into small slightly flat, rounds. 5. Heat oil in a deep frying pan and deep fry the ambode to a reddish brown colour.

12. Biscuit ambode

2 cups black gram dal
a handful chopped coriander leaves
½ coconut gratings
groundnut oil or cooking fat to deep fry
6-8 green chillies (chopped)
a few curry leaves
salt to taste

1. Wash and soak the dal in water for 3 to 4 hours (in the morning). 2. Drain off all the water, and grind it fine, into a thick dough. 3. Add chopped green chillies, coriander leaves, curry leaves, coconut gratings and salt to the dough. Mix well. 4. Heat the cooking fat in a deep frying pan. 5. Take portions of dough and drop them carefully into the pan. Deep fry until reddish brown. Serve them hot with or without coriander leaves chutney.

13. Sweet undlakal

milk extract of ½ coconut
1 tsp jaggery
½ coconut gratings
6 cardamoms (powdered)
½ tsp salt
2½ cups rice flour (fine)
½ cup jaggery (chopped fine)
cooking fat to deep fry

1. Mix together coconut milk extract, salt and jaggery in a vessel. 2. Keep the vessel on a medium flame and allow it to simmer. 3. Pour in the rice flour gradually into the mixture stirring all the time until it blends well. 4. Allow it to cook on a low flame for a few minutes and thicken well to a soft dough. 5. Remove the vessel from the flame, and allow the dough to cool slightly. 6. Take very small portions of the dough and roll them into tiny balls. 7. Heat the fat in a frying pan and deep fry the balls until reddish brown. 8. Mix the coconut gratings, jaggery flakes and cardamom powder together, and add the fried balls to the mixture.

14. Salty undlakal

¼ cup bengal gram dal
¼ coconut-sliced pieces (small)
2 cups water
cooking fat to deep fry
¼ coconut gratings
2 tsps salt
2 cups fine rice flour

1. Wash and soak the dal for an hour and drain off the water. 2. Heat the water in a vessel. Add the soaked dal, coconut gratings and sliced pieces and salt to the water. Bring it to boil. 3. Pour in the rice flour gradually, stirring all the time. Allow it to thicken and cook for a few minutes. Remove the vessel from the flame. 4. When the mixture cools slightly, prepare tiny balls. 5. Heat the fat in a deep frying pan and fry the balls to a light brown colour.

15. Vegetable samosas

250 gms potatoes (boiled, peeled and cut into small pieces)
6 green chillies (sliced)
½ tsp turmeric powder
1 tsp pepper powder
2 tbsps cooking fat
a few tsps onion seeds
125 gms cauliflower cut fine
125 gms green peas (shelled)
250 gms onions (chopped fine)
a handful coriander leaves (cut fine)
salt to taste
½ tsp onion seed powder
2 cups flour (maida)
cooking fat to deep fry

1. Heat 2 tbsps fat in a pan and fry the chopped onions until light brown. 2. Add turmeric powder, green chillies, pepper powder, cut vegetables, peas, salt, coriander leaves, onion seed powder. Allow the peas and cauliflower to cook on a low flame. Remove the pan from the fire. 3. Knead the flour into a stiff dough with some water. Take portions of the dough, roll into small balls, mixing in a few onion-seeds. Roll each ball into a thin flat round. Cut each round into two. 4. Fill each covering with the vegetable bhaji filling. Shape the covering into a triangular samosa,pressing the sides carefully. 5. Heat the cooking fat in a deep pan and fry the samosas to a light brown colour.

16. Batata vade

½ kg potatoes (boiled peeled and chopped fine)
6 green chillies (chopped)
a handful chopped coriander leaves
1 cup gram flour (sieved)
¼ tsp turmeric powder
a pinch asafoetida
a pinch soda bicarb (optional)
cooking fat to deep fry
a small piece of ginger (chopped)
salt to taste
salt and chilli powder to taste

1. Crush chopped chillies, ginger and salt together, add coriander leaves and finely chopped potatoes, mix together and blend it well. 2. Make small balls of the above mixture and keep them aside. 3. Make a batter of bengal gram flour, salt, chilli powder, turmeric, asafoetida and sodabicarb (optional). 4. Dip the balls in the batter and deep fry in oil and serve.

Rice Dishes

1. Khichdi (sweet)

1 cup rice
1 cup green gram dal
1 ½ cups jaggery
4 cups water
1 cup grated coconut
8 cardamoms
1 ½ tbsps ghee

1. Wash the rice and dal and keep it aside for 15 minutes. 2. Heat 1 tbsp ghee in a vessel and roast the rice and dal in it till the rice is whitish in colour. 3. Add four cups of water and cook in the cooker. 4. Remove the vessel from the cooker after the mixture of rice and dal is cooked well. Add jaggery, grated coconut and powdered cardamoms. 5. Stir it on a low fire till the khichdi thickens and the jaggery is absorbed. Then remove the vessel from the heat. 6. Coat a deep thali with the remaining ½ tbsp ghee and spread the khichadi evenly in it. 7. When it cools, cut it into large rectangular pieces and serve.

2. Khichdi (savoury)

1 cup rice
½ cup green gram dal or red gram dal
2 tbsps ghee or any other cooking fat
2 cloves
1 cm. piece of cinnamon
1 pinch of turmeric
3 cups water

1. Wash rice and dal together and drain in a colander. 2. Heat the ghee or oil in a vessel and prepare a seasoning adding cloves, cinnamon and turmeric. 3. Add the rice and dal to the seasoning and stir for a few minutes. 4. Add water and salt to taste. 5. Cook on a low fire or in a cooker.

For variations: 1. Vegetables like cabbage, french beans, peas, potatoes, cauliflower, carrots may be added. 2. Instead of cloves and cinnamon, the seasoning may be prepared with mustard seeds, green chillies, asafoetida and turmeric, or with mustard seeds and green chillies only.

3. Brinjal bhaat

- 1 cup rice (washed and drained)
- 250 gms brinjals cut into large pieces
- 1/4 cup ghee or any other cooking fat
- 1/2 tbsp salt
- 4 cloves
- 2 pieces of cinnamon
- 3 large onions chopped (optional)
- tamarind (a small ball)
- 1/4 grated coconut
- 1/4 cup chopped coriander leaves
- 2 tsps garam masala
- 2 cups hot water

1. Heat 1 tbsp of fat in a vessel. Add cloves and cinnamon. 2. Add rice to this seasoning and stir till the rice becomes whitish. 3. Add brinjal pieces and stir. 4. Add salt and tamarind juice and 1 tsp garam masala. Stir well and add the hot water. 5. Cook on a low fire or in a cooker. 6. Put remaining ghee or fat in a large (broad) vessel, heat it, add the chopped onions and fry till light brown. 7. Add the cooked bhaat to the onions, sprinkle the remaining 1 tsp garam masala, and stir lightly. Cover it and cook for a few minutes on a low fire, till the rice is fluffy. 8. Add grated coconut and coriander leaves and mix it well.

For variations: 1. Instead of brinjals any vegetable like peas, cabbage, cauliflower, potatoes, kovai or cucumber can be used. 2. In stead of onions, the seasoning can be prepared of mustard, green chillies and asafoetida.

4. Cauliflower bhaat

- 500 gms cauliflower washed and cut into pieces
- 3 cups good quality rice washed and drained
- 1 coconut (grated, ground and squeezed out). This coconut milk + enough water to make about 6 cups
- 4 tbsps cooking fat
- 5 cloves*
- 1 tbsp coriander seeds*
- 1/2 tsp black cumin seeds*
- 2 cm. cinnamon*
- 3 to 4 red chillies
- 2 large onions sliced
- 1/2 cup coriander leaves chopped
- salt to taste

* Pounded to a powder

Seasoning:

4 cloves, 4 cardamoms, pinch of caraway seeds.

1. Heat the fat in a large vessel. Add the seasoning. 2. When the cloves become brown and caraway seeds splutter add onions chopped lenghtwise and fry till light brown. 3. Add the rice and stir till it turns whitish. 4. Add cauliflower pieces and stir. 5. Add the

mixture of coconut milk and water. Add salt and powdered masala. Stir well and simmer on a low fire. **6.** After the rice is cooked and all the water is absorbed sprinkle the chopped coriander leaves and stir lightly. Remove it from the fire.

NOTE: If the rice is cooked in a cooker only 5 cups of liquid (water + coconut milk) is enough.

5. Biranji (biryani)

2 cups rice, washed and drained
2-3 onions chopped fine
3-4 green chillies, chopped fine
4-5 garlic cloves crushed
1 small piece of ginger
2 tbsps cooking fat
4 cups hot water
salt to taste

pinch of saffron*
6 cardamoms*
6 cloves*
1/4 nutmeg*
2 cms cinnamon*
small piece of mace*
1 tsp caraway seeds*
2 tsps poppy seeds*

* Roasted and powdered

1. Roast the rice in a tbsp fat in a vessel, till the rice turns whitish. **2.** Add the hot water, salt and the powdered masala. Stir well and cook on a low fire or in the cooker. **3.** Heat the remaining fat in another large vessel and add for seasoning the chopped green chillies, garlic and ginger. **4.** Add onions and fry till light brown. **5.** Add the cooked rice to the fried onions and stir well on a low fire till the rice is dry and fluffy. **6.** Serve with the special curry (saar).

NOTE: 1. Brinjals, cabbage, potatoes, or any other vegetable can be used. 2. Seasoning can be added before cooking the rice.

Saar (curry) for biranji

3/4 cup red gram dal
2 onions chopped
2 tsps chilli powder
tamarind, size of a small lemon, soaked and juice squeezed for use

2 cloves of garlic*
1 cm piece of ginger*

*Ground to a paste

1. Cook the dal in a cooker with 2 cups of water. Drain out the liquid from the cooked dal to use for saar. (The dal can be used for any other preparation.) **2.** Add all the ingredients to the saar (liquid) and make it into about 6 cups. **3.** Cook until the onion is soft. (Note: Lemon juice can be added instead of tamarind juice.)

Chutney for biranji

- ½ grated coconut
- 4 green chillies
- a bunch of coriander leaves (about 1 cup)
- 1 cm piece of ginger
- ½ cup roasted bengal gram dal
- salt to taste
- juice of lemon
- 4 garlic cloves

1. Grind all the ingredients together. 2. Add lemon juice and mix well.

6. Pulav

- 2 cups good quality rice
- 2 cups chopped vegetables (all or any — potatoes, green peas, cauliflower, cabbage, etc.)
- 4 cups hot water
- 4 tbsps cooking fat
- 4 cloves
- 2½ cm piece cinnamon
- salt to taste
- 2 onions sliced
- 10 almonds/cashew nuts
- 2 tbsps raisins
- 10 green chillies*
- ½ cup chopped coriander leaves*
- ½ coconut grated*

*To be ground into a chutney

1. Wash and drain the rice. 2. Heat 1½ tbsps fat in a vessel and prepare a seasoning adding cloves and cinnamon. 3. Add rice and stir to roast it a little. 4. Add the chopped vegetables and stir. 5. Pour hot water into it, add salt and stir and cook it on a low fire or in a cooker. 6. When the rice is cooked, remove it from the cooker, add the ground chutney, mix it well and again keep it on a low fire for a few minutes. 7. Fry the sliced onions, almonds or cashew nuts and raisins in the remaining fat. 8. Add the fried things to the pulav just before serving.

Kadhi (to serve with pulav)

- ½ coconut grated
- 3 green chillies
- 1 bunch coriander
- 6 cloves garlic
- 1 cm piece of ginger
- ½ tsp mustard seeds
- ½ tsp cumin seeds
- ½ tsp turmeric
- 3 potatoes cut into cubes
- salt to taste

1. Grind the coconut fine. 2. Add all the ingredients except potatoes and grind again to a fine paste. 3. Cook the potatoes in salt water. 4. Add the ground masala and bring to boil. 5. Serve with the Pulav.

7. Keshar bhaat (saffron flavoured sweet rice)

2 cups good quality rice
3 to 4 cups sugar
½ cup ghee
½ tsp saffron
6 cardamoms*
½ nutmeg*
3½ cups hot water
4 cloves
2 cm piece of cinnamon
10 almonds soaked, skinned and chopped lengthwise
¼ cup raisins cleaned and washed
juice of ½ lemon

*Powdered

1. Wash and drain the rice and keep it aside to dry. 2. Heat a little ghee in a large vessel and add cloves and cinnamon for seasoning. 3. Add rice and stir till the rice is whitish. 4. Add 3½ cups of hot water and cook it. 5. Soak the saffron in 1 tsp warm milk or water, crush it well and mix with the cooked rice. 6. Add sugar, ghee, powder of nutmeg and cardamom. Add raisins, chopped almonds and lemon juice. Stir well. 7. Cook on a low fire until the rice comes to dry consistency and serve.

Rasayan

Banana rasayan

1 dozen ripe bananas
½ cup grated jaggery
4 to 5 cardamoms powdered
½ litre coconut milk (extracted from one grated coconut) or ½ litre fresh milk

1. Peel the bananas and cut them first lengthwise and then into slices. 2. Mix them with jaggery. 3. Add coconut milk and cardamom powder. 4. Chill and serve.

NOTE: 1. Jaggery can be added to the coconut milk first and when it dissolves banana pieces and cardamom powder can be added. 2. Instead of coconut milk and jaggery fresh milk and sugar and saffron for flavouring can be used.
3. For rasayans of mango, squash and honey-dew, follow the instructions as for the recipe above.

Kheer

1. Coconut kheer

2 cups rice
2 cups sugar/jaggery
6 to 7 cups water
turmeric leaf, fresh/dry for flavouring
milk of 1½ coconut

1. Wash and cook the rice with 6 to 7 cups of water and the turmeric leaf, on a low fire or in a cooker. 2. Add sugar or jaggery after the rice is completely diffused in the water and cook for a while. 3. Add the coconut juice and remove from the heat immediately.

NOTE: This kheer can be made without sugar or jaggery. This plain kheer with salt to taste is served with puran poli or sukaroondas.

2. Rice and green gram dal kheer

1½ cup rice
½ cup green gram dal (roasted lightly in 1 tsp ghee)
2 cups jaggery (grated)
1 coconut (large) milk extracted
1 tsp cardamom powder
10 cups water

1. Cook the rice and dal together in 10 cups of water. 2. Add the grated jaggery and simmer for 10 minutes. 3. Add the coconut milk and cardamom.

NOTE: The consistency of this kheer should be thick like porridge.

3. Wheat kheer

2 cups wheat
2 cups jaggery-grated
7 cups water
2 cups coconut milk
1 tsp cardamom powder

To make wheat samolina: 1. Sprinkle water on the wheat and rub. 2. Pound and remove the husk or thick skin of the wheat. 3. Dry the skinned wheat on a cloth in the shade. 4. Grind it in a grinder or pound and make it into course samolina(rawa.)

NOTE: Ready made 'Lapsi' or broken wheat can be used. 1. Cook the wheat samolina in 7 cups water. 2. When cooked, add 2 cups jaggery. Go on stirring on a low fire until the jaggery is completely absorbed. 3. Add the coconut milk (squeezed and extracted from one grated coconut) and cardamom powder. 4. Bring to boil and remove from the fire immediately.

4. Bengal gram kheer (madgane)

½ cup bengal gram dal
1 cup jaggery, grated
10 cardamoms (powdered)
2 cups coconut milk (extract of 1 large coconut)
½ cup cashewnut pieces
½ cup rice flour or roasted wheat rawa

1. Cook bengal gram dal and cashew pieces in 3 cups water. 2. When cooked, add jaggery and 2 cups water and cook well again. 3. Add the rice flour paste or fried wheat rawa paste and stir well to avoid lumps. 4. Add coconut milk and cardamom powder.

5. Kadhailyen (rice flour kheer)

1 cup jaggery
½ cup coconut milk
4-5 cups water
½ cup rice flour (fine)
1 tsp cardamom powder
½ cup cashewnuts (optional)

1. Cook jaggery (and cashewnuts) in 3 cups of water for 10 minutes. 2. Mix the rice flour in a little water to make a fine paste. 3. Pour the rice paste slowly into the jaggery syrup stirring constantly to avoid formation of lumps. 4. Add the coconut milk and cardamom powder. Bring to boil and remove from the fire immediately.

6. Jeebrutee (rice balls) kheer

2 cups jaggery
10 cardamoms (powdered)
1½ cup rice*
½ cup beaten rice*
½ coconut (grated)*
1½ coconut grated and squeezed to prepare coconut milk

*For jeebrutee

1. Soak the rice and the beaten rice in water for 2 hours (about 2 cups water). 2. When soaked well, grind the rice and beaten rice mixture with grated coconut, to a fine paste. 3. Remove the ground mixture and add enough water to make a thick mixture. 4. Cook it on a low fire stirring it all the time till the mixture thickens into a thick dough. 5. Rub a little ghee on your fingers and make small balls (size of large beads) from the dough. 6. Either fry them in ghee or steam them. 7. Make syrup with 2 cups of jaggery. 8. As the syrup boils add the rice balls. 9. When it boils for about 5 minutes, add coconut milk and cardamom powder.

NOTE: The water needed is approximately 3 to 4 cups for grinding and preparing the dough).

7. Botnevri kheer

For Nevries (karanjies)

1 cup rice (washed) and ½ coconut grated, grind together to a fine paste or 1½ cup rice flour added to ½ coconut grated and ground to a paste with about 1½ cup water. Cook it and make a dough like jawar bhakri dough.

For filling

1 coconut grated and ½ the measure jaggery. Cook together and make a dry filling and allow it to cool.

For kheer

- 2 large coconuts grated and squeezed
- 1 tsp cardamom powder
- 2 cups jaggery
- ½ cup fine rice flour
- 2 cups thick milk + 2 cups thin milk, squeezed after grinding again with 2 cups of water
- 6 cups water

1. Apply some oil or ghee to your fingers and knead the dough till smooth. 2. Take a small quantity of the dough (size of a betelnut) on the left palm and pat it with your right hand fingers or palm into the shape of a round puri. 3. Put ½ tsp of the filling on half puri and close it, pressing on the sides firmly to form a nevri or karanji. 4. When all the nevries are ready steam-cook them. 5. Cook jaggery in 6 cups of water for 10 minutes. 6. Mix ½ cup of rice flour to the thin coconut milk. Add this mixture of the jaggery syrup and cook. 7. Gently add the steamed nevries to this mixture and cook for five minutes. 8. Add the thick milk and cardamom powder and remove from the fire.

NOTE: The dough can be made by steaming the ground paste with about 1½ cups of water in the cooker without weights.

8. Green gram dal kheer

- 2 cups green gram dal (moong dal)
- 1 coconut-grated, ground and milk extracted
- 1 tbsp ghee
- 1½ cups jaggery
- cardamom powder
- 6 cups water

1. Roast the dal in ghee. 2. Add 6 cups water and cook. 3. When well-cooked, add jaggery. 4. Cook for ten minutes more, add coconut milk and cardamom powder, and remove from heat.

9. Jackfruit kheer

15 to 16 finely chopped jackfruit sections
4 cups water
½ cup rice flour
2 cups coconut milk (of 1 large coconut)
1 tsp cardamom powder
2 cups jaggery

1. Cook the jaggery in 4 cups water. 2. Add the chopped jackfruit sections to the jaggery syrup and cook till jackfruit is soft. 3. Add the rice flour paste and cook the rice till it is cooked. 4. Add coconut milk and cardamom powder. Bring to boil and remove from the heat.

10. Shevayi or vermicelli kheer

1 cup broken shevayi or vermicelli
1½ litre milk
¾ to 1 cup sugar
4 to 6 cardamoms powdered
raisins
2 tbsp almonds or cashewnut pieces
1 tbsp ghee

1. Roast cashewnut pieces and vermicilli in 1 tbsp ghee, till light brown. 2. Add milk, stir on low fire till it boils (or heat milk, add the vermicilli, stir on a low fire). 3. Add sugar, saffron, cardamom powder, raisins etc. Boil for 7 to 10 minutes and remove from the fire.

NOTE: 1. Adding condensed milk, fried raisins and almonds will enrich taste. 2. For home-made shevayi, crush it, put in hot water, cover and keep aside for ten minutes. Drain the water when the shevayi is soft. Then add it to the heated milk, and other ingredients and boil for a few minutes.

11. Samolina (rawa) kheer

1 cup samolina (rawa)
2 litres milk boiled and thickened a bit
1 cup sugar
½ tbsp ghee
almonds peeled and chopped, raisins, cardamom powder
nutmeg powder

1. Roast samolina in ghee. 2. Add milk stirring to avoid lumps. Cook well for 7 to 10 minutes. 3. Add almonds, raisins, cardamom and nutmeg powder.

12. Sabudana (sago) kheer

¾ cup sago
1 cup sugar
½ tbsp ghee
saffron
nutmeg powder
2 litres milk
almonds chopped
raisins
cardamom powder

Method: The same as for the recipe of samolina kheer above.
NOTE: The kheer tastes better when chilled.

13. Doodh pak

½ cup good quality rice
¾ cup sugar
10 gms charoli
2 litres milk
1 ½ tsp cardamom powder
10 gms pista

1. Wash, drain and dry the rice on a cloth. 2. Cook rice in the milk. Then follow the method for samolina kheer. This kheer is served with puris.

Puris

3 cups wheat flour
2 tsps butter
cooking fat to deep fry
salt to taste
water

1. Mix salt, butter, wheat flour and water and knead well to make a stiff dough. 2. Make into small balls, roll out, not very thin. 3. Heat ghee well and deep fry the puries until they puff up and become light brown.

14. Masala milk

3 litres milk
1½ cup sugar
2 cups cashew nuts or almonds
cardamom and nutmeg powder
pista
charoli
saffron

1. Grind to a paste half the cashew nuts and almonds. 2. Boil and thicken the milk a bit by simmering it for about 30 minutes on a low fire. 3. Add the ground paste and stir. 4. Add sugar, flavouring and other ingredients and boil for sometime stirring all the while, and remove from fire. This can be served hot or chilled.

15. Basundi

4 litres milk
1 to 1½ cup sugar
½ tsp cardamom powder
¼ tsp nutmeg powder
½ tbsp almonds-chopped
½ tbsp pista-chopped

1. Boil and thicken the milk until it is ¾ to 1 litre. 2. Add sugar and boil it. 3. Simmer for sometime until the milk thickens again. 4. Add flavouring and chopped almonds and pistas. 5. Serve hot or chilled.

Shreekhand

3 litres milk and 1 tsp buttermilk/curds for chakka
cardamom*
charoli and pista for decoration
sugar equal in quantity to chakka
saffron*
nutmeg*

*Powdered

1. Boil milk and cool it down. 2. When it is tepid, add butter milk or curd and mix lightly, cover it with a lid and leave it overnight to make thick curds. 3. Next morning, pour all the curds on a thin muslin cloth, tie it and hang it for an hour or two, until the whey is drained off. 4. Remove the thick curds or chakka from the cloth and mix well with the sugar (ground sugar mixes well). 5. Strain the mixture through a thin cloth or strainer. 6. Add saffron, cardamom and nutmeg powder and mix well. 7. Sprinkle charoli and pista slices for decoration.

NOTE: 1. Shreekhand can be made without saffron. 2. Fresh fruit can be mixed in Shreekhand before serving.

Puddings

---

1. Idli pudding

idli batter
ripe bananas
lemon
sugar

1. Steam-cook idli in a greased round and shallow vessel or cake pan. When cooked take out the big cake like idli and place it on a flat tray. 2. Cut ripe bananas into slices and arrange them on the upper surface of the idli. 3. Make sugar syrup of one string consistency. Add to it lemon juice to taste. This is called sudharas and can be preserved like 'moramba'. 4. Pour this sudharas syrup on the layer of banana slices. 5. Cut the cake with a knife and serve.

2. Rawa pudding

½ cup fine rawa
2 cups milk
½ tbsp butter
½ cup sugar
almonds*
pistachio*
2 tbsp cornflour
vanilla essence

* Optional

1. Cook the fine rawa in 1 cup milk adding butter. 2. Add sugar and cook until it is thicker than rawa kheer. Then pour it on a flat greased tray and spread it evenly. 3. Add almonds and pistachio cut fine. Allow it to cool. 4. Cook cocoa and cornflower in 1 cup milk. When it is thick add 7-8 drops of vanilla essence. Mix it well and spread a layer of it on rawa dish and serve.

NOTE: This can also be served chilled in the refrigerator.

3. Orange pudding

1 dozen oranges
china grass approx. 50 gms
1 cup milk
sugar to taste

1. Take a dozen oranges. Wash them well, scoop out the core of the oranges carefully, preserving the shape of the orange. Keep aside the empty oranges. 2. Prepare jam using the core and keep it aside. 3. Cook the china grass in milk. Add sugar. 4. Fill the empty oranges with alternate layers of china grass custard and orange jam. 5. Cool them in the refrigerator and serve when chilled.

4. Bread pudding

½ cup milk
½ cup sugar
1 cup bread crumbs
6 tsps ghee
10 raisins
vanilla

1. Dissolve sugar in milk. Add the bread crumbs, mix well and allow them to soak for one hour. 2. Heat ghee in a vessel. Add raisins when they puff up. Add a little vanilla mixed in a little milk. Add the soaked bread crumbs. Do not stir it. 4. Then bake the pudding in an oven till it is reddish. Or steam-cook it.

Tea-Time Snacks

---

1. Chaklies

6 cups (1 kg) rice flour
2½ tsps salt
2 tbsp white sesame
1 cup butter
1 kg coconut oil/refined oil for deep frying.
1½ cups black gram (roasted and ground)
approx. 3 cups milk/water

1. Dissolve salt in the water, add butter. 2. Add the flours and knead well. 3. Add white sesame and knead again. The dough should be soft but not sticky. 4. Take a little dough at a time, to fill the special chakli press (gadget). 5. Press it in small circles on a brown paper to make four to five chaklies at a time. 6. Heat the oil and dip the chaklies carefully in the oil (do not put too many chaklies in the oil at a time). 7. Deep fry them on both sides on a medium fire till they are crisp.

NOTE: 1. If the fire is too low, the chaklies become oily. 2. Milk used instead of water for the dough makes the chaklies more brown. 3. Chaklies become soft if the dough is left unused for a long time.

2. Tengodle

6 cups rice flour
1 cup roasted black gram flour

1. Other ingredients — same as above but add cumin seeds or ajma instead of sesame seeds. 2. Use tengodle plate instead of chakkli plate in the press. 3. Instead of full circles, two layers are to be pressed one over the other partially and lengthwise.

3. Katla pedhe

6 cups rice flour
½ cup roasted bengal gram flour
½ cup roasted beaten rice flour
½ cup black gram dal (roasted and ground)

The dough is to be prepared in water as for the recipe for chaklies but without adding sesame seeds and should be pressed in the special press. Deep fry the katla pedhe till crisp.

4. Murku (gadget same as for chaklies)

½ kg wheat flour
½ kg bengal gram flour
½ kg rice flour

For 8 cups of the mixture of the flours:

1 cup butter
2½ tsps salt
8 tsps chilli powder
2 tsps turmeric powder

Method: Same as for chaklies.

5. Potato chaklies

250 gms potatoes
1 cup butter
5 tsps chilli powder
¼ tsp asafoetida
6 cups rice flour
2½ tsps salt
2 tsps sesame seeds

1. Boil, peel and mash the potatoes. Mix all the ingredients (after dissolving salt well) with enough water, to make a soft dough. 2. Knead well, press chaklies and deep fry till crisp.

6. Kadboli

4 cups rice flour/jawar flour
1 tsp cumin seed powder
1 ¼ cups milk
1 cup butter
1 ½ tsp salt

1. Dissolve salt and mix butter properly in the milk. 2. Add rice flour, cumin seed powder and make a dough like that of chaklies. 3. Take small portions and roll on a hard surface and shape into kadbolies. Press the ends of each kadboli well with a little milk. 4. Deep fry in oil or ghee, until the kadbolies are reddish brown and crisp.

7. Shev

3 cups of bengal gram flour
2 tsps salt
½ tsp turmeric
½ tsp asafoetida
1 cup water
oil for deep frying
½ cup butter/¼ cup oil
½ tsp cumin seeds and pepper powder

1. Mix well salt, asafoetida and butter in water until they dissolve. 2. Add all the remaining ingredients and prepare the dough. 3. Heat oil for deep frying. 4. Fill the mould with enough dough and press out directly into the oil. 5. Deep fry on medium heat till crisp and golden yellow.

Ladu (Unde)

1. Soft bundi ladu

for syrup 4 cups water and 5 cups sugar
1 ½ cups water
6 cups fine bengal gram flour
ghee or dalda for deep frying
2½ gms saffron
18 cardamoms powdered
10 cloves, slightly powdered
10 gms raisins
10 gms almond
10 gms pistas

Soft bundi

1. Mix bengal gram flour in 1½ cups water and prepare paste for bundi. Add a little hot ghee to the paste. 2. Place a frying pan, with ghee on a low fire. When the ghee is hot, hold the special bundi strainer with the left hand over the hot ghee and with the right hand pour a little paste at a time with a deep spoon on the strainer. 3. Spread the paste with the back side of the spoon, so that it falls in the oil in drips. 4. Fry the drops or bundis thus dropped in the oil, to a light golden colour but not very crisp. 5. Wash and dry the strainer every time you drop the paste through it. 6. Fry all the bundis and keep aside.

Ladus

1. Put 4 cups of water in a broad vessel, add sugar and place it on a medium fire. 2. Stir constantly and remove the layer of black dirt formed on it as the syrup gets ready. 3. When the syrup is of one string consistency add saffron (soaked and crushed), cardamom powder, slightly pounded cloves, raisins, chopped almonds and pistas (optional). 4. Add the bundies, stir well and remove the vessel from the fire and allow it to cool. 5. When the mixture cools take small portions of it in your palm and turn it into balls or ladus.

2. Moti choor ladus

sugar syrup
5 cups soft powdered (or castor) sugar
2½ cups water
18 cardamoms
10 gms almonds
10 gms pistas
saffron

Bundi

6 cups besan
ghee or dalda for frying
4 cups water

1. Prepare bundies as for 'soft bundi ladus' but fry very crisp. 2. Add almonds and pistas (cut fine) to the bundi and mix well. 3. Prepare sugar syrup of a thick consistency (a drop of syrup dropped on the ground should remain round like a pearl and not spread out). 4. Add cardamom powder and saffron paste to the syrup and stir. 5. Take another broad vessel. Put about 6 tbsps sugar syrup in it and place the vessel on a low fire and stir the syrup till it is frothy (a drop of syrup put in cold water should become hard like a bead). 6. Add 2 full cups bundi to the syrup, stir and mix well and remove the vessel from the fire. 7. Coat your palm with a little rice flour. Take portions of the syrup-coated bundies on the palm and turn them into ladus. 8. Repeat this process until all the ladus are ready.

NOTE: Use two broad vessels, turn by turn for the 5th step of the process and onwards, so that the first vessel can be cleaned to repeat the process. If the syrup sticks to the vessel the bundies cannot be turned into ladus.

3. Churmi ladus

½ kg cashew nuts
1 cup fried peanuts
1 cup roasted bengal gram
water
1 cup maida
¼ cup poppy seeds, fried
2½ kg soft castor sugar
ghee for deep frying

1. Prepare a dough of maida, roll out big puries, cut them with a knife into diamond shapes and fry them crisp in ghee to prepare shankarpali. 2. Prepare sugar syrup of 1 string consistency and keep it aside. 3. Mix together fried peanuts, cashew nuts, roasted bengal gram and shankarpalis. 4. The same as the 5th step of moti choor ladus. 5. When the syrup is frothy, add to it 1 cup mixture of peanuts etc., ¼ tsp poppy seeds, mix well, remove the vessel from the fire and make ladus. 6. Repeat the process.

NOTE: 1. The same as for moti choor ladus. 2. If the balls or ladus cannot be formed easily, heat the syrup a little more or add chikki (sticky) jaggery to the sugar in the proportion of 1 betelnut size jaggery to 2½ kg. sugar, while making the syrup.

4. Besan (bengal gram flour) ladus

6 cups bengal gram flour
2½ cups ghee
2 to 3 tbsps milk
50 gms almonds sliced (optional)
3 cups castor sugar (or ground sugar)
18 cardamoms (powdered)
50 gms raisins

1. Fry bengal gram flour in the ghee till it is slightly reddish in colour. 2. Sprinkle milk on it, stir and leave it to cool. 3. Then add all the remaining ingredients, knead well and make ladus.

5. Wheat flour ladus

6 cups wheat flour
1½ cups ghee
4 cups castor sugar
18 cardamoms (crushed)
50 gms raisins
6 cloves (fried in ghee and powdered)

1. Fry the flour in ghee to a reddish colour and allow it to cool. 2. When cool, add other ingredients and knead well and make ladus.

6. Besan and wheat rawa ladus

3 cups bengal gram flour (fried in 1 ½ cups ghee)
other ingredients the same as for besan ladu.
3 cups wheat rawa (fried in ¾ cup ghee)

Mix together bengal gram flour and wheat rawa and follow method given for 'besan ladus'.

7. Wheat rawa ladus

6 cups very fine wheat rawa
1 ½ cups ghee
18 cardamoms powdered
2½ gms saffron
4 to 5 cups sugar
3 cups water
almonds cut lengthwise

1. Fry the rawa in ghee to a reddish colour. 2. Prepare sugar syrup of 1 string consistency like that for 'soft bundi ladus' 3. Add rawa, saffron paste and the remaining ingredients, mix well and make ladus, when the mixture cools enough.

8. Raghavdas ladus

1 coconut grated fine
other ingredients including sugar—same as for 'rawa ladus'
sugar ½ the measure of the grated coconut,extra if required

1. Grate the coconut fine and fry coconut gratings in a shallow vessel, to a reddish brown colour. 2. Measure the grated coconut before frying and take ½ the measure sugar and add it to the rest of the sugar before preparing the syrup. 3. Add all the ingredients to the syrup and make ladus when the mixture cools enough.

9. Cashewnut ladus

6 cups crushed cashewnuts (peeled and cut into pieces)
4 cups sugar
grated coconut (optional)

1. Prepare sugar syrup of a thicker consistency (hard ball). 2. Add crushed cashew-nuts and make ladus.

NOTE: 1. If grated coconut is to be added, the process is as for Raghavdas ladus. 2. No raisins or almonds. 3. Chikki jaggery can be used instead of sugar.

10. Gulpapadi ladus

6 cups wheat flour
1 ½ cups ghee
3 cups white jaggery
2 tbsps water
10 cardamoms powdered
½ cup fried gingelly or sesame seeds
½ cup fried and crushed peanuts (optional)
1 tbsp ghee

1. Fry the flour in the ghee to a light brown colour. 2. Prepare a syrup of the jaggery (with a little water) to one string consistency. 3. Add cardamom powder and fried flour to it and make ladus when the mixture is fairly hot.

NOTE: Instead of making ladus, the mass may be poured on a greased thali, levelled and cut into cubes.

11. Til (sesame seed) ladus

6 cups white sesame seeds
1 kg patni or chikky jaggery
½ cup fried and crushed peanuts
1 tbsp ghee

1. Soak the sesame seeds overnight. Strain them in the morning and spread them on a cloth to dry (crush with a cloth and winnow them to remove the skin if necessary). 2. Fry them, a little at a time, in a tall vessel and keep aside. 3. Prepare jaggery syrup with ghee (no water). The syrup is ready when a drop in water forms a hard ball. 4. Add the other ingredients and make the ladus when fairly hot, applying a little ghee to the palms.

12. Boondi and puffed rajgira (amaranth seeds) ladus

½ kg boondi (crisp)
1 kg puffed rajgira (puffed amaranth seeds)
1 tbsp ghee
½ kg chikki jaggery

1. Clean the puffed rajgira. 2. Prepare a syrup of the jaggery adding ghee. 3. Make it thick (ball consistency) like the syrup for sesame seed ladus. 4. Add puffed rajgira, boondi, mix well and make ladus.

Halwa

1. Tilgul (halwa)

1 kg good quality sugar
3 measures water
1 tsp lemon juice
½ cup almonds and pistachios (slurry)
handful white sesame seeds (polished or washed, dried and skinned)
½ cup pumpkin or cucumber seeds (dried and skinned)

1. If the white sesame seeds are not polished, clean, wash and soak them overnight. In the morning, drain them thoroughly, (optional — crush them a little at a time with a rough cloth to skin them. Remove the skin by winnowing) and dry them on a cloth in the shade. 2. Add 3 measures of water to the sugar and make a syrup. When it starts boiling add to it 1 tsp lemon juice so that the syrup clears. Strain it and boil it again till it becomes sticky and is of right consistency. (A drop dropped on the flour remains round like a pearl without spreading). Fill it in a jar when cool and keep it covered tightly. 3. Take a shallow and thick brass thali. Heat it on a low fire, add the sesame seeds and stir them lightly with finger tips. 4. Sprinkle 5 to 6 drops of warm syrup and stir again till all the grains are evenly coated. 5. When the syrup dries add 5 to 6 drops again, keeping the thali moderately warm and stirring constantly. 6. If the tilgul starts sticking to the surface, remove the tilgul and wipe the thali clean with a damp napkin. Reheat the pan and put back the tilgul and continue. 7. When the tilgul is half done (size of a green gram) remove a little for colouring, and add almonds, pumpkin seeds and cardamom etc., and continue increasing the quantity of syrup to ½ tsp gradually as the size of tilgul increases. 8. Add saffron to a cupful of syrup and use this for colouring the half done tilgul kept aside and continue till they are of the size of the fully done tilguls. Mix them together with the rest.

NOTE: 1. The thali should always be moderately warm. 2. Clean the thali often. 3. Use a wick stove or segari. 4. Stirring with a motion of the fingers first up and down and then in a circle constantly, gives the tilgul egg like shape.

2. Bottle gourd halwa (variety 1)

2 cups skinned and grated bottle gourd
1 tsp crushed cardamoms
1 tsp ghee
2 cups sugar
1½ cups mava or thickened milk
1 tbsp pistachio or almonds

1. Cook the grated gourd in the pressure cooker, till it is soft. Remove from the cooker. 2. Add sugar and cook till the water is almost absorbed. 3. Add the mava (thickened milk) and cook till the mixture forms into a ball. Add the cardamom powder and mix. 4. Pour it into a thali greased with ghee. Spread evenly with a rolling pin. 5. Sprinkle with chopped nuts and press with your palm. 6. When fairly cool, cut into cubes with a knife and allow it to cool well. Serve.

3. Bottle gourd halwa (variety 2)

2 cups bottle gourd small cubes (skinned and chopped)
½ tsp cardamom powder
½ cup milk
1 cup jaggery (chopped fine)

1. Cook the cubes in milk till soft. 2. Add jaggery and cook till all the water is absorbed and the mixture thickens. 3. Add cardamom powder. 4. Cool and serve.

4. Rajali banana (ripe) halwa

1 dozen ripe rajali bananas (approximately 2 cups pulp)
1 cup sugar (½ the measure of pulp)
4 tbsps ghee

1. Cook the banana pulp and sugar together in a thick, flat vessel, stirring all the time, till the mixture starts thickening. 2. Add 2 tbsps ghee. 3. When it thickens more, add the rest of the ghee. 4. Continue stirring over the fire till the mixture forms into a ball. 5. Test it,rolling a small quantity into a ball. It should not stick to the palm. 6. When it is of the right consistency pour it into a greased thali and spread it evenly with a greased rolling pin or the back of a flat ladle. 7. When cool, cut into cubes.

NOTE: More sugar can be used as per taste.

5. Rajali banana anjir (figs)

½ dozen half ripe bananas
½ cup chopped jaggery*
1 tsp poppy seeds*
ghee for deep frying
½ coconut grated*
½ tsp powdered cardamom*
1 tbsp raisins

*For the filling

1. Steam the bananas. 2. Cool and skin them and grind to a smooth paste. 3. To prepare the filling, cook the rest of the ingredients together till the jaggery is dissolved and syrupy. Allow it to cool. 4. Take about 1 tbsp banana paste on your greased palm,

flatten it, put about 2 tbsps of the filling in the centre of it and fold the sides together shaping it into a fig or modak. **5.** Deep fry in cooking fat or ghee.

6. Arrowroot halwa

2 cups arrowroot powder (kachra pitto)
1 cup grated fresh coconut
1 cup sugar/jaggery
¼ to ½ cup small pieces of cashew
8 cardamoms, powdered

1. Soak the arrowroot powder in 3 cups of cold water for ½ an hour. **2.** Pour out the water once the powder settles down. **3.** Add sugar/jaggery, grated and ground coconut, cashew nuts and cardamom powder to the aararoot. Add 2 cups of fresh water to the mixture and keep it on a medium flame. **4.** Go on stirring till the mixture is translucent and thick like halwa. **5.** Pour it into a greased thali, spread and cut into cubes.

NOTE: **1.** This halwa is soft and lasts only for a day. **2.** This halwa prepared without coconut and cashew is good for a diarrhoea patient. **3.** Similar halwa can be prepared from wheat flour soaked and drained like aararoot. Eating it early in the morning is good for nutrition.

Burfies

1. Cashew nut burfi

½ kg cashews (soak for ½ hour and grind with milk to a fine, thick paste)
1 tbsp ghee
1 ¼ cup sugar for 1 cup cashew paste
pinch of saffron
1 tsp cardamom powder

1. Mix the cashew paste, ghee and sugar (1 ¼ times the quantity of paste) and cook on a medium fire, stirring constantly. **2.** Add saffron crushed in a little milk. Add cardamom powder when the mixture is moderately thick. **3.** Stir the mixture constantly till (a little portion cooled, can be made into a ball and is not sticky), it is of the right consistency. **4.** Pour it into a greased thali, flatten, cool and cut into cubes.

2. Almond burfi

½ kg almonds (soak in warm water, skin and grind to a paste).
1 pinch of saffron
1 to 1 ¼ cup sugar for 1 cup almond paste
1 tbsp ghee
1 tsp cardamom powder

For this recipe follow the instructions for cashewnut burfi.

3. Potato burfi

1 kg potatoes (boil, peel and grind to a paste)
1 tbsp ghee
½ kg almonds (soak and grind)
1 ¼ cup sugar for 1 cup mixture of the pastes.

For this recipe follow the instructions as for almond burfi.

NOTE: **1.** Pista, charoli, pumpkin seeds also can be used to make burfi. **2.** Potatoes, raw papayya, turnip, white gourd, red gourd etc. can also be skinned, grated, washed and drained and used to make burfi but the quantity of sugar must be 1 ¼ times the quantity of the grated pulp. **3.** Jaggery can be used instead of sugar for these vegetable varieties.

4. Bottle gourd burfi

1 cup skinned and grated bottle gourd
1 ¼ cup sugar
1 tbsp ghee

1. Remove the core and seeds and grate the bottle gourd. Mix grated bottle gourd, ghee and sugar and cook over a medium heat, stirring all the time. **2.** Follow the instructions as for the burfies mentioned above.

5. Coconut burfi

2 fresh coconuts, preferably tender (grate and grind coarsely)
1 cup sugar for 1 cup gratings
1 tsp cardamom powder
1 pinch saffron

Instructions — the same as for other burfies.

NOTE: For coconut burfi, jaggery equivalent in quantity to grated coconut + fried sesame seeds (½ the quantity of grated coconut) can also be used.

6. Wheat rawa burfi

2 cups rawa
1 ½ to 2 cups sugar
½ cup ghee
10 to 12 cardamoms (powdered) optional

1. Fry rawa in ghee on a low fire until rawa is brownish. **2.** Make a syrup of the sugar, of one string consistency. **3.** Add fried rawa and cardamom powder and stir constantly until it is of the right consistency (not sticky and can be formed into a ball). 4. Spread evenly on a greased thali and cut cubes when fairly cool.

7. Milk and rawa burfi

2 cups milk
1 cup wheat rava fried in ghee
3 cups sugar
10 to 12 cardamoms (powdered)
¼ cup ghee
¼ nugmeg (powdered)
1 pinch saffron
or 1 tsp vanilla

1. Mix all the ingredients except saffron or vanilla, and stir on a low fire till half done. 2. Mix vanilla or saffron and stir until the mixture is of the right consistency. 3. Pour on a greased thali, spread evenly and cut when still warm.

8. Curds burfi

1 litre milk for curds
10 to 12 cardamoms crushed and powdered
1½ cup sugar for 1 cup drained curds
¼ nutmeg powdered
saffron, optional

1. Make thick curd, tie it in a cloth and hang it to drain the water. Remove from the cloth when all the water is drained and measure the curds. 2. Mix drained curds and sugar, stir the mixture till it blends well and cook on a low fire, stirring constantly. Follow the instructions for other burfis.

9. Gupchup burfi or nankatai

1 cup ghee
1 cup castor sugar or ground sugar
1 tsp cardamom powder
3 cups wheat flour/maida
1 tsp ginger powder or nutmeg powder
raisins/charolies

1. Melt the ghee. Add sugar and blend well. 2. Add the flour and flavourings and knead well. 3. Put into a greased thali or baking tray, spread evenly and cut into cubes. Press a raisin on each cube and bake it in an oven till crisp and light brown.

OR

Make small balls, press each ball a little, press a raisin or charolies on each ball, arrange in a baking tray and bake in an oven, till crisp and brown.

10. Mesurpak

3 cups bengal gram flour
6 cups ghee
3 cups sugar

1. Roast the flour in 1½ cups ghee till it is brownish and fragrant. 2. Make a syrup with 1½ cups water and 3 cups sugar. 3. When the syrup is of 1 string consistency pour it in the roasted flour and stir well. 4. Pour slowly and gradually the rest of the 4½ cups hot ghee into the mixture, stirring constantly over a medium flame. 5. When all the ghee is added and the mixture is reddish and bubbly with ghee oozing out from sides, pour it into a deep, large and flat tray. Spread it evenly. 6. Tilt the tray slightly by keeping the tray raised on one side and allow the ghee to drain out. 7. Cut into cubes when the layer is moderately cool. Collect the extra drained out ghee in a cup.

11. Chocolates

4 cups milk
½ cup cocoa
1 tsp vanilla essence
1 tbsp crushed nuts
½ cup maida (fine wheat flour)
½ cup ghee or butter
4 cups sugar

1. Mix all the ingredients except vanilla and cook over a medium flame. 2. When the mixture starts thickening to the right consistency add vanilla and cook on a low flame, stirring vigorously. 3. When it becomes thick enough to form a ball, and is no more sticky, remove it from the fire, stir a little more and pour it into a greased flat tray. Allow it to cool and cut into cubes when it is still warm. 4. When it is cool, wrap the cubes in silver paper.

12. Toffees

6 cups milk
1 cup chikki jaggery
1 cup maida (fine wheat flour)
5 cups sugar
½ cup ghee
1 tsp vanilla essence

1. Mix everything together and cook over medium heat. 2. When moderately thick add vanilla. 3. When it is of the right consistency, remove it from the fire, stir well for sometime, then spread it into a greased flat tray. 4. Cut cubes when fairly warm and allow to cool. For all these recipes of burfies etc., the mixture when removed from the fire should be stirred well, collected cleanly and then poured into the flat tray.

13. Groundnut chikki

3 cups of groundnuts (roasted, skinned and crushed)
2 cups sugar or chikki jaggery
2 tbsps ghee

1. Mix sugar/jaggery and ghee and cook on a low flame till it is caramalised rich brown and bubbly like the syrup for sesame seed ladus. 2. Add the crushed nuts and stir well. Mix properly and pour out into a greased flat tray. 3. Even it out with a greased rolling pin and when fairly warm, cut into cubes and allow it to cool.

NOTE: 1. Castor sugar can be used instead of chikki jaggery. 2. A little sugar added to chikki jaggery syrup makes the chikki or cubes more crisp.

14. Puffed rice chikki

Roasted bengal gram dal, puffed rice or roasted beaten rice also can be used to prepare chikki or ladus of the same mixture.

15. Coconut chikki

2 tender coconuts (grate and grind roughly)
½ cup roasted sesame seeds
12 cardamoms powdered
1 cup sugar for 1 cup ground coconut paste (equal measure)
1 cup roasted bengal gram dal

1. Grind the roasted bengal gram dal to a rough powder and fry it in a little ghee. 2. Mix jaggery and the roughly ground grated coconut together and put it in a big, thick, deep frying pan. Keep it on a low fire and stir till the mixture is syrupy. 3. Add the remaining ingredients when the mixture thickens to the right consistency (i.e. can be rolled into a firm non-sticky ball). Mix them well. 4. Remove from the fire and pour the mixture in a greased flat tray, roll out and allow to cool. 5. When fairly warm, cut into cubes and cool again.

Some More Snacks

Cake (eggless)

2 cups raisins
2 cups fine wheat flour (maida)
½ cup butter
½ tsp soda-bi-carb
1 cup sugar
2 level tsp baking powder
½ cup orange juice
1 ½ cup water

1. Cook the raisins in 1½ cup water till soft. 2. Sift the flour, baking powder and soda-bi-carb together. 3. Add butter to the flour mixture and blend it well. 4. Add orange juice and the cooked raisins along with the water used to cook them. Mix well. 5. Bake it in an oven for about half an hour on medium heat.

Salted or khari biscuits

2 cups fine wheat flour (maida)
½ tsp soda-bi-carb
salt to taste
½ cup butter
½ tsp caraway seeds (shaha jira)

1. Mix all the ingredients with a little water and prepare dough like the one for puries. Keep it overnight. 2. Next morning roll out and cut it into desired shapes and bake the biscuits till crisp.

Sweet biscuits (variety 1)

2 cups fine wheat flour (maida)
½ cup castor sugar
½ cup butter

1. Mix all the ingredients together, knead well and keep overnight. 2. Next morning roll out the dough and cut into different shapes. 3. Bake till crisp.

Sweet biscuits (variety 2)

1 cup ghee
1 cup rice flour
½ tsp baking powder
1 cup castor sugar
2 cups fine wheat flour (maida)
1 cup sugar*
1 tbsp cocoa*
½ tsp vanilla*

*Icing Syrup

1. Heat ghee and beat in rice flour, castor sugar, and baking powder. 2. Mix together and knead without adding water. 3. Make small balls, flatten them on one side and bake for about ½ an hour, till crisp. Allow them to cool. 4. Make a thick syrup with sugar. Add cocoa and vanilla and blend well. 5. Spread the icing syrup with a teaspoon on the biscuits.

Karanji (samosa)

1 coconut (grated)
1 cup rawa
2 to 2¼ cups sugar
2 cups water (for syrup)
12 cardamoms (powdered)
½ cup roasted sesame seeds
2½ cups maida
2 tbsps hot ghee
milk/water to knead
refined oil for deep frying
¼ cup cashew nuts (chopped fine)

1. Roast the grated coconut on a low fire, till it is dry and pinkish in colour. 2. Similarly roast rawa in a little ghee on a low fire. 3. Make a syrup of the sugar and 2 cups water, boil it to one string consistency. 4. Add roasted rawa, coconut, cardamom powder, chopped cashewnuts and roasted sesame seeds, stir well and cook for 5 minutes. Remove from the fire, stir well and allow it to cool. This filling stored in a steel container and kept in a fridge can be used as and when needed. 5. Make dough (like that for puries) with maida and ghee and adding enough water to knead. 6. Make small thin puries of this dough. 7. Spread a tbsp of the filling on half the side of the puri (leaving a margin all around the semi circle), cover it with the other half and wet the edges with milk or water and press them firmly together and cut the edges with a zig-zag cutter. The karanji is ready for frying. 8. Take a wet thin cloth (napkin), spread half of it on a flat thali (plate), arrange the karanjis as you make them on the cloth spread on the thali and cover them with the other half of the wet cloth so that they do not get dry. 9. When all the karanjis are made, deep fry them in oil, a few at a time, over a moderate fire, until they are crisp. 10. When cool, store them in a tin with a tight lid.

NOTE: 1. If the edges of the karanjis are not pressed firmly, they open while frying and all the filling gets into the frying oil. 2. The cloth should be wet but thoroughly drained. 3. Karanjis should be fried only when all of them are ready. If fried fresh immediately, they become red and soft and not crisp. 4. ½ cup beaten rice roasted and crushed may also be added to the filling.

Jaggery karanji (nevaryo)

- 1 coconut grated (approx. 1½ cup)*
- ¼ cup roasted sesame seeds*
- ¾ cup jaggery (½ the measure of grated coconut)*
- 6 cardamoms (powdered)*

*For the filling

1. Mix the coconut gratings, jaggery and fried sesame seeds and stir the mixture on a low fire till it thickens and all the liquid dries up. 2. Add cardamom powder, stir, remove from the fire and let it cool. 3. Prepare the dough and karanjis as in the previous recipe (sugar karanjis).

NOTE: 1. ½ cup puffed rajgira may be added to the filling. 2. The karanjis can also be steam-cooked but they last only for a day.

Modaks (jaggery and coconut)

1. Make the filling and the dough as above. 2. Place the filling in the centre of the puri and fold the edges (wetting the edges with a little water or milk) giving it a shape of fig and deep fry.

NOTE: 1. Can be steam-cooked also. 2. For steam-cooked modaks and karanjis the covering can also be made with rice flour cooked in equal quantity of water.

Mande

2 cups ground or castor sugar
1 cup beaten rice flour
1 cup puffed rajgira flour
½ cup roasted sesame seeds
12 cardamoms (powdered)
3 cups flour (maida)
¾ cup milk
2 tbsps ghee
ghee for deep frying

1. Mix the first five ingredients for the filling (do not cook). 2. Bind in the rest of the ingredients into a hard and firm dough. 3. Roll out thin puries (flat rounds—12 cms in diameter) from the dough. 4. Fry each puri briskly soft and white (not crisp or brown). Remove quickly and spread 1 tbsp of the filling on ½ side. Fold the other half side on it. 5. Again sprinkle ½ tbsp of the filling in the 2nd fold. Again fold it into a triangle. 6. Keep all such triangles or mande separately (not over one another) in a thali and allow it to cool. 7. Then store in a tin with a tight lid.

Surli holgi

1. Same as 'mande' but add ½ cup dry grated coconut roasted and 1 tbsp roasted poppy seeds instead of sesame seeds. 2. Instead of folding the briskly fried, soft puris, spread the filling on one side and roll them (first folding the sides so as not to allow the filling to drop out).

Chirote or Lakhote

3 cups flour
4 tbsps ghee
3 tbsps rice flour
pinch of salt
1 cup castor sugar
cardamom powder
ghee for deep frying

1. Heat 4 tbsps ghee. Add the rice flour and salt. Beat the mixture well. Add the flour and a little water and bind into a hard dough. Knead and pound it well. 2. Divide the dough in small portions (size of a big playing marble). Roll out each portion into a thin round like puri. Smear each with a little ghee and sprinkle a little rice flour on it. 3. Cover it with another such puri. Smear it with ghee and sprinkle again with rice flour. 4. Keep three layers like this. Then fold in the two opposite sides towards the centre. Again fold these two sides one over the other, so that the whole thing has an oblong shape. Cut this across into equal pieces with a knife.

5. Roll out each piece towards the open side with a rolling pin, into a square shape. 6. Deep fry each piece on a low fire. 7. Remove when crisp and press sideways so that the layers separate. 8. Sprinkle castor sugar mixed with cardamom powder inside and outside. 9. When cool, store in a tight container.

NOTE: As a variety salty chirote can be prepared without using sugar but with a little more salt to taste, in the dough.

Phenori (sweet)

3 cups flour
5 tbsps ghee
1 cup milk or water
pinch of salt
2 cups sugar
9 cardamoms powdered
oil for deep frying
2 tbsp rice flour

1. Make a hard dough with flour, 4 tbsps ghee and a pinch of salt, knead it well and pound it to make it pliable. 2. Divide it into 24 equal portions and roll each portion into a thin round shape, of the size of a chapati. 3. Heat the rest of the ghee a little. Add rice flour to it and mix. 4. Take a chapati and smear it with a little mixture of ghee and rice flour. Place a second chapati on the first one, but a little lower from the upper edge. Again smear it with the mixture. Arrange 8 layers of chapaties like this, each chapati a little lower than the previous one. Roll them into a tight roll. Tuck in the edges at the two sides inside the roll firmly. 5. Cut the roll into thin slices. 6. Roll out each piece into a thick puri. 7. When all the slices of one roll are rolled into puries, deep fry them in oil, on a medium fire, till crisp and brownish. 8. Prepare a thick syrup of the sugar with a little water and cardamom powder. Place it on a low fire to keep it warm. 9. Dip three to four phenories at a time in the warm syrup. When they are well coated, drain the extra syrup, remove them and keep them on a flat tray, till the syrup dries. 10. Store in a tight container.

Phenori (savoury)

1. Make a dough as for sweet phenories, but adding a little extra salt, 1 tsp turmeric powder, 4 tsps chilli powder, 1 tsp cumin seed powder. 2. Do not dip them in syrup.

Saath

3 cups flour (maida)
½ cup bengal gram flour
½ cup rice flour
½ cup hot ghee or oil for frying
2 cups sugar
9 cardamoms powdered

1. Make a thick syrup of the sugar and cardamom powder. 2. Mix all ingredients with just enough water to make a soft but firm dough. 3. Knead the dough well, make small balls, flatten each in the centre and fry in hot ghee over a low fire. 4. Arrange in a flat tray, after dipping in syrup. Dry and serve.

NOTE: For all these recipes, the ghee that is added to the flour should be made very hot so that the layers are crisp when fried.

Jalebi

- 1 cup rawa
- 1 cup flour
- 4 tsps rice flour
- saffron/orange colour
- 4 tsp curds
- 4 tsps ghee
- ghee for deep frying
- 2 cups sugar*
- 2 cups water*
- 1 tsp lime juice*

*For syrup

1. Make a syrup with the sugar and water. Let it be sticky but not thick. Add 1 tsp lime juice and saffron for flavour or orange colour (consistency — a drop on the floor should maintain its shape). 2. Mix together rawa, flour, rice flour, ghee and curds on the previous night. The batter should be thick (like that for bhajias). 3. Heat ghee/cooking fat in a deep frying pan. Prepare jalebies on a low flame, squeezing the batter through a piping bag, into circular rounds, with a quick movement of the hand, into the heated fat. 4. Fry the jalebies crisp. Dip the jalebies in syrup until they absorb the syrup. Drain them and keep in a flat tray. 5. Serve hot.

NOTE: Jalebies should not be piled together when hot. Otherwise they become soft and turn into one mass.

Malpuris

- 1 cup flour
- 1 cup rawa
- 1 cup sugar
- ½ tsp soda-bi-carb
- 1 pinch saffron
- cashew nuts

1. Mix together flour, rawa, soda-bi-carb and sugar on the previous night and allow to ferment. 2. Add saffron and nuts and pour a tbsp of mixture slowly with a spoon, in the hot ghee and fry till crisp and brown.

NOTE: As a variation, batter prepared with butter-milk, maida, sugar and saffron can be used for making malpuris immediately (need not be mixed the previous night and allowed to ferment).

Shankarpali (tukde) (variety 1)

2 cups flour
2 tbsps hot ghee
1 pinch of salt
ghee for deep frying
1 cup sugar
cardamom powder
water

1. Add hot ghee and salt to the flour and make a hard dough with just enough water. 2. Roll out thick 15 cm. diameter rounds. 3. Place two rounds one over the other. Roll them out again into a thin round and cut it into diamond shapes or squares with a cutter. 4. Deep fry the diamond shaped or square pieces in the ghee, till crisp and light pinkish in colour. 5. Make a syrup (not very thick) of the sugar and cardamom powder and water. 6. Dip the fried pieces (tukde) or shankarpali in the warm syrup, drain and allow to dry (like sweet phenories). Store in a tight container when they cool.

Shankarpali (variety 2)

½ cup castor sugar
2 cups flour
½ cup ghee
a pinch of salt
2 tbsps rice flour
¾ cup milk or water
ghee for deep frying

1. Cream ghee and sugar together till the sugar dissolves and the mixture is light. 2. Add salt, the flours, and milk or water, mix well and knead the dough. 3. Roll out small portions into slightly thick rounds. Cut each round into cubes or diamonds and deep fry them in ghee.

Shankarpali (salty)

3 cups flour
1 tsp salt
4 tsps chilli powder
2 tbsps hot oil
water
1 tsp turmeric powder
½ tsp coriander and cumin seed powder
oil for deep frying

1. Mix all the ingredients in water to form a hard dough. Knead well. 2. Roll out into thin 15 to 20 cm. diameter rounds. Cut each round into diamonds or squares. 3. Deep fry these pieces in oil on a moderate fire, till they are crisp.

Masala Puri (savoury)

- 1 ½ cups wheat flour
- 1 ½ cups wheat flour roasted in ½ cup ghee
- 1 tsp coriander and cumin seed powder
- 1 ½ tsps salt
- 4 tsps chilli powder
- water for kneading
- oil for deep frying
- 1 tsp turmeric powder

1. Mix all the ingredients and bind into a hard dough with just enough water. Knead well. 2. Divide into portions and roll each portion into small thin rounds and give cuts on the rounds with a knife or fork to prevent the puries from puffing up. 3. Deep fry them in oil, till crisp.

Bhubhus Roti

- 2 cups maida
- ½ cup curds
- ½ cup sugar (powdered)
- ½ tsp soda bi-carb
- 2 tsp ghee
- 1 banana (mashed) - optional
- a pinch of salt
- refined oil for deep frying

1. Mix ingredients into a hard dough. 2. Roll into puries and deep fry.

Biscuit roti (variety 1)

- ½ coconut grated
- ½ cup chopped coriander leaves
- 7 to 8 chillies chopped fine
- salt
- ½ cup bengal gram flour
- 2 cups fine rawa or wheat flour
- 2 tbsps hot oil
- oil for deep frying

1. Mix salt, fine rawa or flour, hot oil and enough water and make a dough a little softer than the dough for puris, about two hours in advance and keep it aside. 2. Mix the first five ingredients to prepare the filling. 3. Knead the dough well. Divide into small portions. Apply oil to the right hand fingers. Take a portion of the dough (double the quantity of the filling) on the left palm and flatten it a little with the greased fingers, place a little filling in its centre and cover the filling completely with the sides of the flattened round. 4. Roll the ball in a little flour, roll it like a puri and deep fry in oil.

Biscuit roti (variety 2)

- 1 cup black gram dal
- 2 tbsps bengal gram dal
- salt to taste
- 2 tbsps grated coconut
- 4 green chillies
- ¼ cup chopped coriander

1. Prepare the dough with fine rawa or wheat flour, hot ghee, salt and water as for the first variety. 2. Soak both the dals for 1 to 1½ hours. Then grind them coarsely. (These dals soaked for 6 to 7 hours have a better taste.) 3. Mix all the ingredients to prepare the filling. 4. For filling and making puries follow the instructions given for the first variety.

Chivda

- 1 cup roasted bengal gram dal or 1 cup fried (in oil) bengal gram dal
- 1 cup roasted peanuts
- 1 cup slices of dry copra (coconut)
- 2 tsps salt (powdered)
- 2 tsps chilli powder
- 3 tbsps coriander and cumin seed powder
- curry leaves
- 6 cups beaten rice
- oil for deep frying
- 2 tsps sugar (or more to taste)
- 1 tsp turmeric powder
- 2 pinches asafoetida
- 8 green chillies cut lengthwise
- 1 tsp mustard seeds

1. Deep fry the first four ingredients separately (using the wire strainer available) and keep them aside. 2. Mix together all the powders, salt and asafoetida. 3. Deep fry the beaten rice (using the strainer) a little at a time. Put it in a big vessel or a big deep frying pan and sprinkle a little of the mixture of the powders and mix well lightly. Continue this process until all the beaten rice is fried. 4. Prepare a seasoning in a big vessel or a big deep frying pan with oil, mustard seeds, slit green chillies, a pinch of asafoetida and curry leaves. When the mustard seeds splutter remove it from fire and add the fried ingredients, the remaining mixture of powders and the fried beaten rice and mix well. 5. Store in a tight container when cool.

NOTE: Fried cashew nuts and fried raisins can also be added to the chivda.

Potato chivda

1. Wash the potatoes, peel and grate them. 2. Put the grated potatoes in cold water to which a little alum is added. 3. Remove after 5 minutes, dry on a cloth or in a colander and deep fry till crisp. 4. Add spices and seasoning as for beaten rice chivda.

NOTE: 1. Alum makes the grated potatoes more crisp and white. 2. Fried bread crumbs and corn flakes can also be used to prepare chivda.

Shevaya usal (dried wheat noodles upama)

1 cup shevaya
1 tsp sugar
salt to taste
1 tbsp ghee/refined oil
1 tsp black gram dal*
1 handful grated coconut
3 or 4 red chillies*
curry leaves*
mustard seeds*

*For seasoning

1. Soak the shevaya in cold water for 10 minutes or put them in boiling water and drain after 1 minute. Shred them into small pieces with the fingers. 2. Add salt and sugar to taste and mix well lightly. 3. Prepare a seasoning in a deep frying pan with ghee/oil, mustard seeds, black gram dal, red/green chillies and curry leaves. Add the shevaya, stir lightly and keep it covered for two to three minutes on a very low fire. 4. Add the grated coconut, mix well and cover and remove from the fire after one or two minutes. 5. Serve when it is warm.

Bhel

½ kg puffed rice
½ kg fine sev or ¼ kg sev + ¼ kg chivda
½ kg potatoes boiled and chopped
½ kg onions chopped fine
2 cups coriander leaves finely chopped
raw mangoes grated or chopped (optional)
¼ kg ripe tomatoes
hot and spicy chutney
sweet chutnev

Chutney (hot and spicy) (variety 1)

1 cup grated coconut
5 to 6 green chillies
coriander leaves
mint leaves (optional)
tamarind*
salt*
4 to 5 cloves
2 cm. piece of cinnamon
1 tsp coriander
½ tsp cumin seeds
2 cm. ginger
1 small bulb garlic
a small onion

* To taste

1. Grind the coconut, tamarind and chillies, add other ingredients and grind again to a fine paste. Add a little water and make a semi-fluid chutney.

Chutney spicy (variety 2) (optional)

1 cup grated coconut
5 red chillies
1 tbsp peanuts
1 tbsp roasted bengal gram dal (optional)
2 cm. ginger
½ tbsp cumin seeds
amchur (optional)

Grind into a fine semi-fluid chutney.

Chutney sweet

1 cup tamarind juice	1 cup dates
¾ cup jaggery	2 tsps salt

1. Soak and grind the dates and tamarind, add jaggery and salt and boil and cool.

To prepare Bhel

1. Add all the ingredients of Bhel and the chutnies together, only a small quantity at a time, and serve. **2.** Mix just before serving and in small quantity only, otherwise it becomes soggy.

Poha (beaten rice) usal

2 cups of beaten rice	½ tsp mustard
1 cup grated coconut	1 tbsp ghee
4 green chillies sliced	½ tsp black gram dal
2 tsps sugar	curry leaves
1 tsp salt	1 red chilli-broken

1. Clean and wash the beaten rice briskly to avoid sogging. Add salt and sugar (preferably both powdered) to it and mix well. **2.** Prepare a seasoning (in a dry deep frying pan) of ghee, mustard seeds, black gram dal, red chilli and curry leaves. Add the salted and sugared beaten rice and half the grated coconut. Mix well and keep on low fire, covered with a lid for five minutes. Mix the rest of the grated coconut and serve hot.

Green (garden) peas poha

2 cups beaten rice (poha)	mustard
7 to 8 green chillies (chopped)	asafoetida
chopped green coriander	turmeric powder
1 cup green peas shelled	2 tbsps ghee or oil
½ cup grated coconut	1 tsp sugar
juice of 1 lemon	1 tsp salt

1. Wash the beaten rice and add salt and sugar and mix well. **2.** Heat oil and prepare a seasoning of mustard seeds, green chillies, asafoetida and turmeric (add chillies etc., only when mustard seeds splutter). **3.** Add the green peas, fry them a little, add a little water and cook. **4.** When cooked add beaten rice and coriander. Stir well and keep it covered on a very low fire only for 3 to 4 minutes. 5. Add lemon juice and grated coconut, mix well, remove from fire and serve.

NOTE: 1. Potatoes chopped into thin and long pieces or boiled potato cubes, cauliflower, brinjal etc., can be used as substitutes for green peas. 2. Onion can be added for seasoning. 3. 1 tsp garam (amti) masala can be added reducing the number of green chillies.

Jaggery poha (jaggery and beaten rice)

2 cups of beaten rice
¾ cup light coloured jaggery
2 tsps ghee
4 cardamoms powdered
½ coconut grated

1. Chop the jaggery fine. Add ½ portion of grated coconut and cardamom powder and mix it well. 2. Add the beaten rice and a little water and mix well again. 3. Put some weight over it so that the beaten rice absorbs all the jaggery and its flavour. Cover and leave for 15 minutes. 4. Add the remaining grated coconut and ghee, mix well and serve.

Roasted sweet poha

6 cups roasted (puffed) beaten rice
½ cup grated dry copra
2 cups jaggery
1 tsp cardamom powder
2 tsps ghee

1. Clean the puffed beaten rice. 2. Roast the copra. 3. Make a thick syrup of the jaggery. When it is of 1 string consistency add cardamom powder and the roasted copra and the ghee. Stir well and remove from the fire and serve.

Spiced or masala poha (variety 1)

3 cups beaten rice
4 red chillies, 2 green chillies
1½ tsps coriander
1½ tsps cumin seeds
½ tsp turmeric
1¼ tsps salt
tamarind (size of a small marble)
2 onions chopped
green coriander*
sugar to taste*

* Optional

1. Dampen the beaten rice, cover and keep it for 10 minutes. 2. Grind a chutney with ½ portion of the grated coconut, red and green chillies, tamarind, coriander and cumin seeds, turmeric, salt. 3. Mix the chutney, remaining grated coconut, finely chopped onion and the dampened beaten rice. Mix well and serve. Add a little sugar to taste and chopped coriander (optional).

Masala poha (variety 2)

The beaten rice can be roasted in a tbsp of ghee (instead of dampening) and mixed.

Masala poha (variety 3)

Instead of onion add seasoning of ghee, mustard seeds, red chillies, asafoetida and curry leaves.

Savoury poha

2 cups beaten rice
1 tsp sugar
3 green chillies
salt to taste
¾ cup grated coconut

1. Dampen the beaten rice with a little water. 2. Slice green chillies and crush them with salt and sugar. 3. Add beaten rice and mix well. Add grated coconut. Mix and serve.

Curds poha

3 cups of beaten rice
3 cups curds
¼ coconut grated
2 tsps powdered sugar
2 tsps ghee (for seasoning)
8 green chillies
1 cm piece ginger chopped fine
salt to taste
mustard
curry leaves
coriander (optional)

1. Wash the beaten rice and squeeze out the water. 2. Grind the coconut, chillies and ginger coarsely. 3. Mix the masala, salt and sugar with the curds, beat well and add the beaten rice. 4. Prepare a seasoning with ghee, mustard seeds and curry leaves and add it to the above mixture of beaten rice. 5. When the beaten rice soaks well in the curds and becomes thick, make small balls of the dahi pohe and serve.

NOTE: Dahi pohe balls are offered to Lord Krishna on Gokulastami.

Green peas (garden peas) rawa

2 cups rawa (samolina)
1 cup green peas
2 tbsps ghee or oil
½ cup grated coconut
5 cups water
chopped green coriander
1 tsp mustard
a pinch of asafoetida
6 green chillies-chopped
curry leaves
2 onions (optional)
sugar to taste (optional)

1. Roast rawa in a little ghee or oil till it is light brown. 2. Prepar

the seasoning in hot ghee or oil with mustard seeds, green chillies, curry leaves and asafoetida. (Add onions and fry till light brown — optional). **3.** Add green peas, fry them a little and add 5 cups water, salt and sugar (optional) to taste. **4.** When the peas cook, add rawa, stirring as you add it, mix well. Add lemon juice, stir well, cover and leave it on a low fire for 5 minutes. **5.** When it is done, add chopped coriander and grated coconut and serve.

NOTE: Cucumber, cauliflower, potatoes, tomatoes also can be used separately or in a combination with peas or instead of peas.

Uppit

2 cups rawa
2 tbsps ghee or oil
4 to 4½ cups water
1 tsp lemon juice or 1 cup buttermilk
¼ grated coconut
salt to taste
1 tsp black gram dal
1 tsp bengal gram dal
2 onions (optional)
mustard seeds
6 slit green chillies
curry leaves
asafoetida

1. Fry the rawa in a little oil, till it is light brown. **2.** Prepare a seasoning with mustard seeds, green chillies, curry leaves, asafoetida, bengal gram dal and black gram dal. Add onions and fry till light brown. **3.** Add 4 to 4½ cups water (or 1 cup buttermilk and 3 to 3½ cups water) and salt. **4.** When water boils, add rawa stirring as you add it, add lemon juice and grated coconut and chopped coriander. **5.** Stir well and cook on a low fire for about five minutes and serve.

Savoury rawa (plain)

2 cups rawa
4 cups water
¼ cup ghee or oil
¼ grated coconut
½ tsp mustard seeds
3 red chillies
curry leaves
jaggery/sugar, and salt to taste

1. Fry the rawa in a little ghee. **2.** Make a seasoning with mustard seeds, curry leaves and red chilli pieces. Add water, jaggery/sugar and salt to taste. **3.** When it boils add rawa, stirring well, add grated coconut and cover it and keep on a low fire till it cooks well. **4.** Remove from the fire and serve.

Sweet sanza (variety 1)

2 cups rawa
1 cup ghee
1½ cup sugar
3½ cups water
2 tsp raisins
almonds chopped
½ tsp cardamom powder
1 pinch saffron (optional) soaked in warm milk

1. Roast the rawa in a little ghee. 2. Heat 3½ cups water, add sugar and bring it to boil. 3. Add almonds, cardamom powder, saffron and rawa, mix well. Add raisins and the remaining ghee, stir well and let it simmer on a slow fire till the rawa is cooked. 4. Remove from the fire and serve.

Sweet sanza (variety 2)

2 cups rawa
2 cups ghee
4 cups milk or 2 cups milk + 2 cups water
slices of 2 ripe bananas
1 tsp raisins
almonds chopped
2 cups sugar

Follow the instructions for the 1st variety. This sanza is offered to Lord Satyanarayan at the time of his pooja.

Geen (colostrum pudding)

2 cups 1st or 2nd day colostrum milk of buffalo
4 cups plain milk or 2 cups coconut milk
3 cups jaggery/sugar
6 cardamoms powdered
10 pepper corns (powdered)

1. Mix all ingredients and dissolve the jaggery or sugar well. 2. Test the consistency by steaming a little mixture in a small ladle (2nd day milk requires less plain milk). 3. Put the mixture in a shallow vessel and steam until cooked well.

Geena soyi (colostrum and coconut pudding)

2 cups 2nd or 3rd day colostrum milk of buffalo
1½ cups jaggery
6 cardamoms powdered
½ cup coconut gratings

1. Mix all the ingredients and cook till the mixture thickens and resembles 'halwa'.

Fruit Preserves

Mango preserve or moramba (variety 1)

4 to 6 large semi-ripe mangoes
sugar 1½ to double the weight of mangoes
pinch of saffron
cinnamon

1. Keep the mangoes in cold water for sometime. Then wipe them dry, peel and cut into cubes. 2. Weigh the mango cubes and take sugar 1½ to 2 times that weight. 3. Boil some water, remove it from heat. Add the mango cubes to it. Cover with a lid and keep for two to three minutes. Then drain off the water. Spread the cubes on a dry cloth for a while. 4. Prepare a syrup of the sugar (a drop on the floor should retain its shape). 5. Add saffron, cinnamon and mango pieces to the syrup and heat on a slow fire till the syrup becomes thick again. 6. Remove from heat, cool and pour in a clean jar and store. This moramba lasts for at least one year.

NOTE: Cardamon powder can be substituted for saffron.

Mango preserve or moramba (variety 2)

4 to 6 half ripe mangoes (grated)
sugar 1½ to 2 times measure of mango gratings
1 pinch saffron, or cardamom powder

1. Wash, peel and grate the mangoes. 2. Take sugar 1½ to 2 times the measure of gratings. 3. Mix mango gratings and sugar and keep aside for 15 to 20 minutes. 4. Cook over a medium heat till the mixture is sticky and thick. 5. Add saffron, mix well and remove from heat, cool and store in a glass jar.

NOTE: Rajapuri, totapuri and badami mangoes are ideal for these recipes.

Mango jam

4 half-ripe good quality mangoes
sugar double the quantity

1. Wash, peel and steam the mangoes. 2. Remove the pulp and strain it through a mesh. 3. Mix sugar double the quantity and cook till thick and sticky.

Strawberry jam

1 kg strawberries
1 kg sugar

1. Clean the strawberries, cut into pieces if they are too big. 2. Add sugar and keep aside for some time. Then cook on a medium fire, till the syrup is thick and sticky. 3. Remove, cook and store.

NOTE: Alubukhar, tomatoes, half ripe papaya or any other fruit can be used for the jam.

Pineapple preserve

1 ripe pineapple (peeled, cut into cubes)
sugar equal in measure, saffron, 1 cup water

1. Wash, peel and cut the pineapple into cubes. 2. Measure the cubes and take equal quantity of sugar. 3. Add one cup water to the sugar and make a thick syrup 4. Add pineapple pieces and boil further till the syrup is thick again. 5. Add saffron. Cool and store.

Guava jelly

25 medium size guavas
6 to 7 lemons
2 sticks cinnamon
sugar (by measure)
10 cloves

1. Wash and cut guavas into small pieces. 2. Put them in a steel vessel and add water just enough to cover the pieces and cook on a low fire (or in a pressure cooker) till the pieces are well cooked and soft. Allow to cool. 3. Strain the pulp on a plastic strainer. Collect the liquid and measure it. 4. Take a measure of sugar for 4 measures of the liquid. Add lemon juice and cook on a low fire till the mixture thickens. 5. Add cloves and cinnamon as it thickens. Cook further until a drop on a plate does not spread.

NOTE: 1. The boiled guava pieces can be put on a thin cloth, tied and suspended to collect the liquid for the jelly. 2. The guava pulp left after draining the liquid can be used for a pudding. From this remove the seeds, add sufficient sugar and milk to the pulp, blend well to a thick consistency, cool in a refrigerator and serve.

Indian gooseberry (Amla) jelly

Same as above but lemon juice not needed. Jellies can be prepared from pineapple, papaya, pomegranate, etc., similarly.

Amla (whole) preserve (morawla)

1 kg larga amla (Indian gooseberries — awlas)
saffron for colour and flavouring
sugar 2 to 2½ times the amla weight

1. Wash, dry and weigh the amla. Prick them all over with a fork 2. Put them in boiling water and cover for some time or cook for 5 minutes and drain off the water. 3. Make a thick syrup of the sugar, add the drained amla, add saffron and cook till the syrup is thick and sticky. 4. Cool and store.

NOTE: This preserve is very good for acidity and jaundice. A similar preserve can be made of tender ginger also.

Amla (grated) preserve

Amla grated, ginger grated, sugar double the quantity can be cooked together till thick and sticky, and preserved.

NOTE: If desired amla and ginger may be soaked in lime (chuna) water for an hour before use.

Preserves

1. Wheat papad

6 cups wheat
1 litre water
3 tbsps sugar
1 ½ tbsps salt

1. Take good quality wheat, wash and soak in enough water for twenty four hours (soak in the morning). 2. Next morning wash the wheat again and grind it fine. 3. Strain it through cheese cloth or a strainer. Add a little more water to the residue and squeeze and strain again. 4. Keep the strained mixture in a large vessel and allow it to settle for twenty four hours. 5. Remove the water gently, add 1 litre of fresh water, salt and sugar to the thick sediment. Mix well. 6. Take a large vessel (preferably aluminium or brass vessel). Coat the bottom with a teaspoonful of coconut oil and pour a cup of water into it. Bring it to boil. Gently pour the flour mixture into it stirring all the time. It is of the right consistency if it is soft like butter. Add a little more water if necessary. When the mixture is properly cooked, it will become opaque and bluish in colour. 7. Apply coconut oil to the palms, take large portions of the mixture and make moderately big rolls. Keep these covered. 8. Take out rolls one at a time, and knead properly, divide into small portions and roll out into moderately thin papads (round like puris). Use maida or refined flour while rolling out. 9. Dry the papads in the sun, on a cloth. Cover them with another cloth and weigh this cover down with weight or stones so that the papads do not curl while drying. 10. Store in an air-tight tin when they cool.

NOTE: 1. These papads taste better if roasted rather than fried. They are very good for children and convalescents or the sick people. 2. The sediment can be kept longer by changing the water daily. 3. It can also be dried in the sun and stored. The dry flour can be used to make halwa, chocolates etc.

2. Wheat shevaya (hoppers)

1. Method is the same as above but add a little more water so that the dough after it is cooked is a little softer and can be squeezed out from the shevaya mould more easily. 2. Make shevaya when the dough is warm. Dry them in the sun immediately otherwise they become darker in colour. 3. The mould should be washed clean and coated with oil on the inside. 4. Store in an air- tight tin when well dried.

3. Wheat shetodya

6 cups wheat
1 ½ tbsps salt
2 litres milk
2 tbsps sugar
½ cup white sesame seeds

1. Wash and soak the wheat for twenty four hours. 2. Grind, strain the paste, allow the mixture to settle down for twelve hours. 3. Remove the top water, add 2 litres of water, salt and sugar to taste and sesame seeds to the sediment. (Consistency — thinner than bundi batter). 4. Cook well on a slow fire stirring till it cooks. 5. When cooked, remove from heat, keep in a cool place covered with a cloth. When it cools cover it with a lid. 6. Next morning spread a cloth or a plastic sheet coated with a little oil, in the sun. A spoonful of mixture poured in a round shape in one place makes one shetodi. Pour spoonfuls of the mixture like this, a little away from one another, all over the cloth or sheet. Dry them in the hot sun for four or five days. 7. Remove them from the sheet when they dry well. Turn them over and dry them again in the sun for a day or two. 8. When cool, store in an air-tight tin.

NOTE: If the shetodya stick to the cloth when dry, dampen the wrong side of the cloth with a little cool water and leave for sometime so that they can be easily removed. When removed, dry them thoroughly before storing.

4. Jawar vadyo

6 cups jawar
4 tbsps salt
5 gms asafoetida
1 ½ cup crushed green chillies
3 cups sesame seeds (powdered)

1. Dampen the jawar, pound and winnow to remove the husk and soak it in water early in the morning. 2. In the afternoon i.e. after about 6 to 7 hours, grind the soaked jawar and strain it. 3. In the evening, remove the extra water at the top, retaining enough water to cook the mixture (a little thicker than wheat shetodya mixture).

Add crushed green chillies, salt, white sesame seeds, asafoetida (dissolved in water). **4.** Cook the mixture a little thicker than shetodya mixture, allow it to cool and cover it. 5. Next morning spread out the mixture on an oiled plastic sheet or cloth, dry well, store like shetodya.

Variation: Instead of green chillies, asafoetida and sesame seeds, ½ cup chilli powder can be added while preparing the dough and 2 kg. of onions, chopped fine, can be added in the morning before drying in the sun.

5. Ragi vadyo

Follow the same instructions as above. In this case the residue of starch is less and hence the ingredients added should also be less in proportion.

6. Green chilli vadyo

2 cups black gram dal
4 tsps fenugreek seeds
5 gms asafoetida
1 cup salt
1 cup sesame seeds
2 cups crushed green chillies

1. Soak black gram dal and fenugreek seeds for 2 to 3 hours in the evening. 2. At night grind them dry, yet fine (adding very little water). 3. The next morning add all the ingredients and spread teaspoonfuls on a plastic sheet and dry in the hot sun for 2 to 3 days. **4.** Remove, turn them over and dry again for a day or two more and store.

Variation: Grind the black gram etc. in the morning and in addition to the given ingredients add ½ kg finely chopped green mangoes and 3 cups of chopped green fenugreek leaves. (Do not use fingers to make sandige because the mixture is very pungent and hot.)

7. Ashgourd vadyo

2 kg ashgourd
2 cups black gram dal
¼ tsp fenugreek seeds
½ cup green chillies
2 tsps salt

1. Soak the dal and fenugreek seeds in the morning. **2.** Grind the dal at night along with green chillies and salt, without adding much water. **3.** Next morning, peel the ashgourd, remove seeds and grate. Squeeze out the water and add the gratings to the batter just before spreading out the sandige for drying.

NOTE: 1. The batter must be prepared the previous night. If ground in the morning the sandige do not last. 2. The squeezed out water can be used for ashgourd curry. 3. Cut the skin of the ashgourd into 2 cm. pieces. Smear them and the seeds with the sandige mixture and dry them in the sun and fry them like the sandige.

8. Banana papads

1 kg thick skinned green bananas
salt to taste
jaggery and chilli powder to taste (optional)

Steam-cook the bananas. Skin them when hot. Mash them to a fine paste. Add salt (jaggery and chilli if desired) and knead well. Roll out small papads and dry in the sun like wheat papads.

9. Jackfruit papads

Half ripe jackfruit must be used. Instructions the same as above. Potato and sweet potato papads are prepared similarly. A little chilli powder can be added to potato papads.

10. Black gram papads

8 cups black gram dal
1 cup salt
1 1/4 cups chilli powder
1/2 litre water
15 gms black asafoetida (powder)
40 gms white pepper corns powdered
1/2 cup black gram dal (to be soaked)

1. Clean 8 cups of black gram dal, remove black grains and get it ground (or pulverised) from the mill. Strain the flour through a fine sieve. 2. Keep aside 2 cups of the flour for rolling the papads. 3. Soak 1/2 cup black gram dal at night and grind it to a fine, thick paste. 4. Add salt to 1/2 litre water and bring it to boil. Cool it. Add asafoetida and dissolve it well. Add chilli powder and pepper powder to the salt water. Add the mixture to the ground paste of soaked black gram dal. Blend well. 5. Add 10 cups of the sieved black gram flour to the above mixture and bind into a very hard dough. Coat your palms and the inner surface of a thali with coconut oil, take portions of the dough and knead them well one by one in the thali and roll into balls. 6. Smear the inner surface of the grinding stone (ragda) with coconut oil, put a ball of dough in it and pound it well till the dough is soft and pliable. Repeat this with all the balls of dough. Keep all the balls covered well, overnight. 7. Next morning pound the balls again, knead well, divide into small equal portions and roll out each portion into a papad using the 2 cups flour kept aside. Dry well and store.

11. Green chilli papads

Same as above but take 250 gms of green chillies instead of chilli powder and pepper powder. Boil them in the salt water and grind to a paste. Add 40 gms of papad khar also.

12. Papad khar papads

1. 40 gms papad khar (dissolved in water). 2. Other ingredients same as for red chilli papads. Only take 20 gms salt less as the papad khar is salty. Do not add chilli powder or chillies.

13. Green gram dal papads

8 cups green gram dal (husked) 40 gms papad khar

Get the green gram dal pulverised from the mill. Rest of the ingredients and method is the same as for the papad khar papads.

NOTE: Keep 10 gms of asafoetida in the tin of the papads so that the flavour is not lost during storage.

14. Green chilli kachrya (variety 1)

5 kg green chillies (fresh thick, long and with 1 cm. stem)
sour buttermilk
1 tsp asafoetida
1 tsp fenugreek
1 cup salt

1. Wash the green chillies and dry them with a cloth. 2. Slit the chillies on one side from the tip to the stem, mix them with salt. Put them in a jar and press them down with some weight. 3. Turn them over every day and again keep them pressed with weight. 4. Repeat this for 3 days. On the fourth day press them thoroughly and remove all the salt water and dry them in the sun. 5. At night soak them in sour and thick buttermilk (stale buttermilk will also do) to which a paste of ground fenugreek seeds, asafoetida and salt have been added. Preserve the extra mixture for repeated use. 6. Next morning dry them again in the sun. 7. Repeat this process of soaking them in buttermilk and drying them in the sun, for 2 or 3 days more, till they are no more pungent. 8. Then dry them thoroughly and store them in an air tight bottle or tin. 9. Deep fry them in oil whenever necessary and serve.

NOTE: Even deep fried chillies can be preserved in an air tight tin for a day or two.

15. Green chilli kachrya (variety 2)

5 kg fresh green chillies (thick and long)
2 cups buttermilk
1 cup salt

1. Wash and dry the green chillies with a cloth. Slit them as for variety 1. 2. Dissolve one cup salt in 1 measure water and bring it to boil. Remove from the heat and add chillies to the salt water, cover

and leave to cool. **3.** At night add the buttermilk to the water. Soak the chillies in it overnight. **4.** Remove them the next morning and dry them in the sun. Preserve the solution. **5.** In the evening put the chillies again in the solution and repeat the process of soaking and drying in the sun, till the chillies lose their pungent taste. **6.** Then dry them thoroughly and preserve them. **7.** Deep fry in oil and serve whenever required as a side dish.

NOTE: Fried chillies crushed and mixed with curds only, or with curds and a ground masala of grated coconut, make a good side dish.

16. Seasoned chillies

50 large green chillies
1/2 cup salt
1/2 cup tamarind pulp
1 tsp turmeric powder
1 cup mustard seeds*
1 cup sesame seeds*
1/4 cup fenugreek seeds*
1/2 cup groundnut oil
1/2 tsp mustard seeds
a pinch of asafoetida

*Roast on a dry hot plate and pound

1. Wash chillies, wipe them dry. Slit them into 4 sections. **2.** Mix the pounded ingredients, salt, tamarind pulp and turmeric powder, blend well. **3.** Stuff the chillies with the mixed ingredients. **4.** Heat oil, prepare a seasoning with mustard seeds and asafoetida. **5.** Add the stuffed chillies to the seasoning and allow to simmer, until the chillies are cooked in oil.

17. Methkoot

1 kg bengal gram dal
1/2 kg rice
1/4 kg black gram dal
1/4 kg wheat
20 gms pepper
20 gms fenugreek
175 gms salt
10 gms asafoetida
10 gms dry ginger (soonth)
20 gms cumin seeds
20 gms mustard seeds
20 gms dry turmeric
40 gms red chillies

1. Dry all the ingredients except salt in the sun until they become crisp (i.e. for an hour or two). **2.** Keep a deep frying pan or a shallow vessel on a slow fire and roast each ingredient slowly without using oil and stirring constantly, till crisp and fragrant. Fry them in the following order: rice, wheat, black gram dal, red chillies, bengal gram dal. Add asafoetida, turmeric and ginger cut into small pieces, when the bengal gram dal is almost roasted and then add pepper, fenugreek, cumin and mustard seeds and lastly salt. **3.** Mix all the ingredients and grind them to a fine powder and store in an air-tight bottle.

NOTE: 1. This chutney can be served with rice, adding lemon juice and ghee to the rice. 2. Or mix it with a little curds or buttermilk and season with mustard seed and curry leaves.

Pickles

1. Lemon pickle (variety 1)

100 lemons (fresh and juicy)
1 kg thick juicy fresh ginger
2 kg green chillies
6 measures salt

1. Wash the lemons, chillies, and ginger and dry them in shade by spreading on a thick cloth. 2. Wipe them dry with a clean napkin. 3. Roast the salt for a few minutes (without oil) on a low fire, and pound to a fine powder. 4. Take a little coconut oil, and roast the lemons till the skin gets brownish patches and they are fragrant. Cool and cut each lemon into 8 pieces. 5. Chop the tips and ½ the stems of the chillies. 6. Skin the ginger and cut into thin slices. 7. Wash a large glass or china clay jar, wipe dry and keep it in bright sunlight for 2 hours. 8. Cool the jar well (4 hours). 9. Spread ½ cup of salt in the bottom of the jar and keep another ½ cup aside. Mix the remaining salt with the lemon pieces, chillies and chopped ginger. 10. Fill the jar with the above mixture and sprinkle the remaining salt (½ cup kept aside) on top. Close the jar and tie a piece of clean cloth on top.

2. Lemon pickle (variety 2)

1. Just give the lemons two cuts one lengthwise and another sideways (as for stuffed brinjals and potatoes) without severing or separating the pieces completely. Stuff the lemons with 3 cups of roasted salt. Mix the remaining salt with the chillies and ginger pieces. 2. Sprinkle ½ cup of salt in the jar. 3. Put one layer of lemons, top this with chillies and ginger layer, again put a layer of lemons and repeat. Sprinkle the remaining ½ cup of salt on the topmost layer. 4. Close the jar and tie a piece of clean cloth around the mouth of the jar.

3. Spicy lemon pickle (variety 1)

100 lemons + 25 lemons (for juice)
1 kg ginger
1 measure turmeric
½ measure crushed fenugreek
2 kg green chillies
3 measures chilli powder
20 gms asafoetida
6 measures salt

1. Prepare the lemons, chillies, ginger and salt as per the first lemon pickle. 2. Extract juice from the extra 25 lemons. 3. Mix all the spices, salt, and the juice with the lemon pieces. 4. Fill the jar with layers of the lemon pieces, chillies and ginger alternately. Sprinkle salt on top and close the jar. Tie a piece of clean cloth on the lid.

4. Spicy lemon pickle (variety 2)

1. Slice the lemons on top and sides. Stuff them with spices and salt. Fill in the jar in layers. 2. Do not add the green chillies or ginger. Rest of the method is the same as above.

5. Spicy lemon pickle (variety 3)

25 lemons
1 ¼ measures salt
1 ¼ measures water
5 gms asafoetida
1 measure chilli powder
¼ measure turmeric
1 measure mustard seeds

1. Roast 25 lemons and cut into small pieces. 2. Boil 1 ¼ measure salt in 1 ¼ measure of water. Boil till it condenses to one measure. Grind the above masala with it. Add the lemon pieces to this mixture. Pour into a clean glass jar. This pickle is ready within 10 days.

6. Spicy lemon pickle (variety 4)

25 lemons
1 ¼ cups salt
1 cup of water
same masala as above

1. Wash, wipe and cut the lemons into small pieces. 2. Boil 1 cup of water with 1 ¼ cup of salt. Cool it slightly. Add the chopped lemons to this solution. Keep covered for 15 minutes. 3. Add the ground masala as in variety 3, mentioned above.

7. Spicy lemon pickle (variety 5)

100 lemons + 25 lemons (for juice)
6 measures of salt (roast and powder)
¼ measure pounded fenugreek
1 measure chilli powder
¼ measure turmeric powder
5 grams of asafoetida

1. Wash and wipe the lemons clean, cut into 8 pieces. 2. Mix with salt, all the spices and lemon juice. 3. Fill in a clean glass jar.

8. Spicy lemon pickle (variety 6)

Ingredients same as above plus 1 measure of mustard. Roast the lemons before cutting. Roast the spices and powder. Mix together with salt and then add the lemon juice.

9. Kanchi fruit pickle (wild bitter-lime pickle)

25 bitter limes
2 measures of salt

1. Wash the bitter limes and dry on a cloth at night. 2. Cut these into 3 cm. long and 2 cm. broad pieces. 3. Roast and pound the salt. 4. Mix both the ingredients well and fill in a clean glass jar.

NOTE: All these pickles should be stirred thoroughly every few days till the salt is absorbed. Bitter lime pickle is very good for digestion and is often served to the invalids.

10. Mango pickle

3½ kg raw mangoes (wild appinmidi)
2 measures of chilli powder
5 gms asafoetida
5 gms black asafoetida (for seasoning)
4 measures of salt + 4½ measures of water
¾ measure turmeric
1½ measures of mustard seeds

1. Wash and wipe the mangoes clean. 2. Boil the salt water till its level is reduced by 1 cm. Cool and strain into a large china clay jar. 3. Add the mangoes to the salt water and cover the jar. Go on stirring everyday till the salt is absorbed. 4. Once the mangoes become yellow and crisp, strain out the salt water. Dry the mangoes on a clean cloth. 5. Again boil the salt water, allow it to cool. Grind the spices with this salt water. Grind the mustard seeds with clean water, to a slightly rough paste (not very fine). Wash the grinding stone to collect all the masala with salt water and add it to the paste. The mixture should be thick like fritter batter. 6. Mix the mangoes and the ground masala. Pour in a clean china clay jar dried in the sun. 7. Tie 5 gms of black asafoetida in a clean piece of cloth and drop it in the pickle. 8. Heat ½ cup of coconut oil, add a pinch of asafoetida. Cool it and dip a piece of clean cloth in it. Put the lid and tie with a cloth. Store the pickle in a warm and dry place.

NOTE: 1. Pickle tender ambade or wild mangoes in a similar way. 2. As a variation pickle the mangoes without salting them first. Just grind the spices with salt water and add the mangoes to it.

11. Mango pickle, instant (variety 1)

1. Spices same as above but in proportion to the mangoes. 2. You can add green mangoes (larger ones cut into small cubes) or tender cucumber, cauliflower, tender bamboo shoots, green breadfruit, jackfruit, gerkins, Indian gooseberries (awla).

12. Mango pickle (variety 2)

1. ¾ cup mustard seeds, 1 tsp fenugreek and 5 pinch of asafoetida (roast all these in a little oil). 2. 2 cups of chilli powder, ¾ cup turmeric powder. Grind these in salt water. 3. Add any of the above vegetables or fruits mentioned.

13. Grated mango pickle (kochla lonche)

10 or 12 good quality green mangoes
½ measure mustard seeds
2½ gms asafoetida (powdered)
1 cup green chillies (chopped)
¾ measure ground salt
¾ measure chilli powder
4 tsps turmeric powder
10 gms fresh ginger

1. Wash and skin the mangoes and grate or chop them very fine. 2. Add all the spices (after grinding). Add salt along with the chopped ginger and green chillies. 3. Mix well. This will be ready within 2 hours.

14. Grated mango pickle — variation

1. Roast all the ingredients in a little oil. Grind in salt water and add chopped mangoes, ginger and green chillies.

15. Ukadamba (boiled mango)/amla pickle

1. Boil mangoes/amla in salt water. 2. Add the masala as above (roasted and ground).

16. Mango pickle in oil

10-12 large green mangoes
1½ measure of salt (roast and powder)

Masala:

1 measure of mustard dal (split and husked)
4 tbsps mustard seeds*
1 small piece asafoetida*
1½ measure chilli powder
½ measure turmeric powder
2 tbsps fenugreek seeds*

* Roast and powder

Seasoning:

2 cups of peanut oil (heat)
½ tsp of turmeric powder
¼ tsp of asafoetida

1. Wash and wipe the mangoes, cut into large 5 cm x 5 cm pieces. 2. Add the powdered salt to these pieces. Cover and keep. 3. Remove the salt water after 2 hours. Add mustard dal to this water and beat well with your palm. Mix all the powdered spices and the mango pieces to this. Stir well. 4. Prepare the seasoning, cool it well. Mix with the pickle stirring well. Store in a clean jar.

NOTE: Instead of the home-made masala of step 3, ready-made masala available in shops can be used (Bedekar's etc.).

17. Dry mango pickle

medium size good quality mangoes
chilli powder
turmeric powder
salt
asafoetida*
fenugreek seeds*
red/green chillies (sliced)*
oil*

*For seasoning

NOTE: 500 gms oil for 8 kg pickles.

1. Wash and wipe the mangoes clean. Peel and cut into medium sized cubes. Add salt and keep covered with a weight on it. 2. Squeeze out the salt water and dry the mango cubes in the sun for 2 to 3 days. 3. Prepare salt water (boil the salt in water). Cool it. Add chilli powder and turmeric powder and mix well. 4. Add the dried mango pieces to this mixture. 5. Prepare the seasoning in oil. Allow the seasoning to cool. Then add it to the pickle. Mix well and fill in a clean glass jar. 6. Stir it well again after a week.

18. Sweet pickle (variety 1)

25 mangoes (preferably rajapuri)
salt to taste
2 tbsps groundnut oil*
1 tsp fenugreek seeds*
½ tsp turmeric powder*
jaggery (1 measure to 1 measure mango cubes)
1 tbsp chilli powder
1 tsp mustard seeds*
½ tsp asafoetida powder*

*For seasoning

1. Wash, skin and cut the mangoes into cubes. 2. Measure the cubes and take equal quantity of jaggery. Chop it fine. 3. Prepare the seasoning. Add the mango pieces, jaggery, salt and chilli powder. 4. Cook till the mango pieces cook and the liquid is syrupy. 5. Cool and store in a clean glass jar.

19. Sweet pickle (variety 2)

16 cups mango cubes (large green mangoes)
15 dry dates (wash and slice)
1320 ml vinegar
6 tsps chilli powder
8 tsps salt
2 tsps pepper powder
3 pieces of ginger 7 cm long (cut into thin slices)
25 almonds (soak in hot water, skin and slice)
1 cup raisins (washed and cleaned)
16 red chillies (each cut into two pieces)
16 cups jaggery
5 bulbs garlic

1. Dry almond slices, date slices, raisins. Soak them in 330 ml vinegar about 15 minutes before making the pickles. 2. Peel large green mangoes and cut them into 2½ cm. cubes. Cook 16 cups of cubes into 660 ml of vinegar. Allow it to cool. 3. When it cools take out the cubes and add 330 ml more vinegar to the cooled 660 ml vinegar and heat it again. 4. Add cloves of garlic, chillies, chilli powder, salt, pepper powder, ginger and jaggery. 5. Cook till the mixture starts thickening. 6. Add the mango cubes and soaked dry fruits along with the 330 ml vinegar and boil again until the syrup is thick like that of (muramba) mango preserve. 7. Remove from heat, cool and store in a glass jar. This lasts for 1 year.

NOTE: This pickle is mostly served with western type non-vegetarian preparations.

20. Green Chilli Pickles

50 large green chillies
juice of 15 lemons
1 cup groundnut oil
2 tsps mustard seeds
a large pinch of asafoetida
1½ cups mustard seeds*
½ cup fenugreek seeds*
2 tsp turmeric powder*
¼ tsp asafoetida*
½ cup salt*

*Pound them together

1. Wash chillies. Wipe them dry and slit them into four sections. 2. Mix the pounded ingredients in the lemon juice and blend well. 3. Heat oil and prepare a seasoning with mustard seeds, fenugreek seeds and asafoetida. Keep the seasoning aside and allow it to cool. 4. Stuff the chillies with the mixed ingredients. 5. Pour the seasoning over the stuffed chillies, and store the pickles in a glass jar with a tight lid.

21. Salted mango preserve

25 mangoes (medium sized with stone formed)
2½ cups salt
4½ litres water

1. Wash, wipe the mangoes clean. 2. Boil the water and the salt till its level goes down by 1 cm. 3. Remove from heat, allow to cool. Add mangoes when it is still warm and cool again. 4. Clean and dry a china clay jar and pour in the mangoes with the salt water. 5. Stir every alternate day. 6. After a fortnight take out the mangoes and dry them in the shade. 7. Strain the salt water and boil it till it again reduces by 1 cm. Cool it. 8. Dry the jar again and pour in the salt water and mangoes. Close it with a lid and cover it tightly with a cloth.

22. Boiled mango (ukdambe) preserve

25 mangoes (as for salted mangoes)
¾ measure water

1. Dissolve the salt in water and bring it to boil. 2. Add the mangoes while it is boiling. Cook till the mangoes change colour to white. 3. Cool and preserve in a glass jar.

23. Amla hindi (variety 1)

25 amlas
salt to taste
buttermilk/rice kanji

1. Wash the amlas, cut and remove the stones. 2. Put in a clean glass jar and add buttermilk or rice kanji enough to cover all the pieces. 3. Keep the jar in the sun till the pieces are soft and fluffy. Stir every day. 4. Strain it in a large strainer. Add salt, mix well and fill it again in the glass jar and keep it in the sun for 2-3 days. Store in a warm place. 5. Take out a small portion for use as a side dish, adding green chilli paste and chopped coriander and salt to taste.

24. Amla hindi (variety 2)

1 cup grated amla
2 tsps salt
1 tsp chilli powder
2 tsps groundnut oil*
½ tsp fenugreek*
1 pinch asafoetida*

*For seasoning

1. Mix the grated amla with salt and chilli powder. 2. Add the seasoning. 3. Mix all the ingredients well, fill in a glass jar and keep in the sun till the salt is absorbed and store. 4. Grind a little portion of it with a few green chillies and coriander leaves before serving.

Vegetarian Recipes (non-saraswat varieties)

Bhakarwade

1 cup grated onion
8 cloves garlic
1 cup chopped coriander leaves
½ tsp garam masala or amti powder
1½ cup bengal gram flour*
½ cup coconut (grated)
4 to 5 green chillies
1½ tsps salt
1 tsp poppy seeds (khuskhus)
1 tsp salt*

*Covering

1. Make a dough like chapati dough with a little oil and bengal gram flour and salt. 2. For the filling, crush the chopped garlic and chillies with salt. Mix it with other ingredients. 3. Take a small portion of the dough and roll out like a chapati (flat pancake). Sprinkle 2 tbsps of the filling evenly on the chapati, roll it and press slightly with the palm. Cut into 2 cm. broad pieces. 4. Deep fry in hot oil.

Potato bhakarwade

1 kg potatoes
4 green chillies*
1 cm. piece of ginger*
2 tsps salt
1 tsp chilli powder
½ tsp sugar
2 tbsps lemon juice
1 tsp garam masala or amti masala
1 tsp mustard seeds
pinch of asafoetida
oil for seasoning

*Crush together

Covering:
1 cup of wheat flour
2 tbsps of oil
½ cup of bengal gram flour

1. Make a dough with just enough water. 2. Peel the potatoes and grate them. Squeeze out the water. 3. Prepare a seasoning in hot oil by adding mustard seeds and asafoetida. Add grated potatoes and all other ingredients. Stir well and cook till all the water dries, and the mixture is dry. Cool. 4. Roll out small chapaties of the dough. Spread the filling evenly. Press with your palm slightly and cut into 2 cm. broad pieces. 5. Deep fry till crisp.

Khandvi

1 cup bengal gram flour
3 cups sour buttermilk
1 tsp salt
1 cm ginger and
4 green chillies (grind together)
½ tsp turmeric powder

Seasoning:
1 cup of oil
1 tsp mustard seeds
8 to 10 grains of fenugreek
pinch of asafoetida

Garnishing:
A handful of chopped coriander leaves and grated coconut.

1. Keep 2 or 3 metal dinner plates (thalis) ready by coating them with a tsp of oil. 2. Add buttermilk, all the spices and salt to the gram flour gradually, so that lumps are not formed. 3. Cook on a medium fire till the mixture thickens. Cook for 5 more minutes on a low flame. Remove and spread a ladleful of paste on each thali evenly and thinly. Do this very quickly while the paste is still hot. Even it with a flat ladle or a metal cup coated with oil. 4. Cool. Cut into strips 2 to 3 cm. broad. Roll each strip separately into a small

roll. You can fill this with a little grated coconut, chopped coriander leaves, or with cooked vegetables like carrots, french beans, cauliflower with a little garam masala. 5. Prepare the seasoning in a large shallow pan and put in the rolls. Stir lightly. Garnish with finely cut coriander leaves and grated coconut and serve.

Khaman dhokla

2 cups of bengal gram dal
1 tsp salt
1 tbsp lime juice
1 cm ginger
4 green chillies
1 tsp cooking soda (or papad khar)
pinch of asafoetida *
1 tsp mustard seeds*
½ cup oil*

*For seasoning

1. Soak 2 cups of bengal gram dal in 2 cups of water overnight. 2. Grind it coarse next morning, with 1 cm. ginger and green chillies. 3. Add all the other ingredients just before steaming and make the batter as idli batter consistency. 4. Pour in the batter in a shallow metal container to 1 cm. thickness and steam for 15 to 20 minutes (see that water keeps boiling throughout). 5. Remove the container, cut the dhoklas into big cubes. 6. Prepare the seasoning in a large shallow pan and put in the dhoklas. Stir for 5 minutes and serve.

OR

Spread the seasoning, grated coconut and chopped coriander on the top of the cubes before serving.

Khatta dhokla

1. 3 cups of rice (washed and dried in shade). 2. 1 cup green gram dal, grind coarse in a grinder (dry). 3. Buttermilk enough to prepare the dhokla batter (thick like idli batter). Prepare the batter at night. Rest of the procedure is the same as for khaman dhokla.

Sambharia (mixed vegetables)

½ kg small brinjals (aubergines)
2 radishes (cut in 3 to 4 pieces lengthwise)
2 sweet potatoes
½ kg medium sized potatoes
½ kg kovai (tendli)
3 rajali plantains

Filling:

1 coconut grated
3 tsps chilli powder
2 tbsps limejuice
1 tbsp jaggery
½ tsp soda bicarb (cooking soda)
1 cup bengal gram flour
2 tsps coriander and cumin seed powder
1 tbsp salt
1 tbsp oil

Seasoning:

2 cups oil
pinch of asafoetida
2 tsps mustard seeds

1. Wash and keep ready all the vegetables, cut crosswise to stuff. 2. Bind the filling (without water) and stuff all the vegetables. 3. Prepare the seasoning in a large, shallow vessel. Put in the vegetables. Cover the vessel with a large metal plate filled with water. Do not stir the vegetables often.

OR

Prepare the seasoning in a pressure cooker. Put in the vegetables. Stir well so that all the vegetables are well covered with oil. If not pour in ½ tsp. of oil and ½ tsp of water. Close the lid, **do not put the pressure weight.** Put a katori (a metal cup) on the spout and immediately reduce heat. Cook for 20 minutes.

Osaman

1 cup red gram dal (toordal)
½ radish (cubes)
1 green raw banana cubes (optional)
chopped coriander leaves
1 tsp ghee*
½ tsp asafoetida*
4 amsols
1 tsp salt
2 tsps chilli powder
1 tbsp curds (yoghurt)
1 tbsp grated coconut
1 tsp mustard seeds*,
4 curry leaves*

*For seasoning

1. Cook the dal in 3½ cups of water and take out 3 cups of water after the dal is cooked. 2. Add to the water 4 amsols (kokam), radish cubes, banana cubes, salt, chilli powder, turmeric powder, and grated coconut. Cook well. Add coriander leaves and curds. Remove from heat. Add the seasoning.

Sago (Sabudana) khichdi

1 cup sago
1 cup water
¾-1 cup peanuts (roasted and roughly crushed)
1½ tsp salt
2 tsp sugar
2 tsp lemon juice
or 2 tbsp buttermilk (optional)
3-4 green chillies* (slit and cut)
1 tsp cumin seed*
A pinch asafoetida*
2 tbsp oil or ghee*
corriander leaves (cut fine)

*for seasoning

1. Soak sago in water. 2. Apply salt, sugar and lemon juice/buttermilk and keep aside for 30-45 minutes. 3. Prepare the seasoning and add the mixture of sago and peanuts. 4. Keep on stirring on a low flame until it cooks (do not add water). 5. Add corriander leaves, cover with lid and remove from fire.

NOTE : Boiled and finely cut potato pieces and/or 1 tbsp grated coconut may be added.

Masala supari (betelnut powder)

2 cups betelnut finely shredded (pieces-chikni)
½ cup grated dry kopra (dessicated coconut)
½ cup dried, peeled cucumber magge seeds (optional)
½ cup poppy seeds (khuskhus)
½ cup badishep (dill)
12 cardamoms*
12 cloves*

* Powdered

1. Roast the betelnuts in ghee on a slow fire, till crisp. 2. Add khuskhus, badishep, cucumber seeds, stir well and remove from heat. 3. Roast kopra separately without ghee and add cardamom and clove powder (a little sugar optional). Mix well. Store in a bottle.

Soups

---

1. Barley and tomato soup

1 large onion
½ kg tomatoes
celery 2 stalks (or coriander leaves and mint)
1 carrot
2 tbsps barley
salt and pepper to taste
a little butter

1. Cook onion, carrot and the tomatoes together well. Mash and strain. 2. Add barley, salt, pepper and the celery (chopped) and simmer for another 15 minutes.

NOTE: For a thicker soup, fry 1 tbsp of maida (flour) in the butter, add ½ cup of milk, stir well till it boils. Mix with the soup. Bring to boil and serve.

NOTE: To prepare stock as a base for the soups. Cook mutton or chicken bones, 1 onion, 2 garlic cloves, 1 bay leaf, small piece of ginger and 2 tomatoes (carrots, spinach, bottle gourd, french beans, cabbage, etc. also can be added). Strain the liquid, add salt and pepper, boil. Serve or cool and store in the refrigerator, for use.

2. Beetroot soup

1 beetroot
½ kg tomatoes

1. Cut and cook in 4 cups of water, add salt and pepper and strain. Serve with a little cream.

3. Fish soup

Head, tail and bones of pomfret or any other large fish
parsley
1 onion
1 cup milk
salt and pepper to taste
celery (or coriander leaves and mint)
tomato or 1 tsp vinegar
yolk of 1 egg

1. Clean the fish, wash and cook in 3 cups of water along with the vegetables for 20 minutes. 2. Strain, add salt, pepper and the milk. Bring to boil, add the beaten yolk, stir and remove from the fire. Serve hot with toast.

4. Green peas soup

½ kg green peas
1 bunch parsley (or mint)
1 bunch spring onions
salt and pepper

1. Cook all the vegetables in 4 cups of stock or plain water. 2. Save some cooked green peas, mash rest of the vegetables, and strain, add salt and pepper. 3. Serve with green peas.

5. Irish milk soup

4 potatoes
2 stalks celery
2 cups milk
1 onion
salt and pepper to taste

Cook the vegetables well, mash and strain. Add 2 cups of milk, salt and pepper. Bring to boil. Serve. (This can be served chilled also.)

6. Macaroni soup

½ kg macaroni
120 gms cheese (grated)
salt and pepper
1 cup milk
2 cups vegetable stock

1. Cook the macaroni in water and strain under cold running water. 2. Remove half. Cook the rest of it in the stock, with salt and pepper till it is very soft. 3. Add milk, macaroni, and cheese. Do not boil too much. Serve with hot toast.

7. Cabbage soup

1 small cabbage
120 gms butter
salt and pepper to taste
1 onion
2 cups cold milk + 30 gms cornflour blended together

1. Cut the cabbage and onion fine. Fry these in butter and cook in 1 cup of water. 2. Add the milk and cornflour stirring all the time.

Add salt and pepper. Bring to boil and serve.

NOTE: Soup with any other vegetables (cauliflower, turnips, french beans, etc.) can be made in a similar way.

Egg Preparations

1. Egg stew

4 eggs
6 onions
30 gms butter
1 tbsp flour
a little milk
salt and pepper to taste

1. Hard-boil the eggs, cool and shell them. Remove the yolk gently and slice the whites into thin strips. **2.** Cut the onions into rings and fry lightly in the butter. Remove the rings. Add the flour to the remaining butter. Add a little milk to make white sauce. Add salt and pepper. **3.** Add the slices of egg whites. Cook for sometime. Pour it into a shallow dish. Arrange the yolks.

2. Egg beat

1 beetroot
french loaf or any other bread cut into rounds
butter
3 hard boiled eggs
salt, pepper and lemon juice to taste

1. Steam the beetroot. Skin and slice it. **2.** Slices of bread should be of the same size as the slices of beetroot. **3.** Butter the bread slices, shell and cut the eggs and remove the yolks. Add salt, pepper and a little lemon juice. Beat well. Cut the egg whites into strips. Arrange the beetroot slices on the bread slices, sprinkle the crumbled egg yolk on top and arrange the egg white strips on them and serve. (This dish is served as hors. d'oeuvre)

3. Aspic eggs

1 carrot (boiled)
2 tbsp green peas (boiled)
1 egg (hardboiled)
1 cucumber
aspic jelly packet
2 small moulds

1. Slice the carrot and the cucumber. Cut the egg into two. 2. Arrange the egg-half with the yellow yolk facing down in the mould. Arrange the carrot and cucumber slices around the egg and sprinkle the green peas on them. Pour the prepared jelly onto these and set. 3. Unmould it just before serving.

4. Egg on spinach

2 or 3 bunches of spinach or any other green leafy vegetable
6 eggs
butter
pepper and salt to taste

1. Clean the spinach, wash and cut. Cook in very little water with a little salt. 2. Butter a baking dish. Pour the cooked spinach. Make 6 dents in the spinach with a table spoon. Break egg into each of these dents. Sprinkle salt and pepper. Dot with butter. Bake till the eggs set. Do not overcook.

5. Eggs on potato

4 large potatoes
4 eggs
butter
1 cup grated cheese
2 cups milk
salt and pepper to taste

1. Boil the potatoes. Peel and grate. Add hot milk, salt and pepper to the mashed potato to make a thick batter. 2. Coat the baking dish with butter. Pour in the mashed potato. Make dents. Break on eggs into each of these dents. Sprinkle salt, pepper, and cheese all over. Bake till the eggs set.

Fish Preparations

1. Fish cakes

1 large fish (pomfret, surmai or rawas)
4 boiled potatoes
anchovy sauce, 10-12 drops
½ tbsp butter
2 eggs
lemon juice
salt and pepper to taste
milk (optional)
dry bread crumbs

1. Boil the fish in very little water or steam in a cooker. Remove bones, and mash the flesh. 2. Mash the boiled potatoes, mix with the fish. Add 1 beaten egg, anchovy sauce, salt, pepper and butter (and milk if needed to bind). Mix well after adding the lemon juice. Form into small balls or rolls. 3. Beat one egg, with a little salt and pepper. 4. Dip the fish cakes into the beaten egg, and roll into the bread crumbs. Deep fry in oil.

NOTE: For extra flavour, add little chopped onion and a few finely chopped mint leaves if desired.

2. Macarel (Bangda) Hugga

6 macarels cleaned, with cuts
2 heaped tbsp grated coconut*
10-12 red chillies*
small ball tamrind/6-7 kokum*
2-3 green chillies*
turmeric leaves
½ tsp turmeric powder*
7-8 triphal crushed*
½ tbsp rock salt

* Grind together

1. Apply salt and turmeric powder to macarels, marinate for an hour. 2. Stuff the cuts with ground masala and apply the remaining. 3. Bake in a greased dish, with turmeric leaves in between the layers, for 7-8 minutes.

NOTE : 1. This preparation can be made with any type of fish. 2. Onion, green chillies, ginger, garlic and corriander leaves, chopped fine, can be added to ground masala.

3. Fish moli

fish 8 to 10 pieces (pomfret)
3 onions (chopped)
ginger slices, 10 to 12
1 cup coconut milk
juice of ½ lemon or vinegar
5 green chillies (slit)
¼ tsp turmeric powder
salt to taste
1 tbsp flour

1. Fry the fish pieces after sprinkling a little salt on them. 2. Fry the onions, chillies, ginger slices and turmeric in a little butter. Simmer for some time until the fish is cooked. Add coconut milk Add lemon juice or vinegar just before serving.

NOTE: If vinegar is added thicken the gravy with flour.

4. Fish curry (Variety 1)

1 fish cut into thin slices
6 small onions chopped fine
7-8 green chillies*
2 cm piece of ginger*
salt to taste*
2 tbsps tamarind juice
1 tbsp curry powder
2 tbsps ghee/oil
6 cloves of garlic*

*Grind together

1. Wash the fish and sprinkle some salt. Keep it for at least ½ an

hour. 2. Fry the onions in the cooking medium till light brown. Add the ground paste, tamarind juice, curry powder, and fish pieces. 3. Add a little water if necessary. Simmer lightly until fish is cooked and remove from heat.

5. Fish curry (Variety 2)

fish pieces (marinate with salt for 1 hour)
1 tsp turmeric
2 tbsp oil
garlic 5-6 cloves
1 coconut (grated)
25 red chillies
salt to taste
2 tsp coriander seeds
onions

1. Clean and wash the fish well. Marinate in salt for 1 hour. 2. Grind to a fine paste coconut, ½ onion, red chillies, coriander seeds, turmeric powder, adding garlic last. 3. Fry 2 chopped onions in oil ti'' ''ght brown. Add the ground masala. Bring to boil. Add the fish pieces. Simmer gently till cooked.

NOTE: Chopped onion, ginger and green chillies can be added before removing from the heat. Also add 1 tbsp of coconut oil if desired.

6. Hot and Sour fish curry (aamshe tikshe)

2 large fish or 8 macarels
1 tbsp coconut oil
6 triphal*
25 red chillies*
2 tbsps tamarind juice*
garlic (optional)*

*Grind to a fine paste

1. Clean and wash the fish and marinate with salt for 1 hour. 2. Bring to boil the ground masala. Add the fish pieces and a little salt. Simmer till the fish is cooked. 3. Add 1 tbsp of coconut oil.

7. Fried fish

2 large fish or 8 macarels
salt to taste
rice flour to coat
4 cloves garlic*
4 tsps chilli powder*
1 tsp turmeric*
1 tbsp tamarind juice*

*Grind together

1. Clean and wash the fish. Sprinkle salt and apply the ground masala. Shake well so that all the pieces marinate well. Keep for ½ an hour. 2. Roll in rice flour, and fry in oil, either deep fry or shallow fry.

8. Prawn pickle

1 kg prawns (cleaned)
salt to taste
1 cup oil*
mustard seeds*
asafoetida*
turmeric*
1 tbsp cumin seeds
2 cm ginger
4 tbsps chilli powder
2 tbsps tamarind juice or ½ cup vinegar

*For seasoning

1. Clean and wash the prawns well. Sprinkle salt and keep for 1 hour. Then fry in the oil. 2. Prepare the seasoning in a deep vessel, add the prawns and the rest of the ingredients. Stir, add a little salt. Cook well till the oil separates.

Mutton Preparations

---

1. Mutton curry (Variety 1)

½ kg mutton (cut into small pieces)
salt to taste
1 onion chopped
2-3 tomatoes chopped or 1 tbsp vinegar
2 cm ginger †
10 cloves of garlic †
3 onions (sliced)*
1½ cup grated coconut*
2 tbsps coriander seeds*
8-10 red chillies*
3-4 sticks cinnamon*
5-6 cloves*
10-12 black pepper corns*

*Roast in oil and grind together to a smooth paste.
† Grind together

1. Clean and wash the mutton. 2. Fry the chopped onion in oil. Add the mutton and the ginger and garlic paste. Add salt and 2 cups of hot water and cook well till soft. 3. Add the second masala and chopped tomatoes or vinegar to the cooked mutton. Simmer for sometime.

NOTE: 1. Add potatoes, knolkol or carrots if desired.

2. Mutton curry (variety 2)

Same as above but instead of second masala, add 1½ cups grated coconut, 7-8 cloves garlic, 7-8 red chillies, ground together.

3. Mutton curry (variety 3)

½ kg mutton
ginger and garlic paste
4 onions chopped
salt to taste

1. Fry the chopped onions, add the mutton along with ginger and garlic paste, salt and cook with 1 cup of hot water. 2. Masala, same as for curry no. I but **without** the **coconut**. 3. Add the ground masala and cook, adding water, only if necessary, as this is a dry mutton preparation.

4. Maulavi curry

½ kg mutton
125 gms onions (chopped)
2 tsps chilli powder
1 tsp turmeric powder
salt to taste
1 cup curds (yoghurt)
4 cloves garlic*
2 cm ginger*
6 cloves †
6 black pepper corns †
4 cm stick cinnamon †
¾ cup of ghee

*Grind to a paste
† Pound into powder

1. Clean and wash the mutton. 2. Fry the chopped onions in ghee. Add the mutton when the onion is light brown. Stir for a few minutes. Add ginger and garlic paste, chilli powder, turmeric powder and salt. Add 2 cups of hot water and cook well. 3. Add potatoes, radish, or cauliflower (optional). Add pounded garam masala and cook till the vegetables are done. 4. Add 1 cup of beaten curds just before removing from the heat.

5. Irish stew

125 gms of mutton (preferably boneless from neckpieces)
6 small spring onions (skinned)
8 large pieces of potato
2 onions (chopped)
4 cloves
2 cm cinnamon
6 black pepper corns
1 tbsp flour
½ cup of milk
salt and sugar to taste

1. Fry the chopped onions in 1 tbsp butter. Add the mutton pieces, fry and add the whole onions and potato pieces. Add salt, cloves, cinnamon, pepper (whole). 2. After the mutton is well cooked, add the flour mixed with water and sugar. 3. Cook till the flour is cooked. Add the milk, bring to boil and remove from the heat.

6. Pulav

Pulav or biranji recipes are similar to the vegetarian recipes. Substitute mutton or chicken in place of vegetables.

7. Mince pie

½ kg minced mutton
3 onions chopped
salt to taste
(2cm ginger, chopped fine)
coriander leaves
maida/refined wheat flour*
margarine*
rice flour*
3 green chillies

* For the crust

1. Wash the mince in a strainer. 2. Fry the chopped onion in ghee or oil, till light brown. Add the chopped green chillies, ginger, and coriander and salt along with the mince meat. Cook till the meat is cooked and all the water is absorbed. Cool. 3. Prepare the crust dough by beating the margarine with salt and bind the flourswith very little cold water. 4. Roll out the dough into 2 pancakes. Line the pie-dish with one. Fill in the mince and cover again with another pancake. Press the edges with wet fingers. Brush the top with a beaten egg or milk. Make slits on the covering pancake. Bake till the top is brown and crisp. Serve hot or cold.

8. Potato and mutton chops

4 to 5 large potatoes (boil and mash)
2 eggs
salt and pepper to taste
mince meat same as above, but add 1 tbsp of tomato ketchup to it
bread crumbs

1. Add 1 egg (beaten), salt and pepper to the mashed potatoes. Knead well. 2. Take a portion as big as a lemon, and flatten it on your palm with wet fingers. Put a tbspful of the mince meat in the centre. Cover with the potato batter on it. 3. Dip these rounds in the beaten egg, and roll them in the dry bread crumbs. Shape them into flat rounds or heart shapes or rolls. Fry in hot ghee or oil on a flat frying pan.

9. Mutton and macaroni in tomato sauce

1. Prepare the mince meat same as given in the above recipe, but add a little more of tomato ketchup. 2. Boil ½ kg macaroni. Strain in a colander under running cold water. Add to the mince. Bake for 10 minutes or just heat on the flame.

10. Cutlets

½ kg minced mutton
4 onions chopped
2 tbsps tomato ketchup
salt and garam masala to taste
2 large bread slices (soaked in water)
2 cm ginger
3 green chillies
6 cloves garlic
coriander leaves (chopped)
dry bread crumbs
1 egg

1. Fry the chopped onions till light brown. 2. Add the minced mutton along with the ginger and garlic paste, coriander leaves, and salt. Fry till all the water is absorbed. Add tomato ketchup, soaked bread slices and knead well. Shape into cutlets. 3. Beat the egg. Dip the mince meat cutlets into it, roll in bread crumbs, and deep fry or shallow fry on a frying pan.

11. Baked tomatoes

½ kg tomatoes
125 gms of mince mutton
75 gms onions (chopped)
1 tsp pepper powder
1 tsp cooking sauce
salt to taste
1 egg
1 cup flour

Gravy:
2 tomatoes*
pulp of the ½ kg scooped tomatoes*
2 onions chopped*
1 tbsp flour
salt, sugar and pepper to taste
ghee

*Grind in a liquidiser and strain

1. Wash the tomatoes and slice off the top. Take out the pulp carefully. 2. Fry the chopped onions, add the mince mutton and salt and cook well, till all the water is absorbed. 3. Add a little sugar, pepper, 1 egg, and the cooking sauce. Mix well and fill this mixture into the tomatoes (of which the pulp is removed). 4. Prepare a batter with the flour and a little salt. Dip these tomatoes into it and deep fry. Serve with the tomato gravy.

Gravy:

1. Fry the onions in butter or ghee, till brown. 2. Add 1 tbsp of flour and fry till pinkish in colour. 3. Add the ground pulp of the tomatoes and onions (2 to 2½ cups) and stir well. 4. Add salt, sugar and pepper powder. Boil till the flour is cooked.

NOTE: For vegetarians substitute cooked vegetables in place of mince mutton.

12. Kabab

½ kg mince mutton
4 onions chopped
ginger and garlic paste 2 tsps
4 green chillies
1 bunch coriander leaves
salt to taste
2 tsps coriander seeds*
2 cm cinnamon*
4 cloves*
½ cup thick curds
1 egg (beaten)
bread crumbs to fry

* Roasted and powdered

1. Chop the onions and fry them, till light brown. Add the minced mutton, ginger and garlic paste and salt. Cook. 2. Remove when all the water is absorbed. Add chopped green chillies, coriander, the powdered spices, curds and the egg. Mix well and form small balls. Roll these in bread crumbs and shallow fry them in the frying pan.

Puddings

---

1. Caramel custard

2 eggs
2 tbsps sugar
2 cups milk
½ tsp vanilla essence
few almonds (sliced), optional

Beat the eggs with sugar and vanilla till the sugar is dissolved. Add the milk, beat again. Add the almond slivers. Bake or steam for 20 minutes.

For caramel

Put 2 tsps of sugar in the dry mould, sprinkle few drops of water and dissolve it on a low fire. Cook till the sugar is dissolved and turns rich brown. Coat the mould by slowly turning it round. Pour in the custard mixture and then bake or steam. Cool it before serving.

2. Plain custard

2 eggs
4 tsps sugar
1½ to 2 cups of milk
½ tsp essence (vanilla)
apples, dates, guavas, appricots etc.
a little lemon juice
2 cm. cinnamon
1 tbsp sugar

1. Beat the eggs, sugar and vanilla. Add the milk. 2. Cook on a

slow fire, stirring all the time, till the spoon gets coated with the layer of custard. Do not over-cook otherwise the custard will curdle. Chill in the refrigerator. 3. Stew the fruit with lemon juice, sugar, a cinnamon stick and a little water.

NOTE: Fresh cut bananas, oranges, chikkoo, can be used which need not be stewed.

3. Apple charlotte

3 apples - peel, core and cut into small pieces
stale bread cubes
½ cup of milk
½ cup of butter
sugar and lemon juice

1. Stew the apple pieces with a little sugar and lemon juice. 2. Butter a baking dish. Spread a layer of bread cubes in the baking dish, top it with a layer of stewed apple. Dot it with butter. Go on repeating till all the apple is used up. 3. Top it with bread cubes. Dot again with butter. 4. Pour ½ cup of milk and bake for 30 to 40 minutes. 5. Remove it onto another dish when ready. Sprinkle sugar on top. 6. Serve with sweetened cream.

4. Banana pudding

60 grams butter*
60 gms flour*
¾ cup of milk*
2 eggwhites + 1 tsp sugar (powdered) for decoration
60 gms sugar
2 egg yolks
2 ripe bananas sliced

*Beat together

1. Beat together butter, flour and milk. Mix well and cook on a slow fire till the mixture thickens. 2. Remove from heat, and add sugar and egg yolks. Beat again, and add the banana slices. 3. Pour into a baking tin or a baking dish and bake for 20 minutes. 4. Beat egg whites till stiff, add the powdered sugar and beat again. Spread it evenly or in peaks on the pudding. 5. Bake or grill till it is light brown.

5. Coffee pudding

60 gms butter
60 gms sugar
2 egg yolks
½ cup strong and hot coffee
sponge fingers (type of cakes)
almonds

1. Beat the butter and sugar together till soft and creamy. 2. Beat the egg yolks and add to the above mixture. Pour in the hot coffee. Mix well. 3. Butter a pudding or jelly mould. Arrange the sponge

fingers all around the mould. Pour in the coffee mixture and chill for 2 hours. Unmould onto another dish, just before serving. Sprinkle the chopped almonds on top.

6. Snow pudding

1 pint black raisins or sultanas or any other fruit
60 gms sugar
120 gms rice flour + 1 pint (approx. 2 cups) water or milk
15 gms butter

1. Mix the dry fruit and sugar. Put this mixture into a baking dish (buttered). **2.** Cook the rice flour and water or milk on a slow fire till thick. Pour it onto the fruit mixture. Dot it with butter. Bake or steam.

Cakes

1. Plain sponge cake

4 eggs (weigh them)
½ tsp baking powder
½ tsp vanilla
equal wt.of eggs, butter, castor or powdered sugar and flour

1. Weigh the eggs and take equal weights of butter, sugar and flour. **2.** Cream the butter first till light. Then add the sugar and beat again till the sugar dissolves. **3.** Add egg yolks and beat till the mixture is light and the colour is pale lemon. **4.** Sieve the flour and baking powder together 2-3 times. Slowly add to the above mixture. Add vanilla too, and beat the batter with a lifting movement of the hand. **5.** Beat the egg whites till frothy. Tilt the vessel and see if any liquid is there. If it is there then beat again. Mix stiffly beaten egg white lightly into the cake mixture. **6.** Butter a cake tin from inside and sprinkle 1 tsp. of castor sugar, shake the vessel and spread it evenly. Pour in the mixture and bake immediately until the cake is light brown. Test by inserting a knitting needle inside the cake. It should come out clean.

2. Fruit cake

Batter same as sponge cake. Add 75 gms of sultanas, currants or candied peel to the above mixture. But wash these (except the candied peel) first, dry them and roll them in a little flour so that they don't sink in the cake mixture while being baked.

3. Chocolate cake

Batter same as sponge cake. Add 1 tbsp of cocoa dissolved in hot water or milk to the sponge cake mixture.

4. Coconut cake

Batter same as sponge cake. Add one cup of desiccated coconut, 1½ tsps of lemon essence and 1 cardamom powdered (instead of the vanilla essence) to the sponge mixture. Sprinkle 1 tbsp of desiccated coconut on top of the cake 15 minutes before taking out.

5. Coffee cake

1. Batter same as sponge cake. Add 1 tbsp of instant coffee or strong essence and a few drops of vanilla to the sponge mixture. 2. Divide the mixture into two tins and bake separately. Cool and spread icing on the top. Keep one on top of the other.

Icing: 60 gms butter, 1 large spoonful of icing sugar, 1 tsp coffee essence or instant coffee. Beat together till smooth, and then spread it evenly with a knife.

NOTE: **Variations:** (a) Spread jam and sandwich the cakes. (b) Make small cup cakes with the above recipe mixture.

6. Pineapple cake

120 gms butter
240 gms sugar
180 gms pineapple (chopped)
4 eggs
360 gms flour + 1 tsp baking powder sieved together

1. Cream together butter and sugar till light. 2. Sieve the flour and the baking powder 2-3 times. 3. Break eggs and mix eggs and flour alternately to the butter and sugar mixture. 4. Add the chopped pineapple and bake, either in one large tin or as small cup cakes. 5. To 120 gm of icing sugar, add water drop by drop till the icing is of right consistency and can be spread easily. 6. Pour the icing on the cakes. Allow to dry.

7. Boston tea cake

1 cup milk + 1 tsp soda-bicarb + 1 egg
2 tsps sugar (optional)
2 cups flour
2 tsps cream of tartar and 1 tsp salt,
½ tsp butter

1. Sieve the flour, cream of tartar and salt together. 2. Add the butter to this flour and crumble it with finger tips. 3. Beat the egg and soda-bicarb in the milk, and add to the flour. Bake in two tins.

NOTE: Add sugar if the cake is to be sweet.

8. Red devils cake

90 gms butter
1 cup sugar
3 eggs
½ cup curds
1 tsp soda bicarb
2 tbsps cocoa
1 tsp vanilla essence
1½ cups flour

1. Cream the butter and sugar together. 2. Beat the eggs with a rotary beater and add to the above mixture. 3. Add beaten curds and flour, soda bicarb, vanilla and cocoa dissolved in hot water or hot milk. Mix well and bake for 40 minutes.

Icing: 1. Dissolve 1 cup sugar in ½ cup water and boil to make a thick syrup (of 1 string consistency). 2. Beat 3 egg whites stiff and add to the sugar syrup. Beat till the mixture thickens. Add any flavour of your choice. Spread this mixture on the cake, even it out with a knife. 3. Allow it to dry. 4. Draw lines with chocolate icing or pink icing on the white icing. With the help of a fork or knife pull all the lines in one direction, then in the other direction, at 2 cms intervals. Repeat. This will give a striped effect.

Biscuits

1. Ginger cookies

1 cup butter* + 2 cups sugar*
2 eggs (beat)
½ tsp salt
½ cup buttermilk and treacle (a sweet syrup available in the market)
1 tsp soda bicarb

*Cream together

1. Mix all these ingredients and keep for 2 hours. 2. Drop spoonfuls of batter, spaced out evenly on a greased tray and bake for 20 minutes.

2. Lemon biscuits

2 eggs + 5 tbsps sugar (beat together)
12 tbsps flour
6 drops lemon essence

1. Mix the beaten eggs and sugar with the flour and the lemon essence. 2. Roll out and cut with biscuit cutters. Bake for 15 minutes.

3. Walnut and chocolate cones

8 tbsps sugar
½ cup walnut pieces
1 tbsp cocoa
2 egg whites

1. Mix the sugar and cocoa. 2. Beat the egg whites till fluffy and stiff. 3. Add the sugar, cocoa, and walnut pieces to the egg whites. 4. Drop spoonfuls of batter evenly on a baking tray greased well with ghee, and bake till firm.

4. Macroons

2 egg whites
1 cup desiccated coconut
½ cup slivers of almonds and pistachio
1 cup ground sugar
2 cups cornflakes
½ tsp vanilla

1. Beat the egg whites till fluffy and stiff. 2. Add all the other ingredients gradually. 3. Drop spoonfuls of the mixture on a baking tray coated with ghee.

5. Surprise cookies

1 cup butter
2 tsps baking powder
2 cups cornflakes
dates, apricots (chopped fine)
1 cup demeras sugar
3½ cups flour
½ cup water + pinch of salt
jam

1. Cream the butter and add sugar and beat again till the sugar dissolves. 2. Sieve the flour and the baking powder, and add to the batter and mix. Add water and salt and bind the mixture along with

the cornflakes. Knead the dough. Divide into equal portions. **3.** Roll out into small rounds. Place a little bit of chopped dry fruit on a tspful of jam in the centre of each round. Cover with another round and press the edges firmly. **4.** Bake in the oven for 10 minutes.

6. Nut cookies

200 gms butter
2 eggs (keep aside the white of one of the eggs)
pinch of salt
200 gms sugar
300 gms flour
1 tsp baking powder
walnut bits and sugar

1. Sieve the flour with baking powder and salt. **2.** Cream the butter, sugar and 2 egg yolks and 1 egg white. Add the flour. Bind the dough. **3.** Roll out into small rounds or any other shape. Brush with the other egg white, sprinkle sugar and the chopped nuts. **4.** Bake for 20 minutes.

7. Ginger biscuits

3 eggs (separate the yolks and weigh them)
200 gms powdered dry ginger
sugar, equal weight of the yolks
flour, half weight of the yolks

1. Beat the yolks and sugar together. **2.** Beat the egg whites till fluffy. **3.** Add to this, the yolk and sugar mixture. Add the flour and powdered ginger. **4.** Bind the dough, knead, roll out, and cut with biscuit cutters. Bake in an oven at medium temperature.

8. Kulkuls

½ cup grated coconut (take out juice)
3 eggs
1 tbsp of ghee
2½ cups rice flour
ghee or cooking fat for deep frying
1 cup sugar
pinch of salt

1. Separate the egg yolks from the whites. Beat each separately. **2.** Add the rice flour, sugar and salt to the beaten eggs. **3.** Bind the dough with the coconut milk. **4.** Take a small portion of the dough (as big as a marble). Spread it on a fork coated with ghee and slowly roll it into a roll. This roll will have lines marked on it. **5.** Deep fry in hot ghee. **6.** Sprinkle castor sugar or dip in the sugar syrup.

·HOME REMEDIES

The Care of the New-Born

Infant Feeding

The best is the mother's milk, but if the baby cannot be breastfed for some reason, top feeds may have to be started. The appetite of all babies cannot be the same, and the measures given below may have to be altered according to the needs and appetite of each individual baby. This table has been worked out by Dr. Annajirao Sirur after finding it suitable and successful in a large number of babies that he looked after in his practice.

BUFFALO MILK

Age in Months	Measure of milk	Measure of water	Feeding interval in hours	Measurement of each feed in ml.	Time of last feed at night
1	1	4	2	25 to 50	12 midnight
2	1	3	3	50 to 75	-do-
3	1	2	3	75 to 100	10 p.m.
4	1	same as milk	3	100 to 150	-do-
5	1	–do-	3	150 to 175	-do-
6	1	No water	4	150 to 175	-do-

As mentioned above this chart is for buffalo milk. If cow's milk is to be given which may be preferable, the dilution with water should be lesser than that used for buffalo milk. In the first month water should be double that of milk. In the second month equal to that of milk. After the fourth month half that of milk and no water to be added from the sixth month onwards. From then onwards full cream undiluted cow's milk should be given. Otherwise infants may tend to get rickets. These measures have now changed and the young mother is well advised to consult a paediatrician.

If the baby does not digest the top feed well, a teaspoon of sweet orange (called Mosambi in India) juice should be given immediately following the milk feed and glucose water or water with sugar should be given in between feeds.

If the baby tends to cry at odd times and at night, water with sugar or decoction of caraway seeds (Badishep or Somph) with sugar should be given. The caraway seeds decoction helps in producing a good bowel movement.

Caraway seed decoction – The caraway seeds should be heated on a hot plate and then powdered. A teaspoon of this powder should be added to cupful of water with sugar, boiled and strained before giving it to the baby.

Home Made Baby Food

¾ kg of Ragi (a small brown grain very rich in vegetable protein) and ¼ kg of wheat should be soaked in water for about 48 hours and then tied in a piece of clean cloth for 24 hours when it sprouts. After having sprouted, it should be dried in shade, spreading it on a clean cloth. Once it is completely dry it should be stone-ground or ground in a mixer and strained on a piece of netlike cloth. About 2.5 gms of dried ginger, 5.8 gms of Ashwagandha (a kind of a herbal substance – English name not known), 5.8 gms of wawaling (another herbal) and a pinch of saffron are ground and added to the ground sprouted Ragi and wheat mixture. The herbal ingredients may be omitted if not known or not available adding only the dried ginger and saffron powder after grinding the grain. It is then sifted through a very fine sieve or even a piece of cloth with a wide weave. The sifted mixture is dried in shade again before storing it in a tin or a glass jar. This baby food can be started from the second or the third month.

Preparation of the Ragi malt feed

Take a cup of half diluted milk (half a cup of milk with half a cup of water). Add one teaspoon of the Ragi malt baby food prepared as above. The powder should be mixed well in a small quantity of the dilute milk when cold to avoid forming of lumps. The rest of the dilute milk should be boiled and as it starts boiling the previously prepared cold mixture of baby food should be added to it, stirring all the time. Let it boil twice when it thickens a bit and is cooked. Add a pinch of salt and jaggery or sugar to taste. Addition of a bit of ghee helps to clear the bowels. If this food is started in the second month it should be given only once a day in the afternoon. From the third month onwards it can be given twice a day. The other feeds should be of milk according to the dilution chart.

The measure given above is for one cup but this can be increased or decreased according to the appetite of the baby. Upto the age of 3 to 4 months the feed should be liquid. From the sixth month onwards the feed should be thickened by increasing the quantity of the powder a bit and can be fed with a spoon. If milk is not available or cannot be given for some reason this feed can be prepared in water with no milk added.

When the Baby Cries Incessantly

If the baby cries incessantly one should not get panicky but try to find out the cause. The baby tired out after incessant crying and going to sleep and crying again after waking up is a sign of ear ache or abdominal colic. With an ear ache the baby rubs the painful ear along with crying and if an adult touches that ear the baby screams with pain. With abdominal pain the baby either twists its body or draws up its legs and screams and sometimes its hands and feet get cold. When distension of abdomen, constipation, or dysentry are present with crying episodes they help in concluding that there may be abdominal pain. If the baby cries non-stop almost day and night without the above reasons and does not have its feeds it may be a sign of approaching convulsions and one must be prepared for it and take suitable action, like informing the doctor.

Earache

1. One clove, or one black pepper corn or one clove of garlic to be crushed slightly and heated in half a teaspoon of coconut or sesame oil. Then strain the oil and when lukewarm put one to two drops in the ear and cover with a piece of cotton wool.
2. One teaspoon of grated fresh coconut, a pinch of turmeric powder and one or two large crystals of salt are mixed together and warmed. This mixture is squeezed and one or two drops of it put in the ear and covered with cotton wool.

The above remedies are equally useful for adults.

It is said that the mouth of the baby should be cleaned after each feed. Otherwise the milk residue after each feed tends to collect in the tonsillar region of the throat causing ascending infection and swelling of the Eustachian tube which connects the cavity of the ear to the throat. This sometimes causes an earache. The baby's mouth should therefore be cleaned with a soft wet cloth after every feed.

Abdominal Colic

If due to gases, rub castor oil on the abdomen and foment it with warm castor leaves. If there is distension usually due to constipation and gas, a glycerine syringe should be given and also use the above remedy of rubbing castor oil and the castor leaves. If the abdominal pain is due to cold, wrap a piece of warm clothing round the abdomen.

Vomiting

Dried lemon peal about 1cm. round piece or one pod of cardamom should be burnt and powdered and should be given mixed with a teaspoon of honey.

Stomatitis

Tender seeds of snake gourd should be rubbed in the snake gourd juice to a fine paste and rubbed gently inside the mouth.

Diarrhoea

In infants – pomogranate leaves, six or seven of them should be boiled and cooked in 25 ml. of water. Then strain the water and give it to the baby with a little sugar and milk. Alternatively 1 cm. piece of pomogranate skin with a pinch of heated cummin seed (Jeera) powder should be boiled in water and given to the baby as above.

Green Diarrhoea

Tender leaves, two each of Guava and Pomogranate should be boiled in the milk feed to be given to the baby. Guava leaves should be very tender, and 2 cm. long.

Diarrhoea or Fever due to Teething

A teaspoon of the juice of the innermost tender parts of the banana flower should be given with a little bit of sugar for seven days. Gums may be rubbed with this juice.

Other remedies involve Ayurvedic herbs and roots which are given in the Marathi Edition.

Cold and Cough

When the baby cannot breathe due to a stuffy nose,a cloth wick dipped in cow's ghee or buffalo ghee (clarified butter from cow's or buffaloes milk) should be inserted in the nostrils. This clears the nose and the baby can breathe freely. Instead of ghee a drop of glycerine can be inserted in the nostrils.

1. Half a teaspoon of onion juice added to half a teaspoon of heated Ajwain leaf juice with a pinch of powdered large crystal sugar should be given once in the morning.
2. Nutmeg should be rubbed into a paste in cologne water and applied to the sides of the chest, forehead and neck. If the cold is severe the nutmeg should be rubbed in brandy.
3. Chopped onion should be heated, wrapped in a piece of cloth and the baby's chest should be fomented with it.

Productive Cough

Half of a medium sized onion should be chopped and kept in a sauce pan. A teaspoon of rice and a pinch of cummin seed (jeera) should be cooked in a cup of water. This boiling water should be poured on the chopped onion and the onion covered. After five minutes this mixture should be strained, add a bit of larger crystal sugar to it and this mixture fed to the baby.

Measles and Chicken Pox

For the itching and burning associated with measles and chicken-pox a solution of warm water with one teaspoon of soda bi-carb and one teaspoon of colognewater in one large jug of water should be used to sponge the child which diminishes or removes the itching or burning. The same thing can be followed for prickly heat.

When a healthy child does not sleep well,his or her feet or the lower half of the body should be immersed in warm water for a few minutes. After removing the baby from the water he or she should be wiped dry and put to bed.

Some Common Ailments

Headache

One sided headache or migraine

1. At four O'clock in the morning the migraine patient should eat two Jilebees (a sweet made with white flour soaked in buttermilk) and drink cold water after it and go to bed again. This should be done for three consecutive days. If the headache is not relieved the same thing should be followed for seven more days. Pedhas (another sweet made with dried milk) could also be used instead of jilebees.
2. Alternatively a tablespoonful of cooked rice should be mixed with a quarter cup of milk and a bit of buttermilk added, to set into curds or Yoghurt the next morning. This should be eaten at four in the morning after which one should sleep for about two hours. This too should be followed for three days.

Headache

Jambee oil – 3 kg of lemon juice, ½ kg of vegetable oil and 4 kg of ghee should be boiled together till it turns into mature oil. This oil should be rubbed on the head and is useful for various kinds of headaches.

Conjunctivitis

Poppy pods should be boiled in water and the eyes fomented with this water when it is warm.

For Cooling the Eyes

1. Take 15 ml. of rosewater, add 1 mg of good quality Bhimsen camphor and store it in a clean bottle. Put one to two drops in the eyes two to three times a day.

2. Two teaspoons of green horse gram (chana) and a pinch of cummin seed (Jeera) to be soaked in water for a few hours after washing the two. Then put one or two drops of this water in the eyes or put wet packs dipped in this water on the eyes.

3. One or two drops of mother's milk or fresh unboiled cow's milk should be put in the eyes or wet packs dipped in this milk should be kept on the eyes.

The remedies for earache have already been enumerated in the infant care section.

Mumps

Grind a few leaves of the ladies fingers plant or okra plant as it is called in some places. Warm this ground paste and foment the swollen region of cheeks.

Toothache

1. Alum of the size of a tamarind seed should be dissolved in a cup of water and used to rinse the mouth as a first measure before seeing the dentist.

2. Leaves of Arhar, a fistful of them to be boiled in a cup of water and rinse the mouth with it.

3. Rinse the mouth with tea decoction.

For swelling with toothache, dry ginger should be rubbed in water and the paste applied over the swelling.

Stomatitis

A teaspoon of Castor oil should be mixed in the decoction of dried ginger and should be taken for three days.

Cold and Cough

1. 2.5 gms of dried ginger, same quantity of Jyesthamadh, 1/4 teaspoon cummin seed (jeera) and 4 corns of blackpepper, one chopped small white onion – all these to be boiled in one cup of water and evaporated to 3/4 cup. The top liquid to be taken morning and evening till the cold or cough subsides.

2. One Bale leaf, two leaves of Tulsi, a pinch of cummin seed (jeera), a teaspoon of coriander seed, 2.5 gms of dried ginger or 5.8 gms of fresh ginger, a pinch of Haldi, one small onion and 5.8 gms of Jyesthamadh to be boiled in a cup of water and evaporated to 3/4 cup and to be given twice a day.

3. Four to five leaves of mint, lemon grass four leaves, four to five top tender leaves of Tulsi, two Bale leaves, a small piece of ginger about 2-5 gms and same quantity of Jyesthamadh, a small lump of large crystal sugar or jaggery all to be boiled in a cup of water, evaporated to half a cup and given morning and evening till the cold or cough subsides.

Cough with Cold

Two cm. round lump of jaggery to be melted in a dry pot till it turns into a sticky syrup. Then add a cup of water. Add a pinch of powdered jeera or cummin seed with a pinch of powdered Haldi, 2.5 gms of Jyesthamadh and two black pepper corns, both these powdered. Boil and evaporate to ¾ cup and give morning and evening.

Chronic Dry Cough

1. Finely chopped small onion mixed with jaggery to be eaten twice a day.

2. One small onion to be roasted without oil and one small onion raw, crush both to extract some juice, mix it with large crystal sugar and take it twice a day till the cough subsides.

3. Teaspoon of juice of Ajwain leaves to be mixed with large crystal sugar and given morning and evening. Can also be given to children.

4. One cup of milk added to one cup of water, 2.5 gms of dry ginger and Jyesthamadh, and a pinch of turmeric (haldi). Boil all this together, evaporate to make it one cup and give it before going to bed, for seven days.

5. Cook ladies fingers or Okra in a cup of water. When it is boiled for a few minutes after cooking the ladies fingers or okra, the water should be drained off. Divide this quantity of water into two parts and give one part in the morning before breakfast and the other part before 3 O'clock in the afternoon with milk and sugar.

6. A teaspoon of linseed (Alsee) and half a teaspoon of flattened rice (Poha) to be boiled in a cup of water and evaporated to half a cup and given with powdered large crystal sugar (Khadi Sakhar).

For an Incessant Cough

Two teaspoons of onion juice, two drops of ginger juice and one teaspoon of honey with one teaspoon of powdered large crystal sugar to be mixed together and given once in the morning.

Chronic Allergic Cough

Two dried dates, two dried figs, two lumps of large crystal sugar and 2.5 gms of Jyesthamadh to be boiled in two cups of water evaporated to half a cup and given once in the morning for fifteen days.

Some Useful Hints

1. For gas trouble put a little Asafoetida (Hing) in water or buttermilk and drink it. It feels better after belching.
2. For billious vomiting eat a few pieces of sugared ginger and drink water before breakfast.
3. To clean silverware use VIM.
4. Brute Borax mixed with water, when sprayed, helps to get rid of cockroaches, ants and flies.
5. In a carious tooth put a garlic clove and stuff it in. It relieves the pain.
6. For cold, eat a few cloves and have quarter teaspoon of clove oil with large crystal sugar.
7. To make pickles air tight tie a piece of plastic over the cloth tied to the pickle jartop.
8. Add a few grains of rice to table salt to stop it from getting moist and lumpy.
9. After a superficial burn dip the burnt hand in salt water. The burning is reduced.
10. Silverware if stored in wheat flour, does not tarnish and get black.
11. Tea leaves left in the teapot should be dried and burnt on live coal. This prevents flies.
12. During rainy season the nuisance of flies is reduced if an iron rod is heated and two pieces of camphor kept on it. The smell of melting camphor keeps the flies away.
13. For bed bugs, wash the bed with hot alum water. The bugs and their eggs are destroyed.
14. Floors mopped with phenyle and washing soda reduces the nuisance of mosquitos.
15. To stop little insects in stored grain, add some bitter neem leaves, or ash from burnt cloth, or onion to the grain. This stops the insects.
16. For lice use oil mixed with powdered custard apple seeds which is strained and rubbed on the hair, comb hair with a fine comb after applying the oil. The lice drop off.
17. If there are mice holes in the house fill them up with melted tar. The mice run away.

18. Use coconut oil mixed with camphor for cracks between toes, during rainy season because of wet feet.

19. Use boiled potato skins in water to clean silverware which make it shiny and it does not scratch.

20. Burning of hands due to cutting of green chillies is eased by applying butter.

21. Hands stained due to cutting of banana flower, or raw bananas etc. should be washed with tamarind, lemon or buttermilk.

22. The brown residue left after making ghee can easily come out if boiled with large grains of salt and water.

23. For hoarse voice eat 3 to 4 pepper corns with sugar or eat a berry size piece of jaggery mixed with a bit of turmeric powder and drink a hot cup of milk over it.

24. Fresh coconut halves get yellowish or start smelling if stored for a day or two. To prevent this smear them with salt.

25. To prevent stored turmeric from discolouration, rub some ghee on the inside of the jar before filling it with turmeric powder. This keeps the turmeric yellow throughout.

26. To store chillie powder without getting spoilt add a little salt to it and put some salt at the bottom of the jar. A little groundnut oil smeared on the inside of the jar also stops the chillie powder from getting spoilt.

27. If tomatoes get soft, put them in cold water for some time. They get harder in cold water and are easy to cut.

28. Green chillies remain fresh for a longer time if their stems are removed.

29. To clean a stove use dry ash and wipe it with a piece of dry cloth.

30. Vegetables cleaned and kept in plastic bags remain fresh for a longer time.

Festivals and Religious Days as per the Hindu Calendar

As we approach the turn of the twentieth century, we find that old Saraswat joint family system is fast disappearing. As a result, advice and guidance concerning the observance of Hindu religious days and festivals, the special foods to be prepared for offerings to the deities and for feasts on such special occasions, the 'Vratas' and fasts to be observed by the religious minded, which were traditionally given by the experienced elders in a joint family home are rarely available now-a-days. Taking this into consideration and to help those who wish to preserve our religious culture and traditions, we have attempted to give here the correct information concerning the commonly observed and important festivals and religious days of the Saraswat Community.

Our Hindu Year commences with Chaitra Shuddha Pratipada.

Note: Shuddha – Bright fortnight of moon
Vaddya – Dark fortnight of moon.

1. Chaitra Shuddha Pratipada – (Gudi Padva)

The day dawns with prayers to Mangal Murthy (Vinayak) to usher an auspicious new year. Priests are invited to read the forecast for the new year from the Hindu Almanac (Panchang).

In some areas, the early morning programme on this day is to mount the Dhwaja or Gudi. Tender neem leaves and flowers fried in ghee and mixed with pepper powder, cumin seeds and sugar are offered to God and then distributed and eaten by all members in the family to ward off all diseases.

For lunch at noon green gramdal kheer and black gram dal dosa are served to guests and family members, clothes and money are also distributed to the needy in accordance with the belief that this act will ward off the evil effects of unfavourable stars in the coming year.

In the evening, puja is offered to God and an offering of mango, jack-fruit, Bengal gram dal Usal, raw mango pachadi (Koshimbir), panak or Sherbat (of ginger and jaggery) are made and distributed as Prasadam.

2. Chaitra Shuddha Navami (Shri Ram Navami)

Passages from Shri Valmiki Ramayana describing Lord Rama's birth are read out, one or two sweets and a mixture of powdered ginger and sugar are offered to God after Pooja and distributed as Prasadam.

3. Chaitra Poornima

It is also called Hanuman Jayanti in honour of Shri Hanumanji's birthday. On this day, people offer oil and shendur and some sweets to Shri Hanumanji's idol.

4. Vaishakha Shuddha Tritiya (Akshaya Tritiya)

Considered as very auspicious, especially if it falls on a Wednesday with Rohini Nakshatra, for weddings and for starting any new enterprise.

5. Jyestha Poornima (Vata Poornima)

It was on this day, that Satyavan died and regained life under the Vata or Banyan tree as a result of his wife Savitri's penance under this tree. Hence Vata Vriksha or Banyan tree is supposed to be sacred and is worshipped by Suvasinis on this day and Vata Savitri Vrita is observed by fasting and an offering of puranpoli to the Vata and distributing to other suvasinis Halad Kumkum, flowers and fresh fruits in cups made from Vata Leaves.

6. Aashadh Shuddha Ekadashi or Aashadhi

(11th day of bright fortnight of Aashadh)

People observe complete fast, spending all the time in repetition of the Lord's name. On the following day i.e. Dwadashi, sprouted green gram Ambat, Chutney of Brahmi leaves or green mango, Surnoli, black gram dal Appe with or without jaggery, are offered to God as Naivedya before meals.

7. Aashadh Poornima

Also called Vyasa Poornima and Guru Poornima – is observed in honour of Guru, offering Pooja and Naivedya.

8. Shravana Shuddha Panchami (Nag Panchami)

Oblations to Cobras offering milk and Yajnopaveet or sacred thread are made for preservation of the family with a long life. Shri Shantadurga devotees offer prayers on this day to the Goddess. And offer Her Halad Kumkum, flowers and food and offer the same to Suvasinis along with betel leaf, areca nut and money (dakshina).

Shri Shantadurga Devotees (Panchamkaris) observe renewal of Yajnopaveet or sacred thread Upakarma on this day. The following dishes are prepared for prasad:- Vada, Bengal gram dal Sukrunde or Puranpoli and coconut kheer.

9. Shravana Poornima (Naarali Poornima)

With Shravana Nakshatra on the day, all men especially devotees of Mangeshi observe renewal of the sacred Thread Upakarma. The scared Thread is also offered to Sea God along with coconut. Preparations for this day are mainly Rice Shevayi and sweetened coconut milk for offering to God. Vayasa Daan (Crow feeding) in honour of the departed is also done and thereafter food is partaken with Brahmins.

10. Shravan Vaddhya Ashtami (Eighth day of the dark fortnight) Termed as Gokul Ashtami

This day is observed as Shri Krishna's Birth day. People observe a fast in the morning and perform Pooja and Aarti to Lord Krishna in the evening or at midnight and distribute prasad mainly of Jaggery ladu, Kadboli, panchkhadya (a mixture of fried sesame seeds, slices of dried coconut, roasted Bengal Gram dal powder, cardamom and sugar powder), jaggery mixed with puffed black gram dosa, green gram kheer, butter, curds, milk curd and beaten rice (dahi poha) etc. along with dried ginger powder mixed with sugar, after naivedya (offering to God).

It is customary to invite newly wedded girls to their mother's place during the month of Shravan, and these girls are personally taught by their mothers, the age old custom of performing special puja to Tulsi plant on Fridays and Sundays in Shravan termed 'Choodiya Offerings'. These Choodiyas are prepared of about 5 types of flowers as several types of scented and colourful flowers are available in Shravan month. Betel leaves, areca nuts along with Choodiyas are offered to elderly Suvasinis and blessings from them are sought. First these Choodiyas are offered to Tulsi plant then Suvashini mother, mother-in-law and only later to other elderly Suvashinis.

Pooja Materials: One Kalasha (Chambu) of water, Panchamrit (honey, ghee, milk, curds, and sugar – 5 ingredients are mixed together for ready use), Flowers, Sandalwood paste, Agarbatti, Camphor, Akshata (rice grains), chalk (or shedi khadu); and for naivedya on Fridays sweet Khichadi and on Sunday, Undlakal etc.

11. Bhadrapada Shuddha Tritiya (i.e. Third day of Bright fortnight in Bhadrapada):

On this day is performed Suvarna Gowri Puja by Suvashini ladies and girls. For every Suvashini – 5 coconuts and for girls 2 coconuts in a basket are decorated. Specially coconuts with Shendi are used. (At first the coconuts are cleaned; washed in turmeric water; lines are drawn all around on the coconuts with a chalk. Eyes of the coconuts are smeared – one with Sindhur, and the other two with Kajal). Sugar cane, fresh areca nut, betel leaves, plantains, areca flowers (Bhingar), Ridged gourd, cucumber, Lady's fingers etc. are kept in the basket, a lighted oil Lamp is also kept in the basket meant for Suvasinis, alongwith Vayana string, black bangles, comb, small boxes of kajal, kumkum, etc.

Three coconuts are specially cleaned, separately washed in turmeric water. Kajal, Sindur horizontal tilak are applied on one and the other two coconuts (one to represent Sri Shiva and the other Sri Ganesha) are be smeared with Sindur alone. This is usually prepared by Suvashinis in the house – while preparing for Vayana.

For naivedya to Gowri, Patholya of Varai or of wheat flour; cucumber kheer (cucumber grated and mixed with jaggery alone *without salt*), cucumber Kochcholi, Upkari of 5 types of green leafy vegetables (without salt) are prepared. After Gowri Puja and naivedya, Vayana is offered. Those ladies who observe Hartalika Vrita, abstain from solid food.

12. Bhadrapada Shuddha Chaturthi (Ganesh Chaturthi)

Earthen idol of Sri Ganesh is brought home from outside, or the one from the house is kept for Pooja.

Naivedya offered to Sri Ganesh are: Khotte, Madgane, Chakly (while kneading the flour into dough, milk is used in place of water), jaggery ladu, Karanjya (Nevryo), Modak or Panchakhadya etc.

Potato Sukki Bhaji (variety 1 - Sukken), bhendi Upkari, Kakdi Kochholi, Aluvadi, Alu (colocasia) Bhaji, Bitter gourd and Ambadi Ghashi, Bitter gourd fritters etc. are prepared. Modak arati is specially shown finally to Lord Ganesh.

13. Rishi Panchami (falls on Bhadrapada Shuddha Panchami)

On this day, Puja of Sapta (seven) Rishis is performed. Food grains produced by the use of bullocks in ploughing are *not* used as food.

14. Bhadrapada Shuddha Ashtami

On this day it is customary to perform Jyeshti Gowri Puja, after the visarjan pooja of Suvarna Gowri. Daily, after Pooja, curd rice and upkari of 5 types of green leaves *without salt* are offered. This Gowri is considered to be older Gowri (Vradha Gowri), also termed Yele Gowri.

15. Anant Shuddha Chaturdashi

Anant Vrita is observed by men only. Mahashesha along with Sri Vishnu is worshipped in the noon. All prasad preparations ought to bear male names (male gender); sweets are of 14 varieties viz. Tukde, Shankarpali, Ladu etc. all bearing male names; and the varieties of vegetable preparations viz. Khotte, Madgane etc. and 14 coconut preparations, are also offered for Prasad in the night.

16. Mhala Paksha

On the full moon day (Poornima) following Anant Chaturdashi, certain Sanyasis end their Chaturmasa. The fortnight that follows is termed Mhala Paksha i.e. dark fortnight of Bhadrapada – Pratipada to Amavasya – also called Pitru Paksha. During these 15 days usually no auspicious ceremonies are performed. In honour of all departed souls i.e. in memory of the departed relatives, far and near, Shradha ceremony is customarily performed. During this fortnight, the 9th day i.e. Navami is termed 'Avidhava Navami', as it is on this Navami Day, in honour of and in the name of the Departed Sowbhagyavatis in the family, Vayasa is offered (crow feeding). Likewise, Suvasinis are invited and offered flowers, plantains, coconut, Dakshina, Khan (blouse piece) or Saree along with betel and areca. It is customary to offer these as "Voti". Any day of this Mhala Paksha, Shradha may be performed, and if not possible till the end of the fortnight, on Amavasya day (Mahalaya Amavasya) Vayasa is offered to propitiate the departed. Cattle are also offered food. For general death anniversaries or "Mhal", the following preparations are made:

1. Sprouted green gram Ghashhi
2. Saar of the green gram
3. Sukkhi Bhaji of tender bamboo shoots
4. Upkari of any vegetable
5. Raita of raw plantains
6. Chutney of green mango soaked in brine
7. Phodiyas of raw plantains, tender bamboo shoots, sweet potato, bhendi, tendli etc.
8. Black gram Ambode
9. Kheer of wheat lapsi or of green gram dal
10. Plantain (ripe) Shikran (Hashale)
11. Puries

On this occasion, it is customary to prepare foods which were the favourites of the departed.

For Pinda Pradan, one measure of rice is cooked. So also, all the above stated preparations are first offered to the Lord before they are offered to the departed souls by serving on a clean plantain leaf as Vayasa – to feed crows outside the house or to be fed to the cattle.

17. Navaratra (Mahanavami) Celebrations

During the bright fortnight of Ashwin, the first ten days are termed Navratri – festival of Nine Nights and on the 10th day is Vijayadashami (Dasra).

On the first day after Amavasya (i.e. on Pratipada of Ashwin), Ghatasthapana is done i.e. Goddess Durga is invoked on the Ghata. On the day that Moola Nakshatra befalls, Saraswati Puja is performed by offering Pooja to sacred books etc. for endowment of education and knowledge. For Sharda Devi (Saraswati) Pooja Prasad, usually cucumber dosa is made. During these auspicious nine days, it is customary to chant Saptashati. Daily different varieties of preparations are offered to Sri Devi with coconut and khan (blouse piece). During all these 10 days, Kumari Pujan, Brahman Suvashini Pujas are performed.

On Vijayadashami Day new rice is obtained for Navanna. Usually new rice Khir is prepared without jaggery and mixed with coconut milk. Round cucumber pudding is also offered. If new rice is not available in sufficient quantity a few grains may be mixed in Khir. Of the new crop, rice sheaves or stalks are obtained, kept near God's idol, offered Puja and tied to the container in which rice is stored, and at the main entrance of the house, treasure chest, milk cooker, cowshed etc.

In the evening, apta leaves or Shami Vriksha leaves are exchanged between friends and relatives wishing them prosperity. N.B. Those who were unable to perform Vayana or Sri Ganesha in Bhadrapada Masa, must observe Tritiya and Chaturthi in Navratra as being equally auspicious for the Pujas of Devi and Ganesh.

18. Ashvij Pournima (also termed Kojagiri Poornima)

After the moon rise, milk and supari (betel nut halves) are offered to Moon God and Prasad partaken by all.

19. Ashvij (Vadhya) Trayodashi to Kartik (Sudha) Dwitiya

Deepavali falls on these 4 days:

1. Dhana Trayodashi
2. Narak Chaturdashi
3. Bali Pratipada, and
4. Bhau-beej

1. *Dhana Trayodashi*: Auspicious Puja is offered to Gold, Silver and Wealth on this day. In the evening, water is collected in freshly cleaned vessels (in olden days water reservoirs were being offered Pujas) that are decorated with marigold – Jhandu flowers and Toran tied round; also sweet Poha is offered, scented sticks are burnt, Aarti performed etc.

2. (a) *Narak Chaturdashi*: Early at dawn, before sunrise, it is customary to take oil bath applying scented "Utna". It is also observed that at the time of bath, to simulate blood of Narakasur, oil mixed with Kumkum is applied on the forehead. After bath, Kareet vegetable is crushed under one's foot and its seed is put into the mouth. Later jaggery mixed Poha is used for breakfast. Usually during Deepavali, specialities that are prepared are Anaras, Bundi Ladu, Phenorya, Chiwda etc. For lunch, some sweet should be served. In the evening at the entrance and at the bathroom etc. oil lamps are lighted to celebrate deepotsava for 3 days at least.

(b) *Laxmi Pujan*: On new Moon day – Amavasya – traders and businessmen open new accounts in their books, after Pooja offered to them, and Prasad distributed.

3. *Bali Pratipada*: On Kartik Shudha Pratipada is observed Go – Puja to cattle (as cattle is deemed wealth in India for centuries together) and also to Bali Chakravarthi and Sri Krishna, the protectors of cattle.

Copra, Jaggery and Poha, and plantains are offered to the cattle at home (after giving them oil bath). The cattle are also decorated with garlands of flowers after or during their Puja.

4. *Bhau Beej*: It is the glorious day on which a sister invites her brothers for food and offers them preparations that they most like. As is customary, after oilbath etc. the sister performs Aarti to brothers, and in turn brothers present her with gifts to mark the occasion.

20. Kartik Shuddha Ekadashi

It is observed in the same way as Ashadhi Ekadashi.

21. Kartik Shuddha Dwadashi: The day Tulsi married Lord Krishna.

It is customary to clean up and decorate Tulsi Vrindavan. Sugarcane is planted in the Tulsi Square – so also Amla and Tamarind saplings are planted. In the evening, Sri Krishna is worshipped and Tulsi wedding is celebrated. For Naivedya, jaggery sweetened Poha (pounded rice) is usually prepared and distributed.

22. Margashir Shuddha Shashti (Kukke Shashti or Champa Shashti)

It is believed that Nagapuja or pujas of cobras on this day assures good benefits to the progeny. Invariably on this day, ash gourd Ambat for curry and sweet Khichdi for Prasad are prepared.

23. Margashira Purnima: Datta Jayanti Day

Celebrated on similar lines to Shri Krishna Jayanti or Rama Navami etc. Datta Bhaktas deem this a great day.

24. Makara Sankranti

In Poushya month, it is a big occasion. On this day, early morning Ladu or Halwa, Tilgul etc. are offered to God. Halad Kumku, flowers and Tilgul are also exchanged between friends and relatives. Khichdi (sweet) is specially prepared on this day, out of rice, Moong dal and jaggery. Black gram dal dosa or Appe are also offered to God.

25. Magha Shuddha Panchami

Supposed to be auspicious. Votaries of Sri Shanta Durga in particular invite Brahmins and Suvashinis for Bhojan, preparing Vada, Sukrunde or Puranpoli andrice kheer (unsweetened) with coconut milk.

Car festivals of Sri Shanta Durga and Sri Mangeshi temple in Goa are conducted on this day, called Rathotsava.

26. Magha Shuddha Saptami (Ratha Saptami)

Special prayers to Sun God are offered on this day. Opposite to Tulsi Vrindavan are drawn Rangoli Ratha, and a thali full of water is kept over it. It is also customary to prepare three broad floats from the plantain tree bark, decorating each with 2 eyes drawn with Kajal and a few others with Kumkum and these are allowed to float on the water in the Thali with lighted cotton wicks dipped in ghee.

For Naivedya, broken wheat (Lapsi) Payasa is usually prepared.

27. Magha Vadhya Chaturdashi (Maha Shivratri)

In honour of Sri Shankara, pujas are performed with Bel Patri after observing a strict fast throughout the day.

28. Phalgoon Pournima

Is the day of Holi observed for burning Holika, all over the country.

Kheer from coconut and puranpoli are selected for Naivedya.

In the evening, the yard in front of the house is cleaned, Rangoli drawn, firewood collected and after performing Holi Puja, Holika is set ablaze. Coconuts, ahuti etc. are offered to the burning Holi fire.

GLOSSARY

ENGLISH	KONKANI	MARATHI	HINDI	KANNADA
Allspice (Tail pepper)	Kankol (Gandh Menasu)	Kankol	—	Gandh Menasu
Almond	Badam	Badam	Badam	Badam
Amaranth	Chavli	Chavali	Chavrai	Chavali
Amchur	Amchur	Ambyacha Chur	Amchur	Mavinkai Churu
Amla	Aavalo	Avala	Amvala	Nellikai
Anardana	Dalimba	Dalimba	Anardana	Dalimbari
Aniseed	Badishep	Badishep	Badian (Aawonf)	Sompu
Aniseed leaves	Shepi bhaji	Shepu bhaji	Soumpaki Sabji	Sabbasgi Palle
Asafoetida	Hingu	Hing	Hing	Hingu
Ash Gourd	Kunwale	Kohala	Kumhada (Petha)	Boodi Kumbal Kai
Banana Trunk core	Keli Gabbo	Kelicha Gabha	Keleka Gabha	Bale Dande
Basil (Sweet) Bay leaf	Kam Kasturi	Marva	Kali Tulsi	Kam Kasturi
Beetroot	Beet	Beet	Chukandar	Beet
Bengal Gram	Chano	Harbhara	Channa	Kadle
Bermada grass	Doorva	Durva	Doorva	Ambate Hullu
Bishop's weed	Wonwo	Owa	Ajwain	Owa
Bitter gourd	Karaten	Karli	Karela	Hagal Kai
Bitterlemon	Kanchi	Kanchiche Phal	Kainchi	Kanchikai
Black pepper	Miryakan	Kali Miri	Kali mirch	Menasinkalu
Black cummin seed	Kaljeere	Kale jire	Kala Jeera	Kare jeerige
Black Gram	Udeed	Udeed	Urad	Uddin Kalu
Bottle Gourd (White Gourd)	Ghar duddi	Dudhi Bhopla	Louki	Halu Kumbal kai

ENGLISH	KONKANI	MARATHI	HINDI	KANNADA
Brinjal	Vayangan	Vangi	Baingan	Badnekai
Broad Beans	Papdi	Wal papadi	—	Avre Kai
Capsicum	Donne Mirsang	Phuge Mirchi	Simla Mirch	Donne Menasu
Caraway Seed	Shahajire	Shahajire	Shaha Jeera	Shaha jeerige
Cardamom	Yal	Veldode (Velachi)	Elaichi	Yalakki
Carrot	Gajar	Gajar	Gajar	Gajjari
Cassia leaf (cinnamon)	Tamal Patra	Tamal Patra	Tejpatta	Dalchin yele
Celery Seed	Ajmoda	Ajmoda	Ajmoda	Celery Kalu
Chilli Powder	Mirsange Pitti	Tikhat (Mirchichi Pood)	Mirch	Menasin hudi
Cinnamon	Dalchini	Dalchini	Dalchini	Dalchini
Cloves	Lavang	Lavang	Lavang	Lavang
Cluster beans	Mitake saang	Gawar	Gawar	Chawli
Colocasia Leaves	Alwa Panna	Aluchi Pane	Arooiki Sabji	Keshin Ele
Corn (Maize)	Jonnalo	Makka	Makka	Govin jol
Cottage cheese	Paneer	Paneer	Paneer	Paneer
Coriander leaves	Kothambari Pallo	Kothimbir	Dhania Patta	Kothambari Soppu
Coriander seeds	Kothambari	Dhane	Dhania	Kothambari
Cow Gram (Horse Gram)	Kulith	Kulith	Kulthi	Hurll

ENGLISH	KONKANI	MARATHI	HINDI	KANNADA
Crimson Yam	Kon	Konphal	Kachalu	Suran Gedde
Cuba beans	Alsando	Chawali	Rongi Ki Phalia	Alsande
Cucumber	Tavshen	Kakdi	Kakadi	Savte kai
Cumin seed	Jeeren	Jeere	Jeera	Jeerige
Curry leaves	Phanna Pallo	Kadi Patta	Limda	Kerbevu
Dates	Khajjur	Khajur	Khajjur	Khajjuru
Drum Sticks	Mashinga sango	Shevgyachya Shenga	Suanjani Phalia	Nuggekai
Dry Ginger	Sunthi	Sunth	Soonth	Sunthi
Dry Date	Kharuk	Kharik	Kharik	Uttatti
Egg shaped small bitter gourd	Karit	Karith	Takmak	Puttekai (Halmekhi)
Fennel	Badishep	Badishep	Sounf	Sompu
Fenugreek	Methi	Methi	Methi	Menthe
Fenugreek leaves	Metye Bhaji	Methichi Bhaji	Methi Sag	Menthe palle
Field Beans	Avaro (Val)	Val	Badi Rongi	Avarekai
French Beans	Tingal Avro(Pharasbi)	Pharasbi	Sem	Tingal Avre Kai
Gamboge (Kokum)	Birundasol	Amsoal	Kokum	Hurgin Huli
Garlic	Lasun	Lasun	Lasan	Bellulli
Gingelly Seeds (Seasame seed)	Tilu	Til	Til	Yellu
Ginger	Aallen	Aalen	Adrak	Hasi Sunthi
Gooseberry (Indian)	Rai Avalo	Rajavalo	Amla	Raj Nellikai
Green gram	Moogu	Moog	Moong	Hesarukalu

ENGLISH	KONKANI	MARATHI	HINDI	KANNADA
Ground nut (Pea nut)	Bhui moog	Shengadane	Moong phali	Nelgadle
Honey	Mhovu	Madh	Shahad	Jenu tuppa
Horsegram (Cowgram)	Kulithu	Kulith	Kulthi	Hurli
Indian Spinach	Vaali	Mayalu	—	Basale Soppu
Iron hot plate	Tavo	Tava	Tava	Tave
Jack fruit (Raw)	Kadgi	Kaccha Phanas	Kaccha kathal	Halasinkai
Jack fruit (Ripe)	Phanasu	Phanas	Kathal	Halasin Hannu
Jaggery	God	Gul	Gur	Bella
Jawar	Jolu	Jondhala	Jawar	Jol
Jerkins (Kovai)	Tendli	Tondli	Kundru	Tondle kai
Kalonji	Kandya Biya	Kalonji	Kalonji	Ulla Gaddiya Beeja
Knol-kol	Navalkol	Navalkol	Ganth Gobhi	Knol-kol
Kokum (Gamboge)	Birunda Sol	Amsol	Kokum	Murugin Huli
Kovai (Jerkins)	Tendli	Tondli	Kundru	Tondle kai
Ladies Fingers	Bhend	Bhendi	Bhindi	Bende kai
Legumes	Kaddhanya	Kaddhanye	Dwidal Anaj	Kaddhanye
Lemon (lime)	Nimbuvo	Limbu	Nimboo	Nimbekai (Nimbe Hannu)
Mace	Jaipatri	Jaipatri	Jaipatta	Jaipatri
Maze (Corn)	Jonnalo	Makka	Makka	Govin Jol
Mango ginger	Ambe haladi	Ambehalad	—	Kadu Arasin (Kasturi Arasin)
Millet	Bajri	Bajri	Bajra	Sejji
Mint	Marga Pallo	Pudina	Pudina	Pudina

ENGLISH	KONKANI	MARATHI	HINDI	KANNADA
Magge (variety of Cucumber)	Maggen	Gol Kakdi		Maggekai
Mustard	Sasam	Rai (Mohari)	Sarso	Sasive
Neem	Bevapallo	Kadu Nimb	Neem	Bevin soppu
Negro Coffee	Taikilo	Takla	Chakvand	Togate Soppu
Nutmeg	Jaiphal	Jamalgota	Jaiphal	Jaikai
Onion	Kando	Kanda	Pyaz	Neerulli
Peanuts	Bhui Moog	Shengadane	Moong Phali	Nelgadle
Parsley	Parsley	Parsley	Ajmoda	Achumoda
Poppy seeds	Khaskhas	Khaskhas	Khaskhas	Khaskase
Pulses	Dalyo	Dal	Dal	Bele
Pumpkin (Red pumpkin)	Tambdo Duddi	Lal Bhopla	Kaddu (Lalkaddu)	Kumbalkai (Sarekai)
Radish	Mulangi	Mula	Mooli	Mulungi
Raisins	Draksha	Khismis (Bedana)	Angoor (Khismis)	Drakshe
Raw banana	Harayi Keli	Kachchi Keli	Kachcha kela	Balekai
Raw Mango	Ambli	Kairi	Ambiya	Mavinkai
Red Gram	Tori	1oor	Toor	Togari
Ridge gourd	Ghosalen	Shirali (Dodka)	Torai	Hirekai
Sago	Sabudano	Sabudana	Saboodana	Sabakki
Saffron	Keshari	Keshar	Keshar	Keshari
Sesame seeds	Tilu	Teel	Til	Yellu
Shirkal	Shirkal	Tilvan		Kivikalu

ENGLISH	KONKANI	MARATHI	HINDI	KANNADA
Samolina	Rawo	Rawa	Sooji (Rawa)	Rawe
Snake gourd	Paddul	Padwal	Parora (Chichinda)	Paddul kai
Spinach	Palak/Vali	Palak/Mayalu	Palak	Palak/Basale
Sponge Gourd	Mantav Ghosale	Dodka	Benue (Gilki or Ninva)	Bal Hirekai
Sultana	Kale draksha	Manuka	Munakka	Kare draksha
Sweet Potato	Kanag	Ratali	Sakkar Kand	Genasu
Tamarind	Chinch	Chinch	Imli	Hunasin kai (Huli)
Turmeric	Haladi	Halad	Haldi	Arasin
Turnip	Kon	Salgam	Shalgam	—
Vari	Varai	Vari	—	Varai Akki
Vermicelli	Shevayi	Kurdaya	Shevaya	Shevangi
White gourd (Bottle gourd)	Gharduddi	Dudhi Bhopla	Lauky	Halu Kumbal kai
Wild mango (Hogplum)	Ambade	Ambade	Ambola	Amte Kaai
Yam	Surnu	Suran	Sooran (Jeemi Kand)	Panjar Gadde